Licensing Parents

Can We Prevent
Child Abuse and Neglect?

Licensing Parents
Can We Prevent
Child Abuse and Neglect?

Jack C. Westman, M. D.

University of Wisconsin–Madison
Madison, Wisconsin

With a Foreword by
Judge Charles D. Gill
Superior Court
State of Connecticut
Litchfield, Connecticut

INSIGHT BOOKS

Plenum Press • New York and London

Library of Congress Cataloging-in-Publication Data

Westman, Jack C.
    Licensing parents : can we prevent child abuse and neglect? / Jack
C. Westman ; with a foreword by Charles D. Gill.
        p.   cm.
    Includes bibliographical references and index.
    ISBN 0-306-44766-5
    1. Child abuse--United States. 2. Abusive parents--United States.
3. Children's rights--United States. 4. Parenting--United States.
I. Title.
HV6626.52.W42 1994
362.7'67'0973--dc20   94-22546
                                                                 CIP

ISBN 0-306-44766-5

© 1994 Jack C. Westman
Insight Books is a Division of Plenum Publishing Corporation
233 Spring Street, New York, N.Y. 10013-1578

An Insight Book

Printed in the United States of America

In the hope that we will nurture
and protect all of our children.

Foreword

For years I have traveled across America speaking to thousands of concerned citizens about the need to find new answers to the myriad problems faced by our children.

These formal speeches always contain two references to parenting. The first is that parenting is the most important human-to-human job we will ever have as adults. It is a job for which there is no minimum entry-level standard, no required education, no on-the-job training, no aptitude testing, and no character reference requirements.

The second speech reference was one I delivered with mock sincerity laced with what I thought was humor. I would say, "We need a license to go fishing. We need to be tested physically, intellectually, and fiscally to be licensed to drive an automobile. But to possess, own, operate, and rear a helpless child, there is no test. There is no license. Whoever begets them, gets them."

When the nervous audience laughter subsided, I would continue with my speech. Only fleetingly would a civil libertarian and champion of individual rights such as myself allow such heretical and politically incorrect thoughts to receive thoughtful analysis.

In fact, I would invariably reinforce my aversion to what, at first glance, seemed akin to totalitarianism by loudly declaring: "I, of course, am not really proposing that we license parents." Then, the audience would hear my nervous laughter.

Well, it is no longer a joke to me. I have changed my mind. This is the book that changed it. And this is the book that can change America.

The U.S. Advisory Board on Child Abuse and Neglect issues its annual warning that the state of children in America has reached the point of being a "national emergency." Yet the warning is met with a national yawn.

Apparently, it takes the destruction of children and families in somebody else's country—Kuwait, Somalia—to constitute a real "national emergency."

Passionate people with splendid credentials present us with annual reports of staggering statistics and mind-boggling projections as to the state of America's children. They present no solutions, however. Their message has no effect on policy makers. It is rejected by the average citizen, who has developed a type of psychic numbness in the area of children's issues. It causes no paradigms to shift. When it comes to rearing children, America is losing by forfeit. And the bill for losing gets larger each year. Soon it will bankrupt us.

America is in a true battle for survival, yet we stubbornly prime old mechanisms to solve new problems. In a zany political frenzy, we shout the old, useless slogans: Beef up police! Crack down on crime! Lock them up and throw away the key! Three strikes and you're out! Ban weapons! Limit welfare! Return to basics in education! The list is endless; the paralysis is permanent.

While political leaders can now feel comfortable calling for draconian measures to punish the citizens they describe as "predators," monsters," and "punks," none has the true courage and vision to solve the problem. You might ask our political leaders, "Where do these monsters, predators, and punks come from? Did they parachute from another country? Did they emerge from a spaceship from another planet?"

We know three things about these hated citizens. One, they were all born in American hospitals; two, they were all educated in American schools; and three, they were all reared by American adults. It is a rare predator indeed who has had a successful childhood.

Knowing this, and knowing that proper parenting is the key to a successful childhood, is it not about time that we made proper parenting THE goal of American child policy? Should we not put on the back burner, if not the trash heap, our failing policies that have exclusively focused, after the fact, on adult rehabilitation or personalized child rehabilitation problems that deal with only a single aspect of the myriad bad parenting results? (The latter was aptly dubbed a policy of "disjointed incrementalism" by a colleague.)

My view from the bench during the last decade confirms Dr. Westman's brilliantly presented breakthrough. I have seen the scourge of incompetent parenting manifest itself in child custody proceedings, juvenile hearings, and criminal prosecutions. I have read about the effects of incompetent parenting in the pre-sentencing reports of the thousands of men, women, and children that I sentenced to jails and prisons. The place to fight crime is in the cradle.

In fact, I feel oddly uncomfortable that the first bastion of rights for adults—our courts—is often the last place to look for protective rights for incompetently parented children. Justice is not only blind to the plight of children, but deaf as well. Can we not hear the voice of that young child in Chicago, one of eighteen children living in the filth and poverty engendered by parental drug use? She said to the first arriving female police officer, "Will you be my mommy?" She knows what she needs. Why don't we?

Dr. Westman presents more than an idea here. He presents a Magna Carta for children. Unlike many new ideas that are simply trial balloons to test public opinion or reactions without serious forethought, this proposal has solid statistical, factual, and logical support. It is thoroughly researched and convincingly presented. Dr. Westman will force the traditional children's groups to reexamine their mission, put their turf wars on hold, and scramble back to the drawing board.

Even the legal community will have to reexamine the status of children in America. Are they people or property? I believe that Dr. Westman heads us in the correct direction on this score as well. He acknowledges that the civil rights children need are not necessarily their legal rights at present.

While one may legitimately argue whether children have any real protective rights or not, there would seem to be very little thoughtful argument, after reading this book, that they should not have such rights.

Dr. Westman will startle and provoke you with his hard-hitting scenarios and data. Reading how incompetent parenting created Charles Manson makes an unforgettable statement. (I use that case history in my speeches now.) There are those of us who never questioned a single penny spent to preserve the territorial integrity of

Kuwait, but will question every cent to be spent to preserve the intellectual, physical, and emotional integrity of children. For those in the latter category, the computation that incompetent parenting of a child costs society two million, while a properly parented child yields one million dollars should open some financial eyelids. When Dr. Westman's graphs put the eventual losses of poor parenting in the trillions of dollars, only the most jaundiced would ignore him.

It was personally satisfying to have Dr. Westman remind me that being a parent is just another step in my growth as a person, which, in contrast to its serious responsibilities, is also tremendously rewarding. In fact, most of my parenting efforts were a downright joy. I know I received much more than I gave. I share Dr. Westman's concern that young adults are not told of that wonderful up side of parenting.

Dr. Westman really won me over when he unveiled our newest prejudice—ageism. In his words: "Juvenile ageism is as virulent as racism and as pervasive as sexism." Amen. While we are a nation that professes to love our children, our policies, laws, and actions clearly say otherwise. I have never seen a stronger case for the existence of juvenile ageism than in this book.

The book also takes us to task for forgetting that children who give birth to children are still children themselves. It is a misconception to think that a teenager's childhood stops when parenthood begins.

Dr. Westman justly criticizes us for only looking out for children's needs after they have been damaged by incompetent parenting. By analogy, we are committed to only providing braces and crutches to polio victims rather than an inoculation that prevents the disease in the first place.

The evidence is in. It is incontrovertible. The only possible verdict is to find us guilty of perpetuating a system of incompetent parenting that neglects and devalues our children.

We should be sentenced to seriously examine Dr. Westman's proposal for a new national policy that supports competent parenting.

If this book were mandatory reading for every citizen, the future of America and America's children would be bright. At the very least, it will brighten the future of your children.

JUDGE CHARLES D. GILL
Superior Court, State of Connecticut
Litchfield, Connecticut

Preface

I have worked with abused and neglected children and their parents for over thirty years. Because of this experience, I am keenly aware of children who have three disadvantages which deny them opportunities to become competent citizens and predispose them to crime and welfare dependency. One disadvantage is well known; it is socioeconomic. The second is not as well known; it is personality damage that distorts a child's values and relationships with other people. The third disadvantage may surprise you: many of the interventions intended to help these children actually harm them.

I have been a member of several of the many respected organizations and commissions that have forecast, described, and deplored the decline in the health, education, welfare, and safety of children in the United States in recent decades. This experience has made me aware of our society's lack of genuine commitment to protect and nurture all of its children.

I decided to write this book because the magnitude of child abuse and neglect in the United States far exceeds the ability of professionals to repair the resulting damage to affected children. I am convinced that society itself must assert that every child is entitled to competent parenting and act before children are damaged and placed on the pathways to crime and welfare dependency.

I have struggled with ideas about how we might promote and

support competent parenting. My conclusion is that our society must first explicitly value parenting. Indeed, most adults and teenagers already know that parenting is an important responsibility. For most of the others persuasion and education are sufficient to convince them that it is. But for a small percentage, the only available means of inducing them to function as responsible parents is by enforcing child abuse and neglect statutes *after* they have damaged their children. But children need society's protection *before* they have been damaged. The only way I can see to accomplish this is by setting standards for parenting in the same way that we set standards for everything else we do that affects the lives of other persons—and children are persons.

My central thesis is that we have not set standards for parenting in the United States because of juvenile ageism—a form of prejudice and discrimination against children akin to racism and sexism. One manifestation of juvenile ageism is the way in which we view parenting solely from the perspective of adults rather than from the perspective of children. Another manifestation is the way we tolerate and actually support incompetent parenting while increasing numbers of children are damaged.

I propose that our society counteract juvenile ageism by explicitly valuing parenting through recognizing the civil rights of children so that they will not be required to suffer damage and even death before efforts are made to honor their civil right to competent parenting.

The failure to explicitly identify parenting as a vital social responsibility in the United States has resulted in enormous social and financial costs for our society. In spite of prochildren rhetoric, little public action has taken place to reverse the progressive deterioration of the lives of children in our nation, largely because the civil right of each child to the protection and nurturance of competent parenting has not been recognized and assured.

By focusing attention on the seemingly unthinkable but eminently logical act of licensing parents, my hope is that this book will stimulate thought about the enormous waste of human and economic resources that results from incompetent parenting. In the past setting expectations for parents has been seen as desirable. Now it is a necessity.

The idea of licensing parents brings our rhetorical concerns for children down to reality. Licensing parents would not compromise the right of each woman and man to conceive and each woman to give birth to a child. It would elevate parenting a child to the level of a privilege. It would symbolically set a societal standard that parents may raise children as they desire so long as they do not damage their children's abilities to become contributing members of society. It would convey the message to all elements of society that childrearing is a vital social role. It would heighten public awareness that competent parenting is essential for the well-being and even survival of our society. Most importantly, it would recognize children as human beings with basic civil rights.

Our society cannot afford to continue to subject children to the caprice, neglect, and irresponsibility of incompetent parents. We must see parenting through the eyes of children. If we do, perhaps we can draw upon our compassion and ingenuity to insure that each child has the opportunity to become a responsible citizen.

JACK C. WESTMAN

Madison, Wisconsin

Contents

Introduction

Although Americans generally are better educated and more literate than at any time in our history, an undercurrent of disillusionment in the "American dream" of opportunities for success has been growing in recent decades. In chapter 1, I summarize the evidence that the welfare of so many children in the United States has been declining that the quality of life in the United States has eroded and the productivity of our workforce is in jeopardy.

The gravity of the situation was highlighted in 1991 by the National Commission on Children appointed by Congress and by the President. The Commission called attention to the fact that a small but significant number of parents are failing to fulfill their essential childrearing responsibilities. As will become evident in the pages of this book, there is a definite connection between the damage caused to children by the failings of those parents and our society's educational, health, safety, and economic problems.

A small fraction of the population has reduced public safety for adults and children to unacceptable levels of danger and has sapped the productivity of the nation. Boys are shot in gang wars, school children are slaughtered in crossfire, and many young adults are unemployable. The dangerous and the dependent segments of the population will increase in numbers to further drain public funds and to further decrease the productivity of our workforce.

1

In order to suggest a basic and lasting way to reverse this alarming trend in the United States, I have drawn upon the concept of competent parenting in chapter 2. Competent parenting refers simply to childrearing that does not damage children so that they are deprived of the opportunity to become competent citizens. Simply put, competent parents are people who can restrain themselves from seriously harming their children. In sharp contrast, incompetent parents pursue their own urges and damage their children by ignoring or tyrannizing them or both. More fundamentally, they are unable to manage their own lives effectively.

Although a small fraction of all parents, incompetent parents seriously endanger our society. I estimate that 4 percent of parents in the United States are incompetent and that some 3.6 million children have been neglected by them. This population of children is the source of our society's criminal and welfare dependency problems.

In chapter 3, I describe the benefits of competent parenting to society. Most people regard childrearing as a private matter and do not realize how important parenting is to the health, welfare, and security of the communities and the society in which we all live. In fact the improvement in health and longevity in recent centuries can be traced to the progressive increase in affectionate attachment bonding between children and parents. However, deteriorating family relationships over the last three decades in the United States have led to the decline in the health, welfare, education, and safety of our children and youth. As the quality of parenting has deteriorated, crime, suicide, drug abuse, and teenage pregnancies have increased while scholastic achievement has declined. The relationship between the lack of affectionate attachment bonding between parents and children and these social problems has yet to be widely appreciated.

Parental incompetence in the form of child abuse and neglect has been recognized as a grave national problem. However, its relationship to habitual criminality and to intergenerational welfare dependency is only beginning to be appreciated. In chapter 4, I summarize the evidence that, although many seem to be "invulnerable" because of their remarkable adaptability, the children of incompetent parents are predisposed to become incompetent parents themselves who cannot provide their own children with dependable affection and predictable limit setting. They endanger public safety and the future of our economy by contributing to habitual criminality, welfare dependency, unemployability, homelessness, and self-induced illnesses.

In chapter 5, I estimate the financial costs of incompetent parenting to society. As will be shown, the competent parenting of a child yields $1 million in benefits to society. In contrast the incompetent parenting of a child costs society $2 million.

I describe the trends in our society that I believe make it difficult to deal with incompetent parenting in chapter 6. One of the most important of those trends is the emergence of uncommitted "postnuclear" or "postmarital" families. These unstable parent–child relationships create unstable family units that have difficulty fulfilling their roles as the basic mediating structures between individuals and our society. Then when the family unit breaks down, our society's "crisis-recoil" responses lead to overreactions to the resulting crises followed by recoiling from their underlying causes. In the process parents and children suffer.

In addition, parenting is depreciated because it is not regarded as having economic value in our capitalistic economy. Our traditional markers of economic status and progress do not take into account activities that have no direct financial remuneration.

Even more fundamentally, the generally nurturant and protective attitude of adults toward children has obscured the fact that our society does not regard childhood as a special stage of life deserving protection from adult concerns and responsibilities. Increasingly, children are expected to fend for themselves in a world of hostile strangers, dangerous sexual enticements, and mysterious economic forces that even adults find unsettling. Underlying this situation is the prejudice I call juvenile ageism—the topic of chapter 7.

Juvenile ageism is as virulent as racism and as pervasive as sexism. It is the greatest barrier to recognizing the interests of children in our political processes, in our child-caring systems, and in our households. The most obvious forms of juvenile ageism are violations of children's civil rights that would be recognized in the United States as oppression, torture, enslavement, and murder if they took place with an adult of any race or of either sex.

Although not widely appreciated, I show in chapter 8 that competent parenting is an acknowledged civil right of children. Competent parenting also is a legal right in the negative sense that incompetent parenting is a cause for state intervention and the possible termination of parental rights.

Chapter 9 exposes two misconceptions that dominate popular thinking about parenthood. The first misconception is that a teenager is ready for parenthood in modern society after the attainment of biological puberty. The second misconception is that parenthood consists simply of child care without special responsibility for the child's development and without growth-producing possibilities for parents themselves. In fact, parenthood is an important developmental stage in the life cycle. Because children have a moral right to competent parenting and a legal right to be protected from incompetent parenting, the logical conclusion is that parents have the moral right to be, and to become, competent parents whenever possible.

If we are to reverse the depreciation of parenting and place a high value on competent parenting, a new way of thinking about children in our society is needed. In chapter 10, I suggest that many people have been freed from the "little picture" constraints of personal interests and now are able to engage in "big picture" thinking about common interests. Because of the crisis–recoil nature of political responses to social problems in the United States, there is a compelling need for an overall "big picture" strategy to guide public policies for parenting. That strategy could be based on the goal of achieving competent citizenship for all adults by providing competent parenting for all children. We can reach that goal by articulating cultural values that support affectionate attachment bonds between parents and children as the foundations for social responsibility and for productivity in later life.

Drawing upon current innovative thinking in chapter 11, I propose a national parenting policy based on promoting competent parenting. Licensing parents would be one way to convey society's recognition that parenting is an important undertaking for which there are minimum requirements. One requirement would be that parents be adults who have completed their own growth and development and who are able to assume responsibilities for their own lives and for childrearing. Another requirement would be that parents make a commitment to care for their children and to refrain from abusing or neglecting them.

We need a multilevel approach to families that expresses society's respect for parenting as an important social role and that articulates society's expectation that parents will be competent. For those who are not, financial aid, educational programs, social services, and, when necessary, relief from the responsibilities of parenting are required.

Rather than only focusing our limited resources on trying to repair damaged children and adults, as we do now, a more effective approach would be to increase the general level of competent parenting and positively affect generations to come. Tragically, many of our existing interventions perpetuate and aggravate the very social problems they are intended to alleviate.

In chapter 12, I identify the significant barriers that stand in the way of developing a national policy that supports competent parenting. Those barriers immediately surface whenever concrete action to protect children is suggested, such as licensing of parents. Those barriers can be regarded as insurmountable obstacles, or they can be seen as hurdles to be taken into account in designing and implementing licensing procedures.

The concluding chapter is devoted to a vision for the future. As it now stands, the future holds the demise of public education in a two-class society, the further deterioration of public safety, and the loss of economic productivity. This dire outlook could be reversed if we honored each child's right to competent parenting and each child's right to be protected from incompetent parenting. We could do this by pursuing our cultural objectives that support the development of self-fulfilling parent–child affectionate attachment bonds that, in turn, undergird the capacities of adults to engage in self-fulfilling and productive teamwork. In contrast with societies that depend upon duty to others as the basis for cooperation, America could set forth preparing children for self-fulfilling lives as the motive for the global cooperation required for the survival of humankind.

Chapter 1

The Eroding Quality of Life in the United States

High rates of violent juvenile crime, school failure, and adolescent childbearing add up to an enormous public burden, as well as widespread private pain. Our common stake in preventing these damaging outcomes of adolescence is immense. We all pay to support the unproductive and incarcerate the violent. We are all economically weakened by lost productivity. We all live with fear of crime in our homes and on the streets. We all are diminished when large numbers of parents are incapable of nurturing their dependent young, and when pervasive alienation erodes the national sense of community.

—LISBETH AND DANIEL SCHORR, *Within Our Reach*, 1988[1]

What is happening to our country? Why has our unprecedented material wealth not given us emotional or physical security?

Our young people may well assume that streets and schools inevitably are dangerous places. Yet I can remember walking at night from Washington Square to Central Park in New York City in the 1940s with no fear for my safety. Prior to the 1980s there was no reason to install a security system in my home in Madison, Wisconsin. Now, even in that Midwestern town, drive-by shootings endanger people during the day.

Violent crime and welfare dependency attract our attention, but it is evident to me that the present magnitude of these social problems results from the erosion of the quality of our children's lives in recent decades. In 1989, the growing problems of both our affluent and poor children led President George Bush and Congress to appoint the National Commission on Children to investigate their causes. The Commission's report in 1991 emphatically declared that the United States has neglected the welfare of its children.[2] The consequences of neglecting our children are evident now in the violence of young people and in the decline of the competence and productivity of adults in our nation.

The neglect of children has been seen in past societies, as when children were devalued in the later days of the Roman Empire.[3] During the rise of Rome, children were valued and became productive adult citizens. With the later affluence of Rome and consequent hedonism, children were seen as burdensome and less desirable. Childlessness became an enviable state, so that abortion, abandonment, and infanticide were common when unwanted children were conceived. The parenting and education of children also were neglected. As a result, the failure to prepare the next generation for the responsibilities of citizenship contributed significantly to the fall of Rome.

There are obvious differences between the Roman Empire and the United States. The link between a society's lack of concern for child-rearing and its future demise, however, cannot be dismissed. As in ancient Rome, there is mounting evidence that children of all social classes are not faring well in the United States. The Carnegie Corporation of New York reported in 1994 that millions of infants and toddlers are so deprived of loving supervision, intellectual stimulation, and medical care that their growth into healthy and responsible adults is threatened. David Hamburg, President of the Corporation, pointed out that, although every form of childhood damage is far more prevalent among the poor, adequate income and high social status do not guarantee the healthy development of children in the United States.[4] Alcohol and drug abuse, preventable accidents, child abuse and neglect, and a host of health problems as well as educational deficiencies are plentiful in middle-class and privileged populations as well as among the disadvantaged. Many affluent parents provide their children with material things but neglect their character development.[5] The author James Michener has described the failure of excessively lenient and indulgent contemporary parents to teach their children self-discipline, in part because they want their children to have more material things than they did. As they grow older these children lack the motivation to work. They are preoccupied with self-gratification, lack civility, and regard gifts as entitlements. The frustrations these children pose for their parents were revealed in the following anecdote reported in *Newsweek*:

> Marcia and David Smith have three children, ages 19 to 25, and are wondering when they will grow up. Though the younger two come and go, all three consider their parents' lavish house their own. Each child's bedroom is equipped with a stereo and TV.
>
> "Our kids were spoiled rotten," Marcia admits. For example, last summer his parents promised 19-year-old Brian a Jeep—if he got a job. But Brian just "fooled around," his mother complains, and now he is upset because they won't give him a car.
>
> Shelley, 22, like her brother, has never had to work except for pocket money. The Smiths hit the roof when her recent college bill included hundreds of dollars in parking tickets on her Mustang convertible. "She's so used to having us pay for everything, she has absolutely no sense of values," her mother says.
>
> But the real problem is Craig, the oldest child, who started a limousine business from the home with a loan from his parents. His parents have given him until the year's end to move out and have even offered him the money to buy a house. But Craig refuses to budge. He pays no rent, and his clothes are laundered by the family maid. "I grew up here," he argues, "you are trying to throw me out of my own house."*

Alongside these problems posed by the offspring of affluent parents (for whom it may be difficult to generate much sympathy) are other children who have become literal American "untouchables"— homeless children. Some do not attend school, and those who do are likely to be so tired and hungry that they cannot concentrate on schoolwork. Because of their shabby clothing and poor hygiene, many of them are shunned by their peers.

This situation is not limited to the homeless or to children in urban ghettos, as revealed in the comments of an elementary school teacher in comparatively affluent Madison, Wisconsin:[6]

---

*Reprinted from *Newsweek: The Family in the 21st Century*, Winter/Spring 1990. Copyright 1990, Newsweek, Inc. All rights reserved. Reprinted by permission.

Many children in Madison do not come to school ready to learn. They come hungry, so we provide free or reduced-price breakfasts and lunches. They come without hats, mittens, boots, or warm coats, so the staff donates these items. Their homes lack blankets, books, furniture, toys, school supplies, so we ask for help from others in providing these items. They come physically and mentally abused and neglected, so we provide counseling, a safe haven, and teach protective behaviors about alcohol and other drugs to help them make better choices.

There is no one responsible at home to get them up in the morning, so we assign buddies in their apartment complexes to knock on their doors and get them up in time for school. Or we purchase alarm clocks for them and instruct elementary students on how to get themselves up in time to catch a bus. If they miss the bus, we pick them up to show how important it is to be in school every day.

They come tired, because no one sets down rules at home for times to go to bed. Or no one is home at night to see that they get to bed at a reasonable hour.

We have students who cannot focus on what is happening in the classroom, because their minds flash back to violence they've witnessed in their homes and neighborhoods. Others come with no respect for authority, their parents, their classmates, or themselves, so we try to develop a school climate that fosters respect for others, self-esteem, and discipline.*

The social context these anecdotes reflect is seen at a more general level throughout the United States, where the comfort and safety of everyone is threatened by widespread crime and the abduction of children. This is vividly illustrated by the following experience of Peter Sipchen, a freelance writer living in Missouri:[7]

If the western part of St. Louis County, Missouri, is typical of most fashionable, middle class suburbs, then it is clear that today's American suburbanites are frightened of strangers.

I made this sad discovery recently, when I decided to get some exercise delivering telephone directories. I anticipated cheerful chatting with housewives, laughing with kids, and generally get-

---

*Reprinted with permission from the *Wisconsin State Journal*, February 25, 1990. Copyright 1990 by the Wisconsin State Journal.

ting to know my fellow citizens. Instead, the job turned out to be an experience in alienation I will not soon forget.

The first hints I got that I was not going to be overwhelmed with hospitality were the small but authoritative orange and black signs on nearly every street corner proclaiming, NEIGHBOR-HOOD WATCH PROGRAM IN FORCE. WE IMMEDIATELY REPORT ALL SUSPICIOUS PERSONS AND ACTIVITIES TO THE POLICE DEPARTMENT.

Scarcely ten minutes into my first route, a squad car rolled slowly past me, while the officer at the wheel grilled me with his stare. I waved tentatively, puzzled that the sight of a well-dressed man pulling telephone books from the trunk of a nice-looking car could have spooked someone into calling the militia. The same thing happened six more times in the course of eight routes.

Particularly disappointing was the maximum security atmo-sphere surrounding the children. I often spotted groups of kids in the distance, playing contentedly on the sidewalks and driveways. But almost invariably before I could work my way to their prop-erty line, an obviously nervous mother would herd them inside until I had made my delivery and moved on. I might as well have been hauling nitroglycerin.

The most depressing aspect was the genuine apprehension on the faces of the people when I got to see their faces at all. Many times I would scan a row of homes only to catch a fleeting glimpse of shadowy forms disappearing behind the curtains from which they had been peeping.*

This vignette highlights the fears that many people harbor about their personal safety. As a result, we must teach our children to avoid the many dangers to which they are exposed. They are told to be suspicious of strangers and, now with the focus on sexual abuse, to be suspicious of even their own relatives. Many children are compelled to share apartments with their parents' abusive, drug-selling friends; many more children fear the streets of their own neighborhoods; and most children must be careful in their own school buildings. Because they live in dangerous environments, a generation of children is growing up in fear.

---

*Reprinted with permission from *U.S. News and World Report*, July 11, 1988. Copyright 1988 by Peter Sipchen and U.S. News and World Report.

The Decline of Education, Health, Safety, and the Economy

The inescapable fact is that increasing numbers of children are growing up in this country under circumstances that prevent them from becoming competent citizens because they lack the abilities and the opportunities to learn essential social and work-related skills. A critical number of them swell the ranks of the criminal and the welfare-dependent segments of the population. They become burdens for our society and the sources of our fears.

Even though our children live in the wealthiest nation in the world, they no longer have the highest quality of life. In recent decades their education, health, safety, and economic status have been insidiously eroded through periods of both economic prosperity and recession. The threat they pose to our society has grown through both good and bad economic times.

In 1979, I reviewed the available evidence and found that 16 percent of our children had significant physical, developmental, mental, educational, and social handicaps.[8] Even more striking was the fact that at that time 37 percent of the nation's children were thought to be at risk for maladjustment in later life. The intervening years have borne out that forecast.

The indicators of the well-being of children monitored by the U.S. Department of Education show that there is a glaring disparity between the material welfare of advantaged and disadvantaged children and youth in the United States.[9] But both the advantaged and the disadvantaged pose social problems.

Both affluent and disadvantaged children show evidence of the "syndrome of alienation" described by Urie Bronfenbrenner, a developmental psychologist who has studied our society.[10] The key elements of this syndrome are the lack of attentiveness and misbehavior in school; academic underachievement; smoking and drinking; sexual promiscuity; alcohol and substance abuse; dropping out of school; and ultimately vandalism, violence, crime, suicide, and welfare dependency. The gravity of the situation can be seen by comparing the greatest disciplinary problems rated by public school teachers in 1940 and in 1990. In 1940 they were: talking out of turn, chewing gum, making noise, running in the halls, cutting in line, dress-code violations, and littering. In 1990 they were drug and alcohol abuse, pregnancy, suicide, rape, robbery, and assault.

The quality of life of minority groups has been particularly adversely affected. The Business–Higher Education Forum, composed of corporate and university leaders, reported that the upper third of minority group members have become members of the middle class.[11] The middle third, however, have such limited skills and education that they are only surviving at a marginal level. The lowest third are trapped in an underclass plagued by disorganized families, drug abuse, and crime.

Education

If we look at the money spent on education and the educational level of citizens in the United States, our nation should be doing well.[12] We spend more money on education in proportion to our manufacturing productivity than either Japan or Germany. Since the 1970s the high school dropout rate has dropped from 26 to 15 percent, and the percentage of the population completing college has risen from 11 to 23 percent. From these figures it would appear that the United States is better educated and more literate than at any time in our history.

If we look at how well our educational system is preparing adults for the modern society in which we live, however, a different picture emerges.[13] A study by the Southport Institute of Policy Analysis in Washington, DC, revealed that 40 percent of the nation's small-business workers now are deficient in basic skills. The U.S. Department of Labor's Commission on Achieving Necessary Skills found that more than one-half of our young people leave school without the knowledge and skills required to find and hold more than unskilled employment.

In 1900 nine out of ten youngsters did not graduate from high school, but there was no perceived dropout problem because education was not necessary to find employment. At mid-century, when as many dropped out as graduated, there still was no expression of public concern. Today the impact of an inadequate education can be devastating because of the increasing complexity of available jobs. It will be more so in the next century.

In 1991 the U.S. Census Bureau found that more than one-third of high school age Americans were behind grade level in achievement or had dropped out of school entirely.[14] The U.S. Department of Education reported in 1992 that a quarter of high school seniors and nearly a third of eighth graders were not able to understand grade level material in general. Nearly 40 percent of the students tested on the 1992 National Assessment of Educational Progress failed to reach basic proficiency levels in mathematics, and only 11 percent of 13-year-olds were adept readers. At the present time at least 2 million adults are estimated to be totally illiterate and 30 million to be only marginally literate. The consequences of these kinds of deficiencies are virtually unemployable adults who reduce the nation's productivity.

Children in the United States do not compare well with children in other nations in academic achievement.[15] In 1991 students in the United States were fourteenth behind South Korea, Hungary, Slovenia, Spain, and other nations in science achievement. They were behind Canada, Spain, the United Kingdom, and Ireland in mathematics achievement. A carefully conducted study found that American children lagged behind Chinese and Japanese children in mathematics achievement, and that parental expectations were lower for American students than for the Chinese and Japanese students.

Many high school graduates in the United States are not prepared for college courses.[16] During the 1980s a number of national and international achievement surveys reviewed by the Educational Testing Service of Princeton, New Jersey, warned that something was seriously wrong with our elementary and secondary schools. In 1987 the U.S. Department of Education reported that the Scholastic Aptitude Score averages for college-bound high school seniors were lower than in 1952; in 1992 they were even lower than in 1987. In 1991, 17 percent of all freshmen who entered the University of Wisconsin system needed remedial mathematics courses, and 9 percent needed basic remedial English courses.

Minority groups are particularly educationally disadvantaged.[17] Although African Americans and Hispanics are moving upward into the middle class at unprecedented rates, 26 percent of the Caucasian, 39 percent of the African American, and 44 percent of the Hispanic children in the United States are still more than one grade level behind in school and will be ill-prepared as adults for the labor force. The

Educational Testing Service found that 27 percent of Caucasian, 63 percent of Hispanic, and 77 percent of African American young adults were unable to balance a checkbook or to read a map.

If, as all of these signs indicate, the effectiveness of schools in this nation continues to decline, we will fall behind increasingly in international competition as our society becomes more deeply divided between those who are well educated and those who are not.

Health

Although the quality of health care generally has risen in the United States, the lack of access to health care and the increase in self-induced illnesses and avoidable injuries have jeopardized the health of at least one in four of our children and youth.

The poor health of American children is such a significant problem in the United States that the American Academy of Pediatrics, the American Medical Association, the Congressional Office of Technology Assessment, the Carnegie Council on Adolescent Development, and the Children's Defense Fund all call for immediate action.[18] These organizations note that one-quarter of all adolescents are engaged in behaviors that clearly are harmful to themselves and to others, such as school failure, substance abuse, and unprotected sexual intercourse. Even more strikingly, the National Center for Educational Statistics of the U.S. Department of Education estimates that only one-half of the adolescent population is growing up in a basically healthy manner.

Hunger has grown in the United States since the 1980s, so that in 1991 one in five American children experienced sustained hunger, according to the Tufts University Center on Hunger, Poverty, and Nutrition Policy.[19]

The health problems of the young are evident at the beginning of life.[20] In 1989 the United States lagged behind twenty-three other countries in decreasing their infant mortality rates. Actually, since 1965 the United States has reduced its infant mortality rate. This progress had slowed to a standstill until a recent rise, while other countries have managed to steadily decrease their infant mortality rates. More specifically, infant mortality rates vary widely by race in the United States. In

1990 the death rate for Caucasian babies was 7.7 per 1000 live births, while for African American babies it was over twice as high with 17 deaths for every 1000 births.

The National Commission to Prevent Infant Mortality questions whether government health programs alone can significantly reduce infant mortality rates that are due largely to the low birth weight of babies unless behavioral changes are made by girls and women who use drugs, drink excessively, smoke, and engage in other forms of high-risk behaviors during their pregnancies.[21] In fact illegitimacy and heavy cigarette smoking are more strongly correlated with infant mortality than is poverty. Furthermore, the crack cocaine epidemic threatens an estimated 100,000 infants each year, and the rates of congenital syphilis in babies are at their highest levels in decades.

Sexually transmitted diseases are at an epidemic level among adolescents.[22] In spite of awareness of the consequences, one-third of low-risk and almost two-thirds of high-risk sexually active teenagers do not use contraceptives. Consequently, one in four teenagers becomes infected with a sexually transmitted disease before graduating from high school. Since the beginning of the Acquired Immune Deficiency Syndrome (AIDS) epidemic, more than 5,000 children and young adults have died. In 1991 9,000 AIDS cases were diagnosed in persons under the age of twenty-four, and in many communities AIDS is the leading cause of death among young adults, with an average medical cost of $119,000 for each person. At this rate, by the year 2000, 80,000 children and adolescents will be orphaned by parental death from AIDS.

Adolescent alcohol and drug use has fluctuated in recent years and varies between areas in the United States.[23] According to a study commissioned by the American Medical Association, up to 15 percent of high school youth heavily abuse alcohol and illegal drugs. Experimentation with drugs and alcohol is occurring at earlier ages in elementary schools. In 1993 a University of Michigan study reported an increase in marijuana, LSD, and cocaine use by eighth graders, reversing the trend toward decreased usage of those drugs by twelfth graders during the same year.

Although obscured by the obvious scourges of AIDS and crack in public awareness, alcohol is a far more deadly killer and maimer of adolescents.[24] The National Research Council of the Institute of Medicine determined that motor vehicle accidents are responsible for almost

40 percent of the deaths between the ages of fifteen through twenty-four. According to the National Highway Traffic Safety Administration, one-half of these accidents involve a drunken driver, who is five times more likely to be a male than a female. Compared to those who begin to abuse alcohol after the age of twenty, teenage alcoholics also are much more likely to be depressed, to attempt suicide, and to commit violent crimes.

Mental disorders afflict more then 12 percent of our children and adolescents—7.5 million young Americans.[25] Yet the National Advisory Mental Health Council has pointed out that less than one-fifth receive treatment, and many of those treated fail to recover because their disorders are not adequately understood. A U.S. Centers for Disease Control survey found that 27 percent of high school students thought seriously about killing themselves during the preceding year. Over the last twenty years, suicides have tripled among ten- to fourteen-year-olds and doubled among fifteen- to nineteen-year-olds.

The U.S. Centers for Disease Control reported a seventeen-fold increase in measles cases from 1983 to 1990 with a three times greater incidence for African American and Hispanic than for Caucasian children.[26] Although measles decreased in 1993, whooping cough and tuberculosis are once again on the increase, especially among the homeless, after having virtually disappeared in this country.

Violent injuries and deaths have reached an all-time high among children and youth.[27] Preventable injuries now claim 10,000 lives each year among children to the age of fourteen. Between the ages of ten and fourteen 21 percent of the deaths are because of gun accidents, suicide, and homicide. Homicide has become the leading cause of death among African American adolescents and young adults.

The health of adults is declining in the United States.[28] While Americans generally are living longer lives, there are islands of illnesses, epidemics, and premature deaths in inner cities and in certain rural areas. Although we led other nations in the drop in death rates in the earlier part of this century, we have begun to slip in recent decades. Our life expectancy now trails that of eighteen other nations. In 1988 the life expectancy of African American infant boys decreased by half a year from the peak recorded in 1984.

Although mortality from heart disease is declining in the United States, the prevalence of heart disease is increasing.[29] The frequency of hospitalization and limitations due to disabilities, particularly among children, is increasing. And the homeless mentally ill lack both places to live and medical care.

Most significantly, the majority of deaths in the United States are from preventable illnesses related to smoking, unhealthful diets, poor physical fitness, and stressful working conditions.[30] Although the prevalence of cigarette smoking has been decreasing, obesity, alcohol consumption, and lack of sleep have been increasing.

Their dramatic rise in number has made handgun injuries and deaths a major public health issue.[31] In this time of concern about reducing medical costs, the annual medical costs of gun injuries have risen to more than $4 billion. The average medical cost is over $340,000 for each person wounded by gunfire.

The health of children in the United States has been declining rather than improving. At the same time, most of the serious health problems of adults are preventable and are related to self-defeating habits most likely learned during childhood.

Safety

Although in the past people could walk the streets of large cities of the United States at night without fear, that no longer is possible. Public safety has sunk to intolerable levels as violence rules even during the day time in many urban areas.[32] Calling attention to this situation in 1991, the Senate Judiciary Committee declared that the United States is the most consistently violent nation on Earth.

In some communities law-enforcement institutions are unable to maintain order so that gangs with firepower never before imagined rule the streets. During 1992 there were 2000 murders in New York City alone.[33] Throughout the nation one in four households has been touched by property or personal violence crimes.

The gravity of the situation can be brought home by considering your risk of being a victim of a crime. Your risk is:[34]

Aggravated assault and rape: 1 in 300 a year (1 in 4 in your lifetime)
Robbery: 1 in 500 a year (1 in 7 in your lifetime)
Murder: 1 in 10,000 a year (1 in 142 in your lifetime)

At this rate, only one out of six persons will escape being the victim of a major crime. The chances today of being an innocent victim enormously outweigh the chances of being a falsely convicted, innocent person.

The erosion of public safety in the United States is illustrated by the increases in major offenses between 1965 and 1991.[35] There was a 289 percent increase in robberies, a 320 percent increase in rapes, a 125 percent increase in murders, a 100 percent increase in burglaries, and a 290 percent increase in aggravated assaults. The overall rate of violent acts in the United States increased fivefold from 3.9 in 1971 to 18.5 per 1000 people in 1991. Many of these increases are in juvenile crime.

Estimating the segment of the population that is actively involved in committing all of these criminal offenses is difficult because statistics are available only for those who are apprehended and convicted.[36] Those persons convicted constitute approximately 2 percent of the population. If the number of arrests are included, the total known segment of the population involved in crime is 4.8 percent. In this light about 5 percent of the population appears to be responsible for the deterioration in the safety of the entire nation. As we will see in chapter 5, the greatest threat to society comes from an even smaller, 0.2 percent of the population composed of habitual criminals.

The widespread availability of handguns in the United States has resulted in the highest homicide rate in the world.[37] In 1991 the homicide rate for all ages in the United States was 9.8 per 100,000 compared to 1 in Japan, 2.7 in Switzerland, 3 in England and Wales, and 7.2 in Northern Ireland. The U.S. homicide rate for males between fifteen and twenty-four years of age of 22 per 100,000 contrasts dramatically with the 1 to 3 per 100,000 rate in comparable countries.

The availability of guns is responsible for the increasing numbers of children who are killed while playing with guns and in mass shootings.[38] In 1993 each day fifteen young people under the age of nineteen were killed by guns. For every death an estimated 100 are wounded. Unprecedented numbers of teenagers deliberately gun down their peers. According to the U.S. Centers for Disease Control, the number of youths killed by guns doubled between 1984 and 1990. Juvenile arrests for murder increased by 85 percent between 1987 and 1991. In addition the presence of firearms in homes increases the risk of consummated suicide among teenagers.

Even schools are unsafe, necessitating the Gun-Free School Zones Act of 1990 that made it a federal crime to possess a firearm within the vicinity of a school.[39] According to the National Crime Survey, almost 3 million crimes occur on or near school campuses every year, one every six seconds. As a result, one-fourth of all major urban high schools have metal detectors. A survey of high school youth in Seattle revealed that 34 percent of the students had easy access to handguns, and 6 percent reported owning them and carrying them to school. One-third of those who owned handguns said that they had fired them at someone. A U.S. Centers for Disease Control survey found that 20 percent of U.S. high school students said that they had carried a gun, knife, or other kind of weapon at least once during the preceding month for protection or because they might need it in a fight.

All of this makes it clear that the assertion "guns do not kill people, people do (or guns do not kill children, children do)" should be replaced with the factual statement that "people without guns *injure*; people with guns *kill*."[40]

Another indicator of the extent of violence in the United States is domestic violence that affects 1 in 4 American families.[41] At least 20 percent of women have experienced sexual abuse during their lifetimes. At the same time the safety of children in their own homes has been jeopardized increasingly by the volume of homeless, AIDS, and crack cocaine cases that overwhelm child welfare services nationwide so that their abilities to investigate domestic complaints and provide services are severely limited. The reported cases of child abuse and neglect reached 2.9 million in 1992, leading the United States Advisory Board on Child Abuse and Neglect to conclude that child abuse and neglect is a national emergency.

In 1989 the U.S. House of Representatives Select Committee on Children, Youth and Families pointed out that federal funding for children's services, especially those designed to keep children in their homes, had not kept pace with the need.[42] As a result social workers throughout the nation cannot keep up with huge caseloads, and children are placed on waiting lists rather than provided with services. In urban areas the situation is even worse:

> In the summer of 1989 the backlog of child-endangerment cases numbered 771 in Washington, DC. One social worker revealed that

tragedy is not defined in terms of failure to thrive but whether the child is either maimed or dead. Another social worker in Maryland described a six-year-old boy who begged his teachers to not have to go back to his home, which was a known crack house, but received no attention, because there were twenty similar cases, and the social worker could not take the time to investigate unless there was "imminent danger."

In 1990 the Inter-Agency Council on Child Abuse and Neglect of Los Angeles County described the efforts by overwhelmed social services to help abused and neglected children as "shoveling quicksand." In 1989 one child a week was murdered in Los Angeles County by a parent or caretaker, more than 2,400 babies were born addicted to drugs, and at least 1,800 children were found to have been sexually abused.*

The House Select Committee on Children, Youth, and Families estimated that the number of children placed in foster care, juvenile detention centers, and mental health facilities had grown to nearly 500,000 and at that rate will exceed 800,000 by 1995. In its survey of eleven states with large populations, the number of children in foster care dropped by 9 percent between 1980 and 1985. That number rose 23 percent between 1985 and 1988 while federal funding for child-welfare services aimed at keeping children in their homes rose only 7 percent.

The House Committee further reported that the number of children in public and private juvenile detention centers increased 27 percent from 1979 to 1987, as funding under the Juvenile Justice and Delinquency Prevention Act was cut from $100 million in 1979 to $66.7 million in 1989. The number of children in mental health facilities also increased by 60 percent between 1983 and 1986. Similar trends persist to the present time.

All of these statistics reveal that the most fundamental function of our society to protect its citizens from violent injuries and death has broken down. When law and order disappear, communities are unsafe for children and their parents. Then families become the sources of violence and, in turn, contribute to community violence and disorder.

---

*Reprinted with permission from the *Los Angeles Times*, November 14, 1990. Copyright 1990 by the Los Angeles Times.

The Economy

In addition to these specific indicators that education, health, and safety in the United States have eroded, both children and adults have been affected adversely by the state of the economy. Over the past decade the standard of living has not increased for most families, and for many it actually has declined.

In 1992 the World Competitiveness Report placed the United States fifth in the world in economic competitiveness behind Japan, Germany, Switzerland, and Denmark.[43] Although still leading in the total amount of productivity, the United States lags behind Japan and Germany in its productivity growth rate.

The standard of living in the United States also has been losing ground.[44] The recent low inflation rate is a positive economic indicator. But as the economist Frank Levy points out, in order to maintain the same standard of living family incomes should increase at least with the rate of inflation. This would mean that workers in their forties should be earning 25 to 50 percent more today than a decade ago. In fact they earned little more in 1987 than in 1973, and average hourly earnings actually declined. According to Levy's calculations, the median income for young families with children decreased by 26 percent during that time period.

American families are falling into two extremes with female-headed families on the one hand and two-paycheck families on the other.[45] The middle class is shrinking while the upper and lower classes are growing. This class disparity has grave implications for the future, because one-quarter of the nation's children live in the poorest one-fifth of our nation's families, and some 150,000 children are homeless.

Most American parents find themselves at a financial disadvantage in comparison with adults without children.[46] The Rockford Institute noted that the principle of the "family wage" that guided public policy until recent decades no longer receives much attention. Whereas in the past a single wage earner could maintain an average family, now two wage earners are required, partly because of higher material aspirations, but mostly because wages have not kept up with inflation. Now even two-income families are at the level of the "working poor."

Ironically, Americans are working harder and enjoying life less. The author Juliet Schor documented the fact that Americans generally are overworked, absorbing an additional month of workplace and household work hours in their schedules between 1969 and 1987.[47] The result has been a sharp reduction in leisure time for family and community activities. A Roper survey found that the vast majority of parents report that they do not have enough time to spend with their children. Even the living space for families has decreased across the nation.[48] The average home in the United States now is 1200 square feet in size compared to 1500 square feet a decade ago. Moreover, according to the U.S. Census Bureau, 57 percent of all households are unable to afford to buy a house with a conventional mortgage.

Since 1980 living stipends paid to welfare families with children have dropped to 35 percent below the 1970 level when adjusted for inflation.[49] Since 1980 nearly half a million families have lost all welfare payments. About a million people have been cut off from food stamps. The Women, Infants, and Children Budget, which provides emergency nutrition supplements to low-income babies, young children, and pregnant women, is woefully inadequate and does not reach half of the eligible women and children.

Another repercussion of the financial pressures felt by families and confirmed by the U.S. Department of Labor is the rise in the exploitation of juvenile labor.[50] Many students work beyond the legal limits, fall asleep in classes, skip school, and miss extracurricular school activities.

The economist William J. Baumol and the U.S. Department of Labor's Commission on Achieving Necessary Skills point out that the educational and work skill deficiencies of the young will affect the entire nation adversely if thought, planning, and resources are not deployed to effectively deal with them soon.[51] Consequently, economists are beginning to recognize that economic policies must take into account intergenerational equity so that present decisions will not compromise the lives of future generations and will take into account the real costs of resource depletion and of environmental pollution.

WHY HAVE WE NOT "DRAWN THE LINE"?

All of these adverse educational, health, welfare, and economic conditions that affect children are evident to anyone who does not have an ulterior motive to deny or minimize them. The damage to individuals and to our society has far exceeded the acceptable limits of risk and diversity inherent in a democratic republic. The question is, why have we not "drawn the line" on these intolerable conditions? The journalist Vance Packard addressed this question in 1983.[52] After reviewing the evidence, he described children as endangered in the United States and asked why no action was being taken to reverse the situation. He concluded that the decreasing representation of children in public affairs was a major factor. As more and more households include no children at all, there will be proportionately fewer voters with any direct stake in children. This trend was evident in 1991 when only 34 percent of the households in the United States included children under the age of eighteen, a decrease of 11 percent over the last two decades.

At the same time childbirth is being controlled routinely through the use of contraceptives, sterilization, and abortion. Motherhood and fatherhood have been downgraded as valued careers. Children often are seen as detracting from personal fulfillment, as economic burdens, as impediments to marital happiness, and as undesirable in many housing developments and apartments. The focus has been on where to put children rather than on their developmental needs.

Unless corrective action is taken, all of the negative indicators for children will likely increase because of the growing number of children at risk for living in poverty; at risk for failing in school and dropping out; at risk for having babies as teenagers; at risk for being unemployed in the future; and at risk for perpetuating a cycle of deprivation with the concomitant social problems of crime and welfare dependency.

A small fraction of the population has reduced public safety for adults and children to intolerable levels of danger, and a larger fraction has sapped the economic productivity of the nation. At it now stands, the dangerous and the dependent segments of the population will increase in numbers to further drain public funds and decrease the productivity of our workforce.

As will become evident in the pages of this book, there is a definite connection between our social problems and the damage caused to children by their parents. Because we lack definitive data on the consequences of milder degrees of parental damage to children, this book will deal with the most glaring examples that have been extensively documented.

The way children are parented plays a vital role in the quality of all of our lives. We no longer can afford to avoid defining and confronting incompetent parenting.

Chapter 2

The Proximate Cause: Incompetent Parenting

No other crisis—a flood, a health epidemic, a garbage strike or even snow removal—would be as calmly accepted without full-scale emergency intervention.
—Carnegie Foundation for the Advancement of Teaching, 1988[1]

The way that we think about our social problems differs depending upon our perspectives. Those of us who deal with statistics are guided by what we see on paper. Those of us who deal with people are guided by what we see in human behavior. We need both perspectives, but I am impressed by the way political biases readily influence the interpretation of data. Those biases melt way when we actually work with the people reflected in those statistics.

Sociologists and politicians are accustomed to attributing the major social problems of crime and welfare dependency to societal and environmental causes. While these factors are important, they are susceptible to political interpretations and are at least one step removed from the actual life situations of children in which the foundations of crime and welfare dependency are laid.

Societal and environmental influences are largely transmitted or not transmitted to children in homes and neighborhoods through parent–child relationships. For this compelling reason, the proximate causes of the behaviors of children and adults who become habitual criminals and welfare dependent lie in the parenting of our children. This means that our society has a stake in the way in which children are parented and in the neighborhoods in which they live. Parenting is more than a private, personal matter. It is a vital social role. More significantly, of all the factors that contribute to our social problems, parenting is the most susceptible to remediation, as suggested in chapter 11.

The importance of parenting to society can be demonstrated both in the social benefits of "competent" parenting and in the social costs of "incompetent" parenting. These benefits and costs make defining competent and incompetent parenting a critical public issue.

In a broader sense, questions about what constitutes competent parenting have beco..1e more than academic because of the wide variety of childrearing styles in the United States today. The dramatic social, demographic, and economic changes of the past two decades have fundamentally altered the roles and relationships between many parents and their children, as well as the routines of their daily lives.

Unfortunately, any effort made to define competent parenting can be easily misunderstood. In order to minimize misunderstanding, I will summarize current thinking about parenting.

DEFINING COMPETENT PARENTING

Because we fall short of our ideal images of what we ought to be, most of us who are parents harbor doubts about our own competence. Our initial reaction to even the mention of competent parenting might well be to define ourselves as incompetent. This mistaken impression results in a general reluctance to deal with the question of parental competence, since to do so might adversely judge most parents. This reaction is completely unjustified because the vast majority of parents are competent.

The terms competent and incompetent do imply a spectrum with "super" parents at one end and total failures at the other end, but that is not my intent. As defined in this book, competent parents are simply people who show through their behavior that they care about what happens to their children and who can restrain themselves from seriously harming them. Competent parents are those who do not abuse or neglect their children in a legal sense.

In stark contrast, incompetent parents are "unfit" parents in legal terms. They cannot control their own impulses and either neglect or tyrannize their children. They are unable to manage their own lives, much less the lives of children. Most of them minimize or deny their incompetence. Even with support and treatment, some of them are unable to change in time to become competent parents for their own children.

Just as there are essential dietary elements for physical growth—vitamins, minerals, and proteins—there are essential experiences for the healthy personality development of children. Competent parenting provides those experiences. The way we conceive of those parenting experiences is determined by the way we regard childhood. If we regard children as objects to be shaped by the latest technology, we look to science for guidance in childrearing techniques. On the other hand, if we regard children as the bearers of our culture, we look to cultural values to guide childrearing.

Our present uncertainty regarding childrearing results from a reliance on science and technology instead of on our culture for childrearing aims and methods. Yet it makes no more sense to base parenting on the latest experimental findings than it does to guide our adult lives by them. We can use science and technology to enhance aspects of our lives but not to provide meaning and purpose for our lives.

Fortunately, the pluralistic American culture is a rich source of beliefs about the meaning and purpose of life. When we identify the values and aims shared by the variety of subcultures in the United States, we find that all but a few antisocial subcultures agree that children need a dependable, nurturing environment in early life with a few competent adults with whom the children can identify.[2] There also is little disagreement that the overall objective of childrearing in the United States is the development of each individual's potential to function competently within our evolving, democratic society.

The basic skills we need to competently function in our society include the abilities to learn, to relate to others, and to initiate self-expressive activities. In order to satisfy our desires in an acceptable way in our society, we must develop the abilities to delay gratifying immediate urges, to tolerate frustration, and to work. We also need to adhere to generally accepted values that restrain us from harming others.

Children acquire these skills and values essential for life in our society through the influence of parents who possess those qualities. This does not mean that competent parents are socially conforming persons who raise conforming children who become conforming adults. Our democratic society depends upon parents who initiate changes as well. Our way of life depends upon diversity in opinions and in life styles.

DEFINING INCOMPETENT PARENTING

The quality of parenting a child receives can be compromised, if not overridden, by extremely strong inborn vulnerabilities of the child and by socioeconomic factors. There are also a few "invulnerable" children who seem to survive adversity in their families and in their environmental conditions. But there are certain irreducible aspects of parenting that are needed even by those "invulnerable" children. Incompetent parents do not, and possibly cannot, provide these influences.

Fundamental to competent parenting are the abilities to tolerate frustration and to postpone gratifying immediate urges. Conversely, incompetent parents are incapable of tolerating frustration and of postponing gratification. They are unable to handle responsibility for their own lives, much less for their children's lives. They do not restrain themselves from harming their children. Their incompetence as parents can be the result of immaturity, personality defects, or mental disorders.

Because incompetent parents have difficulty controlling their own impulses, they are vulnerable to substance abuse and alcoholism. They are insensitive to the needs of other people and are unreliable. Therefore, they do not form dependable affectionate attachment bonds with their children. Without the support of spouses, kin, and neighbors, these parents simply are not equipped to meet the demanding tasks of managing their children on a day-to-day basis.

Incompetent parents mishandle the routine behaviors of children. They alternately neglect or overreact to their children's behavior with unpredictable and inconsistent sequences of indifference, idle threats, and severe punishment. They have neither the skills nor the knowledge to balance affection and limit setting in childrearing. Their children's erratic behaviors aggravate their inconsistent childrearing practices. In response to one disappointment after another in childrearing, these parents often coercively abuse and neglect their children, who are confused when what happens to them seems to bear little relationship to what they do. As a result their children's behavior becomes unpredictable, and their children lack sensitivity to the needs of other people. They then become adults who do not know how to control their impulses and who do not care about the effects of their behavior on other people.

The signs of incompetent parenting are inadequate food, clothing, and shelter for the children; the lack of affectionate bonding between parents and their children; the grossly unpredictable and inconsistent reactions of the parents to their children's behavior; and the lack of parental involvement in the lives of their children in their communities.[3] Parental incompetence is indicated by the presence of a substantial number of the following criteria regarding a particular child:

1. *Clothing*: Insufficient to protect from weather.
2. *Hygiene and cleanliness*: Presence of diseases because of inadequate sanitation and bathing.
3. *Health care*: Inadequate routine health and dental care and failure to attend to emergencies.
4. *Nutrition*: Inadequate physical growth or disease due to insufficient nutrition.
5. *Shelter*: Insufficient heating, bedding, and provision for undisturbed sleep.
6. *Supervision and safety*: Overdoses or ingestions of chemicals and accidents related to inadequate supervision; physical or sexual abuse; exposure to injury or property destruction by others.
7. *Attachment to parent*: Lack of affectionate holding, touching, and talking to child; insensitivity to child's initiatives and reactions; and fearful or indifferent attitude of child toward parent.
8. *Parent's support of child's development*: Parent views child as an object rather than as a person; omits care as a result of misper-

ception, preoccupation, or lack of motivation; is sadistic or excessively critical of child; and fails to appreciate child's cognitive and physical level of development.
9. *Socialization*: Parent models irresponsible, sexually stimulating, violent, or criminal behavior.
10. *Continuity of relationships*: Instability of home location and household composition.

These signs of incompetent parenting do not require subtle techniques or tests to detect. No unbiased person who has access to full information about a particular situation would have difficulty concluding that a particular parent is incompetent.

Actually, the neglect of incompetent parents is more harmful to children than is physical abuse because it deprives the children of the opportunity to develop the social skills they need to become responsible human beings.[4] When children are biologically vulnerable, the development of affectionate attachment bonds between those children and marginally incompetent parents also is unlikely. In contrast children who are abused but not neglected must cope with frightening experiences, but at least they can form attachment bonds and thereby acquire the social skills necessary for competent citizenship.

An example of the damage caused by parental neglect is evident in developmentally delayed infants who show nonorganically caused "failure to thrive."[5] Because of the lack of affectionate attachment bonds with their parents, those infants do not feed properly and suffer from obvious delays in their physical, social, and cognitive development.

The number of incompetent parents can be inferred from the cases of reported child neglect. We have data on the annual rates of child neglect; however, we do not have an accurate estimate of the total number of children in the United States who have been subjected to parental neglect. Although about 60 percent of the 2.9 million annually reported cases of child abuse and neglect are not technically substantiated, it is likely that the true incidence is two to three times higher than the number of substantiated cases, because many cases are unreported and because investigations of allegations often are superficial.[6]

Using only the reports of substantiated cases each year, the incidence of child neglect in 1991 was 556,849 cases, or 53 percent of all substantiated cases of both abuse and neglect. If all of the persons under the age of eighteen in the United States are taken into account, a conservative estimate is that 3.6 million of them have been neglected at some time during their childhoods.[7] This suggests that over 5 percent of the young in the United States have experienced parental neglect.

If we assume two children for each family, there would be some 1.8 million households in which neglect has occurred. When single- and two-parent households are taken into account, 2.7 million parents would be incompetent in this analysis. This means that 4 percent of the parents in the United States have been, or are, incompetent. This breaks down to 8 percent of all single-parent and 3 percent of all two-parent households.

Incompetent parenting seldom occurs without a history of incompetent parenting in that parent's own childhood.[8] The public court record of "Mary," the mother in one of my cases, illustrates an intergenerational pattern of incompetent parenting, the ineffectiveness of services she received, and the resulting damage to her children:

> When Mary was born, her mother was a sixteen-year-old alcoholic. Her mother subsisted on Aid to the Families of Dependent Children and was married and divorced twice before Mary was first brought to the attention of the county department of social services at the age of three because of repeated allegations of parental neglect. Mary and her mother were seen sporadically at a child guidance clinic.
>
> At the age of nine, Mary began to be sexually abused by an older brother, but this was denied by him and her mother. When she was ten, Mary was placed in a special class for the emotionally disturbed. At the age of thirteen, she was brought to juvenile court because of alcohol and substance abuse and a year later placed in a county juvenile home. Her destructive behavior led to subsequent placement in two adolescent treatment centers.
>
> At fifteen, Mary was sent to a state correctional facility and thereafter to a state mental hospital. When released at the age of eighteen, she married, and her first child was born. She subsequently was married and divorced three times. Her second child was born when she was twenty. When her children were four and two years old, a county department of social services intervened and placed the children in foster homes because of abuse and neglect. Mary entered two alcohol and substance abuse treatment centers and did not complete treatment. She was arrested several

times for drinking while driving, once in a near-fatal accident, and later for the sale of illegal drugs. She sought and obtained the return of her children after serving three months in jail. Within two months complaints of neglect again were made because Mary had resumed drinking. Her children were placed again in foster care at the ages of six and four. By that time their emotional problems necessitated psychiatric treatment.

When twenty-five, Mary was sentenced to a penitentiary because of drug dealing. Her parental rights to her children were terminated, and they were placed in adoptive homes where the older boy required continued psychiatric treatment and specialized educational services.

Even though not necessarily reflecting parental incompetence, a parent's desire and readiness for parenthood has definite implications for a child's development. For example, Swedish and Czechoslovakian studies revealed that children born to mothers who were denied abortions showed long-term adverse psychological, emotional, and social effects.[9] This does not imply support for abortion as a method of birth control. It does, however, highlight the importance of preventing pregnancies or arranging for the adoption of unwanted children because of the hazards to the children of mothers who are not motivated to raise them.

On the other hand, as we will see in chapter 4, children who have experienced incompetent parenting can break the vicious cycle of continuing incompetent parenting through interventions that improve their life circumstances and through their personal efforts.

The Relationship between Poverty and Incompetent Parenting

Because poverty commonly is associated with incompetent parenting, the troubling possibility is raised that social class and racial biases can operate in judgments about the quality of parenting. This concern is justified because present-day child abuse and neglect interventions evolved from a background of ambivalent public attitudes toward the poor.[10] This has created the false impression that poor people usually abuse and neglect their children.

Governmental Attitudes toward the Poor

The Elizabethan Poor Law of 1601 has been the model for dealing with the poor for the last three centuries in England and the United States. The Poor Law shifted responsibility for aid to the poor from charity to the state. The Poor Law provided for the establishment of tax-supported hospitals and poor houses to shelter the poor who were too old or too ill to work.

Once the public agreed to pay for resources for the poor, it pressed for finding ways to reduce the costs. This led to increasingly harsh and repressive policies toward the poor. The employable poor were compelled to work or were sent to houses of correction if they refused to do so. Poor children were put to work or apprenticed. Many poor men were impressed into service in the merchant marine and shipped to the American colonies. Poor women became indentured servants. The lasting result of this treatment is an ambivalent public attitude toward helping the poor. We want to help the truly needy, but we do not want to be exploited by the "lazy." The dilemma lies in distinguishing the two.

Yet contrary to popular belief, most people who live in poverty today do not rely solely on public funds. In 1987 only 28 percent of poor families with young children relied exclusively on public assistance. Thirty-five percent of them received a mix of earned and unearned income from public sources, private sources, or both; and 37 percent of the families relied solely on earnings from employment.[11]

In spite of these facts, many people believe that the poor live off public funds and abuse and neglect their children. In the United States, this belief has been supported by the evolution in the nineteenth century of child abuse and neglect proceedings from programs for poor, or "destitute," children, presumably to protect them from parental immorality and abuse.

In more recent decades the availability of financial aid to dependent children made the distinction between poverty and child abuse and neglect possible by, at least theoretically, alleviating poverty. Now poverty is a legal defense against rather than a ground for a child neglect finding. This means that child neglect is determined by judgments about parental unfitness (or incompetence) rather than about poverty itself. This appropriately focuses the definition of neglect and of parental incompetence on the quality of parenting rather than on the economic status of families.

The Faces of Poverty

In order to ascertain the relationship between poverty and parental incompetence, I will describe the several faces of poverty. People classified as living in poverty—those with incomes below a threshold calculated by the government to provide a minimal standard of living—are not all alike. According to the U.S. Census Bureau, 9 percent are employed on a full-time basis, 31 percent have part-time employment, and 60 percent are unemployed.[12]

Poverty has been transient for most people in the past, but it is becoming a permanent condition for increasing numbers of people. Earlier in this century the routes out of poverty were imperfect and worked less well for African Americans than for Caucasians, but those routes were available and were often followed. Most poor families believed that ambition, perseverance, and hard work would bring rewards. Their aspirations did not differ qualitatively from those of the non-poor. In those days moving up from a disadvantaged status did not require the personal heroism and the help from others that it does today. In fact the percentage of families defined as living in poverty declined from 19 percent in 1959 to 10 percent in 1970.[13]

Escape from poverty is more difficult and happens less often now than in the past as the wealthy have become more wealthy and as the poor have drifted even deeper into poverty.[14] As evidence of this trend, between 1973 and 1988 the wealthiest fifth of the nation's households saw a 12 percent increase in income, while the poorest fifth experienced an 8 percent drop.

In 1992, 36.9 million people were living in poverty, or 14.5 percent of the population.[15] That figure included 16.2 million males (12% of the male population) and 20.7 million females (16% of the female population). Of particular interest to us is the statistic that 78 percent of the poor live in families.

The largest increase in the categories of people living in poverty in the United States has been in families headed by unmarried mothers.[16] From 1960 to 1990 the proportion headed by an unmarried mother of all poor families increased from 24 to 53 percent. While the total number of children under eighteen years of age decreased from 1960 to 1990, the number living with unmarried mothers increased nineteen-fold from 243,000 to 4.5 million. More strikingly, 59 percent of the children under the age of six living with unmarried mothers lived in poverty in 1991. At the same time, it is important to note that a significant number of parents living in poverty are employed in the workforce. Forty-one percent of unmarried mothers living in poverty are employed on a part-time basis and 10 percent on a full-time basis.[17] This compares favorably with married-couple families in poverty in which 38 percent have one or more part-time workers, and 30 percent have one or more full-time workers.

Children are hit especially hard by poverty. A higher percentage of children than of the elderly are poor. The poverty rate for children fell rapidly from 47.6 percent in 1949 to 15.6 in 1969. From then on, however, it increased to 17 percent in 1979 and to 20 percent in 1991 (to 24 percent for children under the age of six), while the overall poverty rate only increased from 12.5 to 13.5 percent.[18] During the same period the poverty rate for the elderly decreased from 24 to 12 percent. At this rate by the year 2000 almost 13.5 million children will have been raised in poverty.

Most Americans living in poverty are Caucasian, but minorities are disproportionately represented.[19] In 1990, 16.3 million (48%) were Caucasian, comprising 9 percent of that population; 9.8 million (29%) were African American, comprising 32 percent of that population; 6 million (17%) were Hispanic, comprising 28 percent of that population; and 2.3 (6%) million were of other races, comprising 14 percent of that population.

The discrepancies between ethnic groups is particularly evident in large cities. In 1986 the Urban Institute in Washington, DC, identified urban areas of poverty that contained 2.5 million people, or about 1 percent of the U. S. population.[20] In those urban areas 58 percent were African American, 28 percent were Caucasian, and 11 percent were Hispanic. Significantly, 36 percent were children.

For our purposes in relating incompetent parenting to poverty, it is true that children are disproportionately represented among the poor. It also is true that unmarried mothers have increased in numbers, especially among minority groups, and that they are disproportionately represented among the poor. But the poverty of children in minority, single-parent households in itself is not enough to make a convincing link between poverty and incompetent parenting.[21] The critical factors lie elsewhere in the attitudes and behaviors that determine the competence of the parents who live in poverty.

The U.S. House of Representatives Ways and Means Committee collected evidence that indicated that although less than 9 percent of all poor children lived in urban ghettos, they are especially predisposed to chronic welfare dependency and criminality because of the likelihood of parental neglect.[22] This points to the existence of a category of the poor in which parental incompetence is highly represented.

The "Underclass"

The distinction between poor families who do not contribute to criminality and welfare dependency and those who do has been facilitated by the concept of the "underclass." This distinction actually goes back to Victorian times in which "paupers" who were dependent on public assistance for a long time were distinguished from those who were temporarily poor.

In 1982 the journalist Kenneth Auletta focused public attention on an "underclass" that he defined by a pattern of social failure, multiple family problems, and chronic dependency upon public resources.[23]

The typical underclass urban neighborhood is hemmed in by poverty with inhabitants who are unable to find jobs and are largely without hope for the future. They sink into a desperate and vicious way of life. The predator is king. The most admired people are those who most ruthlessly exploit others. Teenage boys with no other way to prove their manhood pride themselves on how many girls they can impregnate and abandon. Drug dealers live by ensnaring others. "Wolf pack" attacks on strangers are justified as sport. Duplicity and trickery abound, even in families and between young couples.

Over the last decade the concept of the underclass has been developed so that its definition now includes three elements:[24] (1) a geographic concentration of individuals; (2) with weak labor force attachment, dependency on welfare, teenage pregnancy, dropping out of school, and criminal activity; and (3) with persistence of these behaviors across two or more generations. This definition reveals that not all poor people belong to the underclass nor are all members of the underclass necessarily poor. In 1990 the Population Reference Bureau estimated that the underclass in the United States numbered 3 million adults.[25] When children are included, the estimate rises close to 6 million. These estimates suggest that the underclass consists of less than 18 percent of those living in poverty.

Unfortunately, the term *underclass* emphasizes the behavior of this group of people rather than the systemic factors that contribute to their behavior, such as persistent unemployment, single-parent families, racism, and poverty.[26] Still it has focused attention on a definable group whose marginal economic position and weak attachment to the workforce is uniquely reinforced by its geographical and social milieu. Because African Americans are "hypersegregated" in urban areas, in part because of the departure of the upwardly mobile, the false appearance is given that they alone constitute the underclass.

Popular attention has been focused on the urban underclass, whose present proportions were forecast in the *Kerner Report* in 1968, but only one in three poor children lives in an urban area.[27] The most rapidly growing number is in the suburbs, where a fourth of all poor children now live. According to the Urban Institute, the majority of the underclass are Caucasian and do not live in large cities. The National Rural Development Institute also indicates that rural underclass children are at greater risk of failure than are comparable urban children. Most of the emphasis of research and of publicity has been on urban poverty, however, where the majority are African American.

The urban underclass has grown out of the wrenching displacement of millions of rural African Americans from the Civil War to the present. Even in urban areas members of the underclass tend to be natives of the region, not recent migrants.[28] Reynolds Farley of the Population Studies Center at the University of Michigan found that census data from 1940 to 1970 do not confirm a sharecropper–underclass link. In fact migrants to the North were more able and ambitious and were less likely to join the underclass than were northern-born African Americans.

The evidence reveals that incompetent parenting is concentrated in the underclass. As will be shown in chapter 4, the children in this segment of the population are at great risk for child abuse and neglect and for subsequent criminality and welfare dependency.

The role of the underclass in the social problems of the United States will not be addressed effectively until we treat people who live in the underclass as part of "us" rather than as "them." As long as the concept of the underclass is used pejoratively to blame poverty on the inadequacies of the poor, it will serve only political purposes.

Fortunately for society, most parents are drawn into the sacrificial process of forming affectionate bonds with their children. But the pressures on a small number of parents to meet their own needs and those of their children are overwhelming. Because the demands of parenthood exceed their capacities, they are likely to abuse and neglect their children. They seriously endanger our society by spawning our criminal and welfare dependency problems. In contrast competent parents contribute to the lifeblood of our society and civilization.

Chapter 3

The Benefits to Society of Competent Parenting

The institution of the family is decisive in determining not only if a person has the capacity to love another individual but in the larger sense whether he is capable of loving his fellow men collectively. The whole of society rests on this foundation for stability, understanding and social peace.

—MARTIN LUTHER KING, Jr., 1965[1]

I would live nowhere else than in the United States if given a choice. I treasure the freedom of opinion and action that our democratic republic allows. At the same time, every day in my work as a psychiatrist I see people who use that freedom to make choices that are contrary to their own interests and that harm other people. I am keenly aware of the heavy responsibility placed on each one of us to make wise choices when our behavior affects other people.

Our freedom of choice as adults places a high premium on competent parenting. This is because we are free to make choices even when our choices are contrary to our own interests. But when parents make choices that are contrary to their own interests and to the interests of their children, they damage themselves and other people—their children. As a result their children have difficulty becoming contributing

41

citizens in the communities and the society in which they live. Instead their children are likely to become burdens for their communities and society.

Most people think of parent–child relationships as private matters and do not realize how important they are to the health, welfare, and security of their communities and to the society in which we all live. Parenting is a vital social role in our democratic society. It provides the context for the affectionate bonding between parent and child that underlies an individual's ability to relate cooperatively to other people and to adopt prosocial values.

In this chapter I will outline the evidence that, in order to become contributing citizens, children need dependable relationships with adults who model competent living. I also will relate competent parenting to preventing illness and to preventing social problems. For these reasons, each one of us has a vital interest in how all of our children are raised. We all gain from competent parenting, and we all lose from incompetent parenting.

THE ROLE OF AFFECTIONATE ATTACHMENT BONDS IN CITIZENSHIP

We live in a strange time. Although we know intuitively that love between parents and children is a good thing, this is not enough to persuade policy makers who need proof that affectionate bonding between parents and children plays a key role in preventing crime and welfare dependency.

One reason why there is skepticism about the long-range importance of early family relationships is that many people do not have loving relationships with their parents now. The emotional scars of their strained family relationships obscure awareness that they really do have attachment bonds with their parents. The strength of those bonds may become apparent only on the death of their parents.

In addition, the deep-seated belief in the American Dream that anyone can succeed in life if given the opportunity to do so washes out awareness that this is not possible for everyone. Accordingly our society idealizes inspiring examples of persons who have risen to prominence from adverse circumstances. The implication is that even the most severe personality damage sustained in early life can be overcome.

Unfortunately, the dream of success for everyone glosses over the fact that most people do not surmount obstacles placed in their way early in life. We now have compelling evidence that children who form affectionate attachment bonds with their parents can overcome early adverse life circumstances whereas those who do not are unlikely to become contributing citizens. This evidence comes from a number of sources.

The first source is from the work of anthropologists who have found that all known cultures employ intimate relationships between adults and children for socializing children.[2] In particular the nurturance of infants is carefully structured around forming affectionate bonds with the kin most intimately involved with the children. Those kin usually are the biological parents. As a result, attachment bonds between adults and children are universally promoted in human cultures. This is empirical evidence of their fundamental significance in human survival.

The second source is ethological research which has shown that, following the instinct to procreate, instinctually based infant–mother attachment bonds are crucial to the survival and normal development of primates and other mammals.[3] By inference those predispositions to developing parent–child emotional ties also exist in humans. The benefits of parenting children are so important for the survival of our species that, whether or not they are activated, there are innate dispositions to form affectionate attachment bonds in both mothers and fathers and in infants. This explains the strong biological urge of human beings to have children and the intense protective emotions that children evoke in their parents.

The third source is the clinical evidence that young children are adversely affected by significant interruptions of their attachment bonds with their parents.[4] This has been gained from extensive studies of the developmental damage to children that results from both short-term and long-term separations of young children from parents with whom they have formed attachment bonds. This is why young children show distress reactions and resist separation from their parents.

The fourth source is knowledge of the harmful effects of the institutional upbringing of infants who cannot form attachment bonds with caregivers.[5] Some children waste away and even die when they do not receive nurturant parenting. This discovery led long ago to replacing the group care of young children in orphanages with the individualized care of children in foster families.

The fifth source is the growing body of research on the positive later effects of strong affectionate bonds between caregivers and infants.[6] The preponderance of this research indicates that sensitive, responsive childrearing promotes the formation of secure attachment bonds in infants and toddlers. It shows that competent social functioning and self-confidence in later childhood are strongly correlated with the formation of secure attachment bonds with adults during the first two years of life.

The sixth source is the weight of the evidence from extensive studies of special populations of children at risk, of the childhood antecedents of adult mental illness, of the causes of childhood mental disorders, and of the factors that produce adult mental health.[7] All of these studies reveal that positive interpersonal influences that create attachment bonds between children and adults during the early years of life foster the mental health of adults.

The seventh source is the study of parent–child relationships across the life span.[8] The results reveal that people who grow up with affectionate parents in cohesive families, and who have had satisfying relationships with their relatives, tend to have high levels of commitment to their own children and to civic activities in later years. They do not become criminals or welfare-dependent people.

The eighth source is an analysis of the childhoods of three hundred eminent people. That study demonstrated that success in life is not precluded, and may even be enhanced by, adversity.[9] Significantly, virtually all of those persons had a devoted parent with an influential personality. A contemporary example is the film actor, Tom Cruise. Born the third of four children and the only son, Tom had the disability of dyslexia, so that he was in remedial classes until his junior year in high school. Because his father traveled from job to job, Tom attended fifteen different schools. His parents divorced when he was eleven, and his mother had to work to support the family. She remarried when he was sixteen. His father died of cancer when Tom was twenty-two. Behind his successful career has been his mother, who supported and tutored him.

All of this research substantiates what we intuitively know. The formation of affectionate bonds with adults during childhood is the most important factor in developing the later ability to form committed relationships with other people and thereby to function cooperatively in society—the foundation of competent citizenship.[10] In essence, the psychological identification of a child with a parent, based on an affectionate attachment bond with that parent, is the most effective and efficient socializing process for developing the values and skills required for cooperative group living.

The core of competent parenting is the affectionate attachment bond that develops between a parent and a child. This bond motivates a parent to care for a child. It also motivates the child to identify with the parent. The damage caused to a child by an incompetent parent occurs because of the weakness or the lack of this bond. Such a child lacks the ability to empathize with and care about other people and, thereby, misses the first rung of the ladder of socialization.

In order to take advantage of the opportunities available in our society, an adult without contravening handicaps must be able to relate to other people and must be able to engage in productive work of some kind. Achieving that ability depends upon having formed affectionate attachment bonds with adults during the early years of life.

COMPETENT PARENTING PREVENTS ILLNESS

Another compelling argument for the importance of parenting to society has been proposed by the public health epidemiologist Leonard Sagan.[11] In his analysis, the present comparatively favorable state of health in Western civilization is due to the progressive increase in the formation of affectionate bonds between parents and children since medieval times, when children were commonly abandoned—the extreme form of neglect.

I will illustrate Sagan's point by briefly reviewing the history of the relationship between public health and affectionate bonding between parents and children.

During the seventeenth and eighteenth centuries, the average life span was less than forty years, even among members of the aristocracy; it is now close to seventy-five in the United States. This increase in longevity is usually attributed to better nutrition, better sanitation, and better medical care. These advances are only part of the story. The dramatic decline in the death rate was well advanced long before adequate diets, clean water, antibiotics, immunizations, and coronary bypass surgery.

According to Sagan, the rise of human hope and the decline in human despair and hopelessness have been more important than technological factors in explaining increased longevity. He attributes this shift in attitude to the progressive formation of affectionate attachment bonds between adults and children as the standard of living has improved.

The increase in parent–child affectionate bonds and the belief that parents have obligations to their children is based on the relatively recent ability of most parents to take care of their children. In medieval times the expectation was that children would be adequately reared but not that all would necessarily be kept. For some the choice was between a whole family starving or disposing of a child. Until the last century, many people were not aware of ways to prevent pregnancy, and no one had access to contraceptives.

The past fragility of the parent–child relationship is illustrated by the situation in eighteenth-century southern Italy.[12] It is likely that in that area 50 percent of the children were abandoned by their parents in desperation, when they were unable to support them; in shame, when they were unwilling to keep them because of their physical condition or ancestry; or in callousness, if they simply could not be bothered with parenthood. The church sanctioned the practice and even helped with it through oblation—the donation of a child to a monastery.

Until the late eighteenth century, the family was primarily an economic rather than an affectionately bonded unit in the Western world. Marriages were arranged for the purpose of preserving the ownership of property, and children were viewed as sources of labor and as hedges against poverty in old age. Beating and whipping were favored, even among royalty, as tools for teaching obedience to children. The attitude toward children then probably was not one of indifference but one of nondifferentiation. Young children were not seen as having distinct personalities. Those who managed to reach the so-called "age of reason" at six or seven were considered merely to be young adults.

Because they were not able to take part in the life led by adults, babies then received little attention. The custom of entrusting them to wet-nurses was widespread; it relieved affluent mothers of responsibilities and enabled lower-class women to earn money. Because of the difficult living conditions and the lack of knowledge about hygiene, the infant mortality rate was high for all social classes. Consequently, emotional detachment from young children on the part of parents was a safeguard against the pain of bereavement.

The idea that children need competent parenting arose from a change in the general attitude toward children in the late eighteenth century.[13] Philosophers, such as Jean-Jacques Rousseau, then argued that, in order to survive in a disorderly and unpredictable world, adults need hope and reasoned judgment. If adults are to develop that capacity, they need affection and guidance as children, not brute discipline. As these ideas took root and as the standard of living rose, childhood came to be recognized as a special stage of life, and affection began to replace duty as the cohesive force among family members. This made it possible for parents and children to express and develop their innate proclivities for affectionate attachment bonding.

The children of smaller families were strengthened emotionally and physically by the nurturance they received from their parents. Children who grew up in circumstances that fostered self-reliance and optimism rather than submission and hopeless despair were larger, brighter, and more resilient. As a result they were healthier and lived longer.

Love, trust, and self-esteem became the keys to health and well-being, probably by enhancing the functioning of the psychoimmune system.[14] People with a sense of well-being could enter lasting relationships and pursue education so as to develop their personal competencies and ultimately become involved in community activities that enhanced the meaning of their lives.

In Sagan's analysis the silent killer of hopelessness was reduced over the last two centuries by affectionate parent–child bonding.[15] The status of the nuclear family as an emotionally satisfying unit improved health because self-confidence and mutual trust were more likely to develop in children whose parents nurtured them as cherished members of the family than in children whose parents perceived them only as economic resources.

We now have contemporary evidence that affectionate bonding

between children and their parents is important in personal health. Research on health and illness is revealing that a feeling of human connectedness with an optimistic attitude is one of the critical factors that distinguishes those of us who remain healthy from those of us who fall ill.[16] This suggests that altruistic self-fulfillment is an important factor in maintaining health.

COMPETENT PARENTING PREVENTS SOCIAL PROBLEMS

My work with patients in the clinic focuses on what has gone wrong in the lives of people. At the same time the help that I can offer really depends upon what has gone right in their lives. What I can do for them depends upon what they can do for themselves, just as the treatment of an infection depends upon the ability of the body's immune system to destroy the invading organisms. Without a healthy immune system drugs in themselves are ineffective. A healthy immune system is a protective factor against infection. In the same way, the coping skills that result from competent parenting are protective factors against stressors in life.

Competent parenting was one of three types of protective factors against criminality and welfare dependency found in a study of high-risk children from birth to adulthood carried out under the supervision of the psychologist Emmy Werner on the Hawaiian island of Kauai.[17] Those protective factors were: (1) predispositions of the individual, such as low activity level, sociability, intelligence, language and reading skills, and a sense of competence; (2) affectionate bonds within a family that provide emotional support in times of stress; and (3) external support systems, such as school, work, and church, that reward an individual's competencies and that provide value systems to guide daily living. Werner's findings confirmed those of other studies that competent parenting has a greater effect on successful adaptation in life than do negative risk factors, such as poverty, birth trauma, parental alcoholism, parental psychopathology, and teenage pregnancy.

The protective effect of competent parenting also was found by David Quinton, a child psychologist, and Michael Rutter, a child psychiatrist, in a comparative study of women subjected to chronic stress and disadvantage in adult life.[18] Those who had not had stable parenting themselves became incompetent parents. Those who had a background of affectionate bonding that resulted in personal competence became competent parents even in the face of adversity. The cause of incompetent parenting was not the stressors; it was the ineffective way in which stress was handled.

The importance of competent parenting in preventing criminal behavior was revealed in Janis Long and George Vaillant's Harvard-based follow-up study of men who were economically disadvantaged but nondelinquent during their childhoods.[19] The vast majority did not repeat their disadvantaged backgrounds during their adult lives. Commonly cited explanations were a mother who maintained standards of hard work and a desire to excel, a man who substituted for an absent father, and a supportive spouse in later years. An additional factor was the entry of this group of men into the workforce in the late 1940s, when employment levels were high.

Studies of vulnerable premature infants have disclosed that the combination of low birth weight, poverty, and incompetent parenting account for high rates of later cognitive and social impairment, whereas competent parenting provides an effective buffer against those same biological and socioeconomic risk factors.[20] For example, the national Infant Health and Development Program demonstrated that cognitive development was enhanced for low birth weight infants by parental support interventions with marginally competent parents but that greater developmental enhancement occurred without the need for interventions with competent parents. The critical importance of competent parenting in brain development is further supported by the observation that affectionate bonding between a parent and child decreases the risk of brain damage from malnutrition in early life.

Evidence for the importance of affectionate bonding during childhood in preventing parental child abuse and neglect even can be inferred from experimental work with rhesus monkeys. As is true with human beings, some monkeys are innately anxious and fearful. The psychologist Stephen Suomi found that when those "high-strung" monkeys were cared for by their mothers in stable environmental settings, they grew up to be successful members of their groups.[21] When "high-strung" females were separated from their mothers during several brief, but critical, periods early in their lives, most of them later neglected or abused their own offspring.

Competent parenting can override the adverse effects of brain damage, birth trauma, malnutrition, and poverty. Conversely, the incompetent parenting of vulnerable and even well-endowed children can produce adults who are ill-equipped for success in our society and who are prone to antisocial behavior and to dependency on others to restrain or to care for them.

Fortunately, some of the adverse effects of early parent–child relationships can be ameliorated by later compensatory and therapeutic experiences. Still, the fundamental human capacity to trust others and to be trusted by others largely rests on the foundation of affectionate bonding with adults in early life.

OBSTACLES TO FORMING AFFECTIONATE ATTACHMENT BONDS

In recent decades there has been a reversal of the public health and social benefits from affectionate attachment bonding in the United States. This can be related to at least four factors in our society that pose obstacles to developing affectionate bonds between parents and children.

The first factor is the reduction in the amount of time parents spend with their children and the resulting dilution of parent–child relationships. The greater priority that vocational careers and recreational activities take over parenting also has contributed to a general devaluation of parenting as an adult role in our society. When parents give them anything but their time and attention, children tend to lack a sense of personal responsibility and sensitivity to the welfare of others.

The second factor is the governmental financial support of incompetent teenage parenting through welfare and educational measures that often operate to the developmental detriment of both the teenage parents and their children. This factor will be the focus of chapter 9.

The third factor is the lack of effective clinical interventions for incompetent parents during the critical early period of life of their children.[22] There are effective therapies for improving parent–child affectionate bonding, but they rely upon motivated parents and are too labor intensive and costly to be made available on the scale that is required. Even optimal education cannot correct the consequences of early incompetent parenting. For this reason, interventions in the schools come too late for most of these children.

The fourth factor is the governmental financial support of intractably incompetent adult parents. When their children are housed, fed, and cared for in day or foster care and at school without parental participation, marginally involved incompetent parents can easily take advantage of the situation. The failure to appropriately terminate the rights of incompetent parents and to provide competent parenting for the affected children perpetuates incompetent parenting by default. Governmental interventions should operate through and with parents, not around them.

Just as the growth of affectionate parent–child bonds was associated with improvements in health over the last three centuries, the deterioration of family relationships in recent decades underlies the decline in the health, welfare, and education of our children and youth. That relationship has yet to be widely appreciated, in part because of a general lack of sustained societal interest in parenting.

A realistic vision for the health and welfare of Americans will need to include their mental health and the quality of their human relationships. It will need to recognize the preeminent role of competent parenting in early childhood in forming the skills, attitudes, and values required for developing self-esteem and affectionate relationships with others—factors that enhance personal and public health. Most importantly for society, it is on these qualities that effective citizenship relies.

Certainly from society's point of view the most efficient and effective social program for any child is a competent parent. It is far more efficacious and far less costly to promote parent–child affectionate attachment bonding than to continue to assume the burden of the educational, clinical, and correctional treatment of those who suffer from the effects of incompetent parenting.

Chapter 4

The Effects of
Incompetent Parenting

My own personal view, as a magistrate, is that our society intervenes far too late in the process of antisocial behavior as this develops in children. It is much easier, and more viable, to make rules in the home and at school and enforce these, than to try rehabilitation programs on adults whose lives have been ruined by society's unwillingness to get involved until it is too late for the life habit of crime to be reversed.

—MAGISTRATE SYBIL B. G. EYSENCK, 1989[1]

Whether we are judges, lawyers, social workers, or mental health professionals, all of us feel the frustrations of trying to intervene in the lives of children after they have been damaged by incompetent parenting. We know that the severity and the prevalence of that damage is far beyond the scope of professional solutions. And we have a responsibility to convey that awareness to the public. The solutions lie in changing the values of our society not in professional services.

As the previous chapter revealed, the most important determinant of competent adult citizenship is the formation during early life of affectionate attachment bonds between parents and children. In contrast, the failure of individuals to form affectionate bonds has dire consequences.[2] Charles Manson is an infamous example of a person who did not form attachment bonds with a parent:

> Manson was born to sixteen-year-old Kathleen Maddox on November 12, 1934, in Cincinnati, Ohio. During the first few years of his life, Charles was cared for intermittently by his grandmother and maternal aunt, because Kathleen left him with neighbors and disappeared for days and weeks at a time. In 1939 she was jailed for armed robbery, and Charles was sent to live with an aunt and uncle, who were harsh disciplinarians.
>
> When Charles was eight years old, his mother was released from prison, and he lived with her in run-down hotel rooms with a long line of men who, like his mother, drank heavily. He ran away and was placed with foster parents for about a year, but his mother regained his custody. In 1947 at the age of thirteen, he became a ward of the county and began to live in a series of juvenile and penal institutions. Prior to his sensational murders at the age of thirty-five, he had spent twenty-two years in institutions.

We can point to individuals like Charles Manson as obvious examples of the products of incompetent parenting. We do not know the true scope of the effects of incompetent parenting because conducting prospective research over the life span of individuals is exceedingly difficult. The constitutional traits and environments of individuals also are important variables that influence their lives.

This chapter will show that, although genetic predisposition, pregnancy and birth complications, malnutrition, disabling illnesses, poverty, and racism all contribute to the vulnerability of children, whether or not children later become habitual criminals or chronic welfare recipients depends largely upon how they were parented. Unstable lives with school and vocational failures are the likely consequences of incompetent parenting.

There are "invulnerable" children who succeed in life in spite of seeming to have been incompetently parented. Careful analyses of those children's backgrounds usually reveal the positive influences of adults other than the children's parents.[3] The invulnerable children who weather child abuse, poverty, and family crises have had constitutional adaptability and competent parent figures. The idealized images of these invulnerable children who surmount adversity and fulfill the American Dream and the fact that children are remarkably adaptable should not distract us from facing the generally devastating effects of incompetent parenting.

In this chapter I will address the products of incompetent parenting in their most extreme and problematic forms—habitual criminality, most notably for males, and welfare dependency, most notably for females. As we will see, a small but highly significant fraction of the population (a minority of those receiving government benefits) is the source of both habitual criminality and continued welfare dependency in subsequent generations.

I also will call attention to the less clear-cut, but still significant, relationship between incompetent parenting and homelessness, public health, and national productivity.

INCOMPETENT PARENTING AND HABITUAL CRIMINALS

In spite of our abhorrence of crime, we tend to have ambivalent feelings about its origins and our society's responses to it. Each one of us knows what it is like to do something wrong. At some level each one of us dislikes submitting to authority. Most of us are fascinated by crime, the staple of our entertainment. It is no wonder that in our open society we are both repelled by and attracted to crime.

For these reasons, before the criminal actions of individuals can be understood, our role in fostering crime must be recognized.

Crime in the United States

The United States leads the world in violent crimes. Cross-cultural studies have shown that, compared to the United States, crime rates are dramatically lower in nations such as Japan where cultural values instilled by families emphasize social obligations as much or more than individual freedom and where families transmit a sense of collective responsibility for each person's behavior.[4]

In addition there is a strong social-class bias in attitudes toward crime in the United States, so that crime is more strongly censured for the lower than for the upper socioeconomic classes. White-collar criminals can become celebrated lecturers and consultants after serving brief prison terms. Upper and middle class youngsters who commit crimes are likely to be diverted from the correctional system and receive mental health services or be sent to boarding schools. In contrast, poor youngsters are much more likely to be incarcerated and initiated into criminal life styles.

Lower class crime rates also vary from one country to another depending upon the degree to which a society reinforces violent behavior, the degree to which it enforces its laws, and the degree to which it restricts the availability of lethal weapons. The easy availablility of guns in the United States provides access to lethal weapons for criminals, for emotionally unstable people, and for children and youths. In societies that do not permit the personal possession of handguns and military weapons, aggressive acts are much less likely to become violent and fatal crimes.

The extent of crime in the United States is documented in the FBI's *Crime in the United States,* the best known source of national criminal statistics.[5] In 1991, 1.9 million violent crimes and 13 million property crimes were reported to law enforcement agencies in the United States. More significantly, when unreported crimes are taken into account, 132 percent more (34.7 million crimes) actually occurred, according to the Bureau of Justice Statistics. Police agencies make arrests in about 20 percent of all the crimes reported to them. Less than one-half of violent crimes are solved by arrests and convictions.

Although the peaks in crime fluctuate from time to time, crime is steadily increasing in the United States.[6] This is reflected in the fact that the number of persons in federal and state prisons more than doubled during the 1980s to the highest number since statistics were kept, totaling 823,414 in 1991.

All of this reveals that public safety in the United States has deteriorated to intolerable levels because the sheer volume of crime has exceeded the capacities of law enforcement agencies to control it.

The Evolution of Criminality

Against this background of crime in the United States, making a distinction between crime, which can be occasional, and criminality, which is a way of life, is important.

Crimes are circumscribed events that can be committed by anyone. Brushes with the law are common in the United States and in England, where one-third of all males encounter the police once or twice as teenagers or as young adults. Still, 70 percent of all criminal offenses are committed by only 6 percent of the male population.[7]

The word criminality refers to the habitual propensity of individuals to commit crimes. Crime is the primary career of these individuals. They are frequently referred to as criminal recidivists.

The number of adult habitual criminals can only be estimated from national statistics on detected crimes, and, therefore, omits those who have not been apprehended. Because of their propensity for crime, it is likely that few habitual criminals escape eventual arrest. Most adult offenders engage in only a few crimes each year, however, in one study the habitual criminals reported that they had committed more than one hundred crimes a year.[8]

Of the prison population in the United States in 1991, 65 percent, or 535,219, were habitual criminals.[9] Fifteen percent, or 123,512 individuals, were "hard-core" habitual criminals with six or more prior terms of probation or prison. They represent the most dangerous chronic offenders, and they are unable to function as competent citizens. They constitute 0.05 percent of the population of the United States. Although tiny in percentage, these "hard-core" habitual criminals still pose a significant threat to society. In a city of 100,000 people, there would be 50.

Habitual criminals begin their careers as juvenile delinquents, although most juvenile delinquents usually commit minor offenses and discontinue doing so after the teenage years.[10] Four percent of the population between the ages of 10 and 17, or 1 million young persons, are estimated to be delinquent. Of that number only 5 to 8 percent, or 50,000 to 80,000, will become habitual criminals. This figure is supported by the some 95,000 arrests for violent crimes by persons under the age of 18 each year and by the fact that 50 to 70 percent of incarcerated juvenile delinquents are arrested again following discharge from correctional facilities.

The early manifestations of criminality are seen in a general pattern of incorrigibility at home, truancy from school, reckless automobile driving, and alcohol and drug abuse.[11] Juvenile delinquents who are destined to become habitual criminals move on to more serious crimes, such as forgery, auto theft, burglary, and assault. According to the FBI, the nature of juvenile crime has become more violent and frequent for all races, social classes, and life styles.

Adult habitual criminals generally have a background of juvenile delinquency, the first incarceration during middle adolescence, and the first adult incarceration by the age of twenty-one. Interventions directed at this small number of individuals during their early lives could dramatically reduce the crime rate in the United States.

The Causes of Criminality

The popular view is either that criminals are born that way or that they are the victims of disadvantaged lives. Even research devoted to the causes of habitual crime tends to emphasize either biological, psychological, familial, socioeconomic, or ecological factors. The false dichotomy between nature and nurture is remarkably persistent because it serves personal and political purposes. All of these elements interact and must be taken into account in each case.

Biological Factors.   The most obvious biological factors in criminality are age and gender. Criminality occurs mostly in young males. Intriguingly, the comparatively small number of female criminals, who represent only 4 percent of the prison population in the United States, may have a heavier loading than males of other as yet undetermined biological predispositions to criminal behavior.[12]

Past explanations of criminality invoked inborn predispositions based on beliefs in criminal types that could be defined by the shape of one's face and head. More recently, this line of thought has suggested genetic predispositions to criminality. The current emphasis on biological factors in mental disorders has revived the long discredited belief that "criminals are born, not made."

Biological factors are involved in crime. Many biomedical conditions do appear to increase the risk of violent behavior.[13] A number of changes in blood chemistry, brain waves, and hormones can trigger violence especially when interacting with drugs, alcohol, stress, noise, overcrowding, and diet. In addition one-third of adult habitual criminals show evidence of mental disorders and 6 percent have psychomotor epilepsy, which in themselves have both biological and psychosocial determinants.

Specific biological factors contribute to violent behavior.[14] Food allergies, refined sugar-induced hypoglycemia, chemical substance abuse, and lead poisoning are examples. There also is evidence that male habitual criminals have deficient biological fear responses and reduced capacities for conditioned learning. Studies of both violent monkeys and violent humans have disclosed low levels of the neurotransmitter serotonin. Yet to expose the nature–nurture oversimplification, each one of these biomedical factors is influenced by psychosocial circumstances, since it has been shown that life experiences, and the lack of them, cause alterations in the structure and the biochemical functioning of the brain.

Environmental factors influence antisocial behavior even when genetic and biomedical factors are operating. For example, the appearance of antisocial behavior in Huntington's chorea is more strongly related to disorganization in an individual's family than to the genetically determined deterioration of the brain.[15]

Studies that compare adopted persons and fraternal and identical twins also indicate that the genetic component in criminality is small.[16] Although temperamental and cognitive style characteristics are inherited, the lack of cooperativeness and the lack of compassion seen in habitual criminals results from life experience not genetic inheritance.

The evidence indicates that criminality as such is not innate.[17] Certain dispositions of the central nervous system are inherited or acquired. Those dispositions interact with certain environmental factors and thereby increase the likelihood that a given person will act in a particular antisocial manner in a given situation. The existence of biological predispositions means that circumstances may trigger violent behavior in one person and not in another; but they are only weak contributing factors to criminality.

The neurologist Richard Restak eloquently described the biological element in violent behavior:[18]

> However one might wish otherwise, neurology will never solve the mystery of why some people kill others, much less explain why some murderers derive pleasure from their actions. Most likely the tendency toward violence, as with most human behaviors, simply follows a bell curve. At one end of the curve are people who, even when faced with a life-death situation, cannot rouse themselves to

violent action. At the opposite extreme are the violent people who represent not insanity, and certainly not brain damage, but only the outer limits of human aggression. In between are the rest of us: gingerly balancing our ethics and our baser instincts, clinging to reason in a desperate world.

Socioeconomic Factors. Attributing crime to socioeconomic disadvantage is the obvious result of the strong association between social class and notorious crime, particularly of the violent type, and the strong association of crime with neighborhoods.

Some urban and rural neighborhoods have been long-standing sites of criminal behavior. Many other neighborhoods have been destroyed by urban blight in recent decades. When disorder goes too far, the social fabric on which the stability of a neighborhood depends is undermined.[19] In such a neighborhood children do not learn that adults hold values that lead them to take responsibility for the condition of their homes and their neighborhoods. Those children seldom acquire a sense of responsibility for their own behavior as well.

Without question disorderly neighborhoods are strongly associated with criminal behavior. When rising levels of disorder are accepted—when broken windows, uncollected garbage, loitering gangs, graffiti, derelicts, and prostitutes are tolerated—a signal goes out that neighborhood residents have lost control of their environment, and criminals then move in. As the level of safety declines, so does the level of civility. Caught in this downward spiral of neglect and crime, neighborhoods succumb to the inexorable forces of decay.

Because of the obvious fact that substandard housing is strongly associated with criminality, it is tempting to assume that providing better housing would solve the problem. The President's Commission on Crime in 1967 made just that assumption and spawned the Great Society programs. Experience with those programs demonstrated that poverty, inadequate housing, and neighborhood conditions are aggravating but not causal conditions of criminality.

Even in the harshest slums, surveys of the residents reveal that most poor people are law-abiding citizens.[20] Attributing criminality solely to economic disadvantage and to disorderly neighborhoods demeans the poor by implying that they are inherently irresponsible people. It invites society to see the poor as morally different, socially distorted human beings. It ignores the fact that a minority of those who live in poverty are responsible for crime. It also does not take into account subcultures in which violent behavior is condoned. Most importantly, it deflects attention from the familial factors that largely cause habitual criminality.

Familial Factors. Criminality runs in families because there are both weak genetic and strong interpersonal factors in its origins. It is transmitted from one generation to the next weakly through genes and strongly through that which is learned, or not learned, from one's parenting. After exhaustively studying the evidence, the criminologists James Q. Wilson and Richard Herrnstein concluded that most of the factors that contribute to criminality can be accounted for by personal traits, by family socialization, and by schooling, with family factors leading in importance.[21]

The sociologist Travis Hirschi convincingly linked criminality to the lack of social bonds with parents, friends, neighbors, and social institutions.[22] The elements of these social bonds are affectionate relationships with other people, parents being the most important; commitment to societal values; involvement in community activities; and shared moral beliefs. Regardless of socioeconomic conditions, a person with weak adherence to moral values is at risk for committing criminal acts.

Habitual criminals begin their misdeeds at very early ages.[23] Although school failure is strongly associated with criminality, habitual criminals begin offending very early in their lives, well before community and neighborhood factors could play much of a role.

The family profiles associated with criminality have been described both statistically and qualitatively.[24] According to the Bureau of Justice Statistics, 72 percent of youths in long-term state-operated juvenile institutions come from other than two-parent homes. Fifty-three percent come from homes in which another family member has been incarcerated. The causes of habitual criminality, however, are related less to family structure and more to the failure to form affectionate attachment bonds and to the inconsistency in limit setting that occurs in severely disordered single- and two-parent families.

The classic Cambridge–Somerville Youth Study carried out in Cambridge, Massachusetts, demonstrated that the most important factors that contribute to criminal behavior lie in parent–child relation-ships, rather than in the disruption of families by death or divorce.[25] Paternal or maternal child abuse and neglect were found to be related to later criminal behavior. The study also found that services provided by the community failed to help the children because the services fell short of affecting their family and peer relationships. There was evidence that those belated interventions did more harm than good.

A number of studies have revealed that the experience of having been abused and neglected as a young child has a substantial impact on the likelihood of later engaging in criminal behavior.[26] A National Center on Child Abuse and Neglect study disclosed that 66 percent of institutionalized delinquents had child abuse and neglect histories. Another study by the psychologist Jose Alfaro disclosed that 50 percent of families reported for child abuse and neglect had at least one child who was later referred to juvenile court. In a long-term follow-up of preschool children carried out by psychologists Lawrence Schweinhart and David Weikart in Ypsilanti, Michigan, 26 percent of disadvantaged child abuse and neglect victims became juvenile offenders compared to 17 percent of the disadvantaged controls. Those who were neglected were even more disposed to delinquency than those who had been only physically abused.

Other studies confirm the adverse consequences of child abuse and neglect.[27] In a forty-year follow-up of abused and neglected children, the psychologist Joan McCord found that one-half had been convicted of serious crimes, became alcoholic or mentally ill, or died at an early age. About one-third of those who were abused later abused their own children. In a related vein, most rapists have histories of sexual abuse in their own childhoods.

A compilation of sixty studies by the psychiatrist J.E. Oliver disclosed that one-third of child victims of child abuse grow up to continue the pattern of seriously inept, neglectful, or abusive parenting; one-third do not; and one-third remain vulnerable to the effects of social stress on the likelihood of their becoming abusive parents.[28] Thus, the majority of abused children who were not also neglected do not grow up to be delinquent, nor have all delinquents been abused. However, having been a neglected and possibly abused child, and even witnessing violence in the home, definitely increases one's risk of becoming a delinquent, an abusive parent, and a habitual criminal. This evidence actually minimizes the long-term effects of child abuse, because research has not addressed the relationship between childhood abuse and the more subtle later manifestations of emotional damage, such as anxiety, depression, personality problems, suicide, and employment failure.

The "hard-core" group of habitual criminals have backgrounds as "children of the state" without parents who were consistently responsible for them.[29] They are called "children of the state" because their guardianships were with agencies rather than with persons. The typical profile of these criminals is one of foster care for over five years and multiple subsequent placements with an ultimate progression through child caring, mental health, and correctional institutions. There now are over 400,000 children in foster care in the United States. About 25 percent have had three or more placements. At that rate 100,000 children are at risk for becoming "children of the state" and later "hard-core" habitual criminals.

The case history of Jack Abbott, another notorious habitual criminal like Charles Manson, further illustrates the typical background of the most dangerous "hard-core" category.[30] Neither Manson nor Abbott ever had opportunities to form affectionate attachment bonds with adults.

> When Jack Henry Abbott's book, *Belly of the Beast,* was published in 1981, he was thirty-seven years old and had been outside of institutions for only 9½ months since the age of twelve.
>
> From his birth Abbott was in a number of foster homes until the age of nine, when he was placed in juvenile detention facilities until the age of twelve. He then was placed in the Utah State Industrial School for boys for all except two months until the age of eighteen, when he was released as an adult. Six months later he was sentenced to the Utah State Penitentiary, where he murdered another inmate at the age of twenty-one. When twenty-six he escaped for six weeks. After his release from the penitentiary to a New York City half-way house in 1982, on an angry impulse he murdered a waiter in a restaurant.

Psychological Factors.   Habitual criminals share certain psychological characteristics. They are unable to form relationships with other people, are unable to adhere to rules, and have varying degrees of educational deficiencies. Their central personality defects are a lack of impulse control, a lack of empathy with other persons, and a lack of an effective sense of guilt.

The psychoanalyst Alice Miller vividly described the attitudes and emotions of habitual criminals who have been incompetently parented:[31]

> When the vital developmental needs of children are frustrated, and children are instead abused for the sake of adults' needs by being exploited, beaten, punished, taken advantage of, manipulated, neglected, or deceived without the intervention of any witness, then their integrity will be lastingly impaired. The normal reaction to such injury should be anger and pain; since children in this hurtful kind of environment, however, are forbidden to express their anger and since it would be unbearable to experience their pain all alone, they are compelled to suppress their feelings, repress all memories of the trauma, and idealize those guilty of the abuse. Later they will have no memory of what was done to them. Dissociated from the original cause, their feelings of anger, despair, longing, anxiety, and pain will find expression in destructive acts against others (criminal behavior, mass murder) or against themselves (drug addiction, alcoholism, prostitution, psychic disorders, suicide). If these people become parents, they will then often direct acts of revenge for their own mistreatment in childhood against their own children, whom they use as scapegoats.

Although the abuse and neglect typical of incompetent parenting often occur together, their respective developmental repercussions for affected children may well differ.[32] Children who have been exposed largely to traumatic abusive events tend to be preoccupied with efforts to master an excess of painful emotions rather than with criminal activities. They attempt to overcome their feelings of helplessness by avoiding dependency on others and by open or subtle provocative acts that elicit abuse from others. They seem to seek abuse.

On the other hand, children who have been largely neglected tend to be preoccupied with a search for recognition and for material things. They lack self-control and the awareness of how to respond to the needs and wishes of others and to legitimately satisfy their desires. Their lives are characterized by continually seeking attention, by testing the limits of acceptable behavior, by doing what they want when they want to, and, ultimately, by adopting criminal careers.

A study carried out by the Minnesota Preschool Project in Minneapolis, Minnesota, disclosed that neglected children learn to expect that their caregivers will be unavailable and unresponsive to their emotional needs.[33] This leads to a sense of themselves as isolated, as uncared about, and as unworthy—in essence as "bad." Other people, in turn, are viewed unrealistically as uncaring and are treated with anger and hostility.

A number of other studies reveal that neglected children behave in ways that elicit confirmations of their "bad" self-images.[34] They continually test the limits of acceptable behavior and exhibit unprovoked aggression, causing other children and adults to reject them. They become disruptive and engage in antisocial behavior, such as lying, stealing, cheating, and sexually molesting other children. They have difficulty controlling their violent tempers and refraining from destructive actions toward others and sometimes toward themselves. As adults they are unable to form lasting and meaningful interpersonal relationships.

In essence, developing the ability to relate effectively to other people rather than being dominated by one's impulses depends upon learning during the early years of life how to restrain oneself out of respect and affection for others. In this sequence, neglected children fail to form affectionate attachment bonds with other people and do not learn to delay gratification and to tolerate frustration. Consequently, they are unable to work in school and to take advantage of opportunities in later life. Their lack of self-control and lack of prosocial values is later reinforced by the values of antisocial peers, often ironically crystallized in institutions intended to treat juvenile delinquency.

Because they feel alienated from other people, neglected children become capable of violent robbery and killing. They have no compunction about taking from the "haves," because they are "have-nots." They do not feel they are in the wrong because they feel that society has deprived them. Therefore, society should give to them. If society does not, they steal, and murder is incidental. They lead irresponsible lives and coerce or manipulate others to satisfy their own needs without regard for the rights or lives of others. Their self-esteem comes from their gangs, from their willingness to commit violent acts, and from venting their hatred on more affluent people and even on each other. They are drawn to crime because it is more exciting and meaningful than any other experience they have known. They are unresponsive to persuasive or educational efforts to change their behavior.

The psychoanalyst Leonard Shengold described the effects of child neglect and abuse as "soul murder."[35] Trapped by their dependence, such children can only identify with their tormentors whom they idealize, hoping for a better outcome "the next time." Such children become estranged from their own feelings and sink into deadened states in which their very existences become roles that are played rather than spontaneous expressions of their own feelings. They are filled with murderous fantasies and overwhelming anxieties, which predispose them either to elicit or to commit acts of violence, whereby they become "soul murderers" or actual murderers themselves.

Most juvenile murderers have been subjected to physical, emotional, or sexual abuse in addition to neglect.[36] In her intensive study of ten juvenile murderers, the psychologist Muriel Gardiner found only one who had lived with his parents in an apparently intact nonabusive home.

The Central Park "wilding" attacks in New York City are infamous examples of the pattern of extreme remorselessness.[37] The youths who raped and nearly killed a young jogger remarked afterward, "It was fun." In Washington, DC, a group of youths sang and joked while they robbed, raped, and brutally murdered a middle-aged mother. In another Washington case, an eighteen-year-old shot a cab driver in the head, because he wanted "to try out a gun." In another, two teenagers killed a third because they wanted his boom box. In New York City homeless people were burned "for the fun of it." The cold-blooded, remorseless nature of juvenile murder is illustrated by the details of an Orlando, Florida, case:

> On June 3, 1986, a nine-year-old boy was charged with drowning a three-year-old boy. After making sure that no one was around, the nine-year-old pushed the younger child into the deep end of a swimming pool and watched him drown. Shortly thereafter he asked another child what the "icky white stuff" was that comes out of someone's nose while drowning. The investigating police officer found the nine-year-old to be nonchalant about the "accident." He

also seemed to be unremorseful and to enjoy the attention he received.

The lack of an effective conscience also is seen in the white collar equivalent of the habitual criminal—the con artist. Because white collar criminals have not been studied as intensively as their lower class counterparts, their backgrounds of neglect and their failures to form affectionate attachment bonds are not well documented.

White collar crimes do not attract as much public attention as street crimes because they do not threaten safety in homes and neighborhoods. A common example of white collar crime is illustrated by a pair of cousins who stole money from teller machines in North Carolina:[38]

> Two young employees of Wells Fargo Armored Services who did repair and maintenance work on automated teller machines stole $700,000 from 16 machines and went on a spending spree to Colorado. They believed that they would get away with their actions and did not regard what they did as crimes.

In an ominous forecast the sociologist Jose Sanches predicts that, if present trends continue, increasing numbers of conscienceless people in the middle and upper classes of American society will create a nation in which expediency, impersonality, narcissistic manipulation, and conspicuous consumption will replace morality and sensitivity to the interests of others.[39] Georgette Bennett also anticipates that traditional criminals—young, male, poor, uneducated—will increasingly be augmented by older, more upscale offenders. At the same time, the underclass will be an increasing source of fear and danger for everyone.

An indication of this trend toward consciencelessness is seen in the increasing number of incidents in which nondelinquent young people participate in sadistic behavior.[40] Examples are the high school youths in Colorado Springs who watched a soldier being kicked to death; a Madison, Indiana, group of teenagers who tortured a twelve-year-old girl to death; suburban Chicago teenagers who viewed a dead body in a woods for several months without reporting it; the shooting of Jose and Kitty Menendez by their sons in their Beverly Hills mansion; and "playing the rape game" by nine to thirteen year olds. It is not unreasonable to speculate that degrees of parental neglect play a role in the behavior of these young people.

The Prevention of Criminality

Children who have been exposed to early and prolonged neglect are largely untreatable in later life by currently available methods. This makes the prevention of criminality the most important strategy by far. Although politically popular, efforts to deal with crime administratively are largely unsuccessful. The reforms implemented following the 1967 President's Commission on Crime included deinstitutionalization, the decriminalization of status offenses, and the diversion of youths from formal court proceedings into public and private treatment programs.[41] Those reforms had the unintended consequences of reaching less serious offenders than those originally targeted, so that community residential programs are now used for individuals who formerly would have been placed on probation. Those who formerly were placed in community residential programs have been shifted into penal institutions with less potential for rehabilitation.

Efforts to use the schools to prevent delinquency usually focus on junior and senior high schools, when antisocial behavior becomes evident. Although interventions with individual delinquents at all levels including predelinquent stages are important, most programs have failed to help those destined to become habitual criminals because the interventions have not improved parenting.

A crucial factor in preventing criminality is the societal support of parents so that children can grow up with hope for their futures. Criminologists agree that children raised by incompetent parents, who lack affectionate attachment bonds with their children and do not set consistent limits, are much more likely to become habitual criminals than those who do not.[42] The prevention of criminality must be based on the family as the unit of intervention.

The more children are affectionately bonded to their parents, the more likely they are to be committed to school and cultural values, the less likely they are to become involved in delinquent acts with peers, and the more likely they are to become competent citizens. Three personality characteristics that result from competent parenting can prevent criminality:[43] (1) a desire to gain the approval of others (initially parents) and a belief that such approval can be reliably expected; (2) the inclination and the ability to recognize the negative consequences of present gratifying actions; and (3) an effective conscience.

The fact that some "invulnerable" children emerge from neglectful and abusive backgrounds resulting from incompetent parenting without becoming criminals should not obscure the undesirability of such a life for them or for any children.

With these factors in mind, a model for the prevention of criminality must take into account the biological endowment of children, opportunities for affectionate bonding of children to their parents, the commitment of parents to educational and moral values, exposure to prosocial peer group values, and adequate educational opportunities.[44] Such a model will be outlined in chapter 11. Little can be done about the genetic and biological predispositions of vulnerable children but much can be done about the quality of parenting and the quality of education they receive.

Multiple factors are involved in the genesis of criminality, but the one that is the most susceptible to remediation or replacement is incompetent parenting.

INCOMPETENT PARENTING AND WELFARE DEPENDENCY

Just as it predisposes males to criminality, incompetent parenting predisposes females to welfare dependency because they bear children. The connection between incompetent parenting and welfare dependency has not received as much attention as the connection between incompetent parenting and criminality. This largely is because criminality is more socially disruptive than welfare dependency. An unfortunate consequence for our purposes is that less attention has been paid to the study of the quality of attachment bonding of welfare-dependent persons than of habitual criminals.

Contrary to popular perception, most people who receive welfare are not dependent on welfare throughout their lives.[45] Only about one quarter of those who receive welfare can be classified as welfare dependent, but that amounts to almost 1 million families. Moreover, according to the American Association for Protecting Children, 53 percent of reported child neglect cases involve families receiving public assistance.

We now know that there are at least three factors that contribute to intergenerational welfare dependency and incompetent parenting: characteristics of the mothers, fathers, and the welfare system itself.

Characteristics of the Mothers

The Urban Institute in Washington, DC, found that (1) being unmarried, (2) being a teenager, and (3) being unemployed are the most important characteristics of mothers who are welfare dependent.[46] Those mothers also tend to have been abused and neglected during their childhoods and to abuse and neglect their own children.

If we look at unmarried female-headed households in general, 60 percent receive public assistance.[47] The sociologists Gary Sandefur, Irwin Garfinkel, and Sara McLanahan found that children raised in those homes were less likely to graduate from high school, more likely to have premarital births, more likely to be unemployed, and more likely to form single-mother households in early adulthood than those from two-parent families. A study commissioned by the Annie E. Casey Foundation found the poverty rate for the children of mothers who finished high school, got married, and reached the age of 20 before having their first child was 8 percent, whereas it was 79 percent for the children of mothers who did none of these three things. According to the American Association for Protecting Children, the alleged perpetrator is a single, female head of household in 51 percent of the reported cases of child neglect.

If we look at teenage childbearing, its relationship to welfare dependency is clear.[48] More than half of all recipients, or over 1.8 million persons, began receiving Aid to Families with Dependent Children (AFDC) when they were teenagers. Most teenage mothers turn to public assistance for support, and most of the long-term welfare dependent began bearing children as teenagers. The Collaborative Perinatal Project of the National Institute of Neurological Disorders and Stroke found that the children of teenage parents were neglected and were living in foster or adoptive homes five times more often than were children of women who began childbearing after the age of eighteen. The socioeconomic index scores of the teenage mothers also revealed their downward social mobility. Other studies of teenage parents reveal that their children often are raised in suboptimal environments and that there is deficient verbal and emotional communication between them and their infants. As a result, many of those children show cognitive deficiencies in later life.

If we look at unemployment, we find it is associated with welfare dependency and with child neglect.[49] According to the American Association for Protecting Children, in 42 percent of the reported cases of child neglect, the child's parent was unemployed. This is highly significant when compared with the small percentage of unemployed parents.

Father Absence

Single motherhood and father absence go hand in hand. Fathers are absent for several reasons that discourage the formation of two-parent families.

The sociologist William Julius Wilson has called attention to the role of male unemployment in contributing to African American, single-parent, intergenerational welfare dependency.[50] He noted that the pool of marriageable males is shrinking in major cities because the available males are either unemployed or are engaged in crime and are in and out of jail. Those who are successful leave the urban ghettos. Out-of-wedlock childbearing and single-parent families are related to the lack of employment opportunities for males, resulting in few men for women to marry.

In addition AFDC policies that discourage marriage and the attractions of the drug trade are factors that promote father absence in underclass families. The cultural factors that contribute to father absence are described in chapter 10.

The Role of the Welfare System

The existence of the welfare system itself cannot be blamed for welfare dependency. The evidence shows that welfare dependency is related more to the characteristics of individuals than it is to the availability of welfare benefits in themselves. The AFDC program is intended to provide temporary aid to parents in order to improve the health and education of their children. This purpose does appear to be realized with most AFDC recipients.

The availability of welfare in itself does not seem to attract most single parents as indicated by the rise in the number of children in single-parent homes while the welfare roles remained steady and by the fact that some of the states with the lowest benefits have the highest rates of unmarried motherhood, and vice versa.[51] The sociologists Sara McLanahan and Larry Bumpass calculated that increases in welfare benefits overall account for from 9 to 14 percent of the increased prevalence of families headed by women. This figure is higher in underclass families, so that sociologists David Ellwood and Mary Jo Bane found that the availability of welfare benefits encourages those mothers to remain unmarried and raises their separation and divorce rates.

The sociologist Greg Duncan and his associates at the University of Michigan also have shown that, for the incompetent parents in the underclass who become long-term recipients, the availability of welfare benefits contributes to out-of-wedlock births, discourages marriage, erodes work effort, and instills attitudes that encourage continued reliance on welfare.[52] The availability of welfare benefits fosters the dependence of incompetent parents by encouraging them to make choices that increase their welfare payments and by fostering an attitude that discourages self-sufficiency in both recipient parents and in their children.

Because federal and state welfare assistance is linked to children, chronic welfare dependency is heavily weighted toward females with children in contrast to habitual criminality which is heavily weighted toward males. This produces a situation in which underclass females, but not underclass males, can receive governmental financial support. In that situation the antisocial behavior of males is more likely to be criminal, and the antisocial behavior of females is more likely to be the abuse and neglect of their children. The welfare system now supports incompetent parents who would not be parents on welfare if they had not been personally damaged and socioeconomically disadvantaged and if they had been educated and had chosen careers.

Although upward mobility is possible for most persons living in poverty, the evidence is that teenage childbearing, single parenthood, and welfare dependency in one generation tend to lead to teenage childbearing, single parenthood, and welfare dependency in subsequent generations. Family economic status and family disruption contribute to this phenomenon, but do not fully account for it, pointing to other factors, such as inadequate affectionate attachment bonding between parents and children.

The evidence indicates that incompetent parenting definitely is associated with the cycle of intergenerational welfare dependency.

INCOMPETENT PARENTING AND HOMELESS CHILDREN

Homelessness is a phenomenon of the last decade that is seen in both urban and rural areas of the United States and Europe.

The relationship between incompetent parenting and homeless children is less clear-cut than it is with habitual criminality and chronic welfare dependency, but it is a factor that needs to be considered. Whatever the reasons for their homelessness, these children are at physical, emotional, and educational risk. Homeless children are society's prima facie neglected children.

Homelessness constitutes a gray zone between bureaucratic welfare and housing lapses and clear-cut parental incompetence.[53] People are homeless because they have no money and no place to live; only about 6 percent are homeless by choice. Twenty-five percent of the approximately 600,000 homeless in the United States are families with young children. There is an obvious need for public assistance and affordable housing for these families. For the some 15,000 children who are abandoned each year by incompetent parents, new families are needed.

Homeless single adults tend to have more mental and addiction problems than do homeless parents.[54] Between one-fourth and one-third of homeless single adults have mental illnesses. In homeless families parental incompetence is involved to varying degrees. A study of homeless families in Boston revealed that more than two-thirds of the homeless mothers grew up in disorganized families and experienced at least one major early family disruption, such as by divorce or death of a parent, that impaired their ability to form and maintain stable relationships. Some were perpetuating a cycle of child abuse.

The Boston study also noted a trend toward a heritage of homelessness in which a second generation of children are growing up on the streets and in shelters. The majority of those children suffer from serious emotional and medical problems and are not being appropriately educated. According to the Institute of Medicine, children who are incompetently parented and who live in chaos during their formative years often develop personality disorders.

A contrast with the Boston study from another part of the country was provided by a Stanford University survey of the homeless in Santa Clara and San Mateo counties in California.[55] It revealed that only 5 percent of the parents reported a history of mental illness and 35 percent of substance abuse. That study did disclose, however, that the homeless children had a high incidence of chronic illnesses and behavior problems.

Another kind of homelessness is seen with youths who run away from families because of conflicts ranging from communication problems to sexual and physical abuse.[56] An estimated 1.7 percent of youths between the ages of ten and seventeen run away from home. The U.S. Department of Health and Human Services reported that up to 1.3 million are known to the Runaway Youth Program each year. The U.S. Department of Justice estimates that there are 130,000 serious runaway and 60,000 "thrownaway" minors. Of them about 176,000, equally representing boys and girls, become truly homeless. The unconscionable exploitation of these young people was vividly described as early as 1969 by Lisa Richette in her book *Throwaway Children*.

Studies of runaway homeless youths reveal that they commonly have a background of school problems, antisocial behavior, depression, and suicide attempts.[57] They have experienced rejection and maltreatment in the past and often avoid help so that they will not be rejected again. A study of runaway youths in New York City revealed that three out of five had a parent with a history of drug or alcohol abuse or criminality. About half had been physically abused by a parent.

The evidence reveals that a theme of alienation and a lack of affectionate bonding capacities in both adults and children runs through the homeless of all ages, many of whom are the products of incompetent parenting.

INCOMPETENT PARENTING AND PUBLIC HEALTH

In chapter 3, I described the relationship of early parent–child affectionate bonding to improvements in public health. Conversely, the lack of affectionate attachment bonding during childhood is related to public health problems.

There is strong evidence that the lack of self-esteem and concern for others resulting from insecure attachment bonding is linked to the way in which people both passively and actively contribute to their own illnesses and to injuries to themselves and to others by drug and alcohol abuse and poor health habits. This relationship is particularly evident when pregnant mothers engage in behaviors that damage both themselves and their unborn children, when parents neglect the health of their children, and when adults neglect their own health.

Maternal Damage to the Fetus and the Infant

There is no doubt that teenage pregnancy, maternal alcoholism, maternal substance abuse, and maternal sexually transmitted diseases are hazardous to fetuses and infants.

The Risks of Teenage Pregnancy. From the biological point of view, the ideal time to give birth appears to be between the ages of sixteen and nineteen. Under fifteen, however, there is an increased risk of maternal mortality, preeclampsia, anemia, low birth weight, and perinatal infant mortality apparently related more to the typical life circumstances and the incompetence of pregnant teenagers than to actual maternal age.[58]

All of these risks can be minimized by adequate health care.[59] The number of low-birth-weight premature infants in Sweden is approximately five times less per capita than in the United States. This can be attributed to the fact that pregnant girls and women in Sweden are well fed, adequately housed, and usually afforded optimal prenatal care. The high-risk factors for teenage mothers and their babies still are found in Cuba, however, where free health care is readily available, so that the availability of health care in itself is insufficient to ensure its use.

Overlooked by focusing only on prenatal care and the biological aspect of pregnancy is the fact that the birth of a child has harmful developmental and social consequences for teenage mothers themselves. Among them is the adverse impact on a teenage girl's life of becoming a mother prior to her own social, educational, and emotional readiness to assume the responsibilities of parenthood. This theme will be developed more fully in chapter 9.

Maternal Alcoholism, Drug Abuse, and Sexually Transmitted Diseases.   The fact that unborn children need protection against the dangerous actions of their pregnant mothers is receiving increasing attention. The height of parental incompetence is seen when mothers damage their unborn babies by knowingly ingesting toxic substances during pregnancy and then neglecting their infants after childbirth with resulting additional physical and developmental damage.

The hazards of alcohol to the unborn have been known since Samson's mother was warned by an angel in the Old Testament to avoid wine while carrying her unborn child. Today some 7500 children are born each year with the fetal alcohol syndrome.[60] This syndrome includes growth retardation, mental retardation, altered facial characteristics, and other physical abnormalities. Since 1981 the Food and Drug Administration has warned that pregnant women should drink no alcohol at all, because even small amounts have been linked to miscarriages, low birth weight, feeding difficulties, mental deficits, attention disorders, and emotional instability in the offspring.

The National Institute on Drug Abuse estimates that over 4 percent of all newborns have been exposed to crack in the womb. In 1988 13,765 infants with mothers who had used drugs during pregnancy were identified in the National Hospital Discharge Survey.[61] A 1988 study at Chicago's Northwestern Memorial Hospital also found that at least 11 percent of 155,000 pregnant women surveyed had exposed their unborn babies to illegal drugs, with cocaine being by far the most common. During the same year, 20 percent of the babies born at Highland General Hospital in the inner city of Oakland, California, were affected by crack.

Cocaine, like heroin and alcohol, is passed from the mother to a fetus with potentially damaging results.[62] For example, a New York City Harlem Hospital study disclosed that 13 percent of the newborns had cocaine in their blood. One-third of them were born prematurely. At the age of five, 15 percent were severely handicapped, and nearly all of the others showed some degree of developmental impairment.

Depending upon the intensity and the length of exposure to crack, fetal growth can be impaired, including head and brain size; strokes and seizures can occur; and malformations of the kidneys, genitals, intestines, and spinal cord can develop. The amount of cocaine used is important since moderate cocaine use during pregnancy apparently does not affect the physical development or behavior of newborns, although those children have not been followed after birth. Later in life many children with high crack exposure have difficulty tolerating being touched, concentrating, learning, and relating to people. Determining the actual effects of the neonatal exposure to drugs on children is complicated by the fact that there usually is abuse and neglect in the picture as well. Still, at the national level the neonatal health care costs of cocaine babies in themselves add up to over $500 million annually.

Another way in which infants are harmed is through the transmission of AIDS during pregnancy.[63] In 1992 the Centers for Disease Control estimated that there were 10,000 HIV-infected children in the United States. Because of the illnesses and deaths of their parents, about one-half have no parents or adult relatives to care for them. The scope of the AIDS problem in the United States in 1992 was seen in the 218,000 persons with the disease and the 1 million persons infected with HIV. Minority groups were disproportionately affected. Twenty-five percent of the population infected with HIV were African American and 13 percent were Hispanic, as compared to their 12 and 7 percent levels in the general population.

As is evident, the babies of incompetent mothers are at high risk for physical and developmental damage.

Parental Neglect of the Health of Their Children

The adoption of mandatory school-entry vaccination laws has protected most school-age children from contagious illnesses. Yet, 90 percent in Dallas to 40 percent in Boston of two-year-old children were not fully vaccinated in 1992.[64] One factor contributing to this situation is that many parents wait until a child must be immunized by law. As a result, until the Childhood Immunization Initiative of 1993, cases of whooping cough, mumps, and measles rose in recent years in step with the drop-off in the number of young children vaccinated against those illnesses.

In addition, the children of the homeless and of families on welfare have more accidents and illnesses and, consequently, incur disproportionately higher medical costs.

Maintaining the health of children is an important function of competent parenting that is neglected by incompetent parents.

Adult Neglect of Personal Health

Because modern medicine has brought spectacular benefits to individuals through the cure and containment of disease, many people believe that more health care expenditures will improve the health of the nation. Overlooked is the fact that most of us become ill as a result of our own personal actions or inactions and as a result of environmental conditions.[65] There is much that adults and children can do to protect their health and to avoid injuries and illnesses.

The major health problems in the United States are the chronic stress-related diseases of middle and later life—heart disease, stroke, and some forms of cancer. Preventing these illnesses and self-induced injuries means forsaking things that many of us choose to do—overeat, drink alcohol excessively, take pills, stay up at night, engage in promiscuous sex, drive fast, fight, and smoke tobacco. The consequent rising health costs of the resulting illnesses and injuries have become a national public health burden that would be substantially reduced if we all assumed personal responsibility for maintaining our own health by exercising regularly, using contraception, promoting a harmonious family life, and avoiding known health hazards.

Competent parents foster their children's sense of personal responsibility and often educate their children in the causes and prevention of illness. Incompetent parents do not do this, so in this way incompetent parenting has an indirect bearing on adult health, which depends upon learning when we are young how to assume responsibility for our own health.

INCOMPETENT PARENTING AND NATIONAL PRODUCTIVITY

I have been told by economists that they do not need to consider the personal lives of individuals in their work because those factors wash out in the overall picture of a nation's economic condition. Yet our nation's economy depends upon the production, distribution, and consumption of goods and the provision of services by people who earn and spend their money. Our economy really does depend upon the ability of individuals to work and to consume goods and services.

At the core of our ability to work is the capacity to sustain effort in productive activity. Beyond inborn qualities, that capacity depends upon having learned to postpone gratification and to tolerate frustration through affectionate bonding to, and effective limit setting by, our parents early in life.

In 1987 the U.S. Department of Labor issued a report *Workforce 2000* which documented an emerging crisis in the American workplace.[66] The report called attention to the adverse implications for our economy of the growing number of young adults who are functionally illiterate and who lack basic work skills, including motivation and perseverance that depend upon the abilities to postpone gratification and to tolerate frustration.

We are confronted with a future workforce in which there will be less young adults and in which more of them will be vocationally incompetent. In 1980 persons between the ages of fourteen and twenty-four numbered over 46 million and represented over one-fifth of the nation's population. Projections by the U.S. Bureau of the Census indicate that by the turn of the century there will be 40.6 million in that age group.[67] That number is anticipated to decline by 2050 to 38.2 million, or only 13 percent of the nation's population.

The evidence indicates that for the foreseeable future, minority groups, particularly African Americans, Hispanics, and Native Americans, will constitute a growing share of the nation's labor force, reaching from one-third to one-half of the entrants by the end of the century.[68] The inadequate parenting and inferior education of these groups will severely compromise the productivity of a smaller workforce then.

At the same time, between now and the year 2000 the majority of all new jobs will require more than a high-school education.[69] Many vocations will necessitate nearly a decade of study following high school, and even the least skilled jobs will require competence in reading, computing, and thinking at levels that have been needed only in the professions. The Hudson Institute concluded that without substantial adjustments in our society that will improve their employability, African Americans and Hispanics will have a smaller fraction of the jobs in the year 2000 than they have today, while their share of those seeking work will have risen.

Whatever the causes, the large and growing proportion of children born in the underclass represent long-term threats to their own lives and to our nation's economic security. Economists no longer can avoid taking personal factors into account. The failure to improve the competence of the parenting of all of our children will further erode our nation's productivity. As it now stands one-half of all newborns in the United States will spend five or more years in a single-parent, female-headed family. One-half of those will live in poverty, and most of those in the underclass will fail to complete high school, will be unemployed, and will be at risk for habitual criminality and dependency upon public welfare.

The vast majority of parents in the United States are quite capable of raising their children without public intervention. A comparatively small but crucial number, however, lack the competence to do so. This lack of competence arises from their own personal qualities, from life stressors, from socioeconomic disadvantage, and from a combination of these factors. Those incompetent parents are prone to abuse and neglect their children.

By far the majority of habitual criminals and many welfare-dependent adults come from backgrounds of child abuse and neglect. Of these two factors that often occur together, the more damaging is parental neglect. This is because physical and sexual abuse can occur in the context of parent–child affectionate attachment bonds—whereas parental neglect does not—and damages the very roots of a person's ability to form relationships with other people and to adhere to social and cultural values.

Although many show remarkable resiliency in spite of adverse early life circumstances, the children of incompetent parents are predisposed to grow up to be adolescents and adults who are unable to control their impulses and who do not care about the effects of their behavior on other people. They do not relate their present behavior to future consequences. Therefore, they do not conduct their lives responsibly and work productively. The males gravitate toward delinquency and ultimately to habitual criminality. The females gravitate toward teenage childbirth and welfare dependency. They become incompetent parents themselves. Many of the less impaired males and females who avoid those outcomes become unemployable and marginally antisocial adults, many of whom suffer from self-induced illnesses and some of whom join the ranks of the homelessness.

Criminality and welfare dependency are not innate qualities of human beings. The foundations for socially responsible behavior and for work skills are acquired in the home. If these foundations are not laid, it is exceedingly difficult and enormously costly for society to repair the resulting damage.

The incredible financial and social costs that result from incompetent parenting cry out for our attention.

Chapter 5

The Costs of Incompetent Parenting

Each of our children represents either a potential addition to the productive capacity and the enlightened citizenship of the nation, or, if allowed to suffer from neglect, a potential addition to the destructive forces of the community.

—THEODORE ROOSEVELT, *Special Message to Congress*, 1909[1]

I tried without success to find out if anyone had placed an economic value on competent parenting and an economic cost on incompetent parenting. I discovered in my quest that most economists do not think of parenting as having economic significance.

The traditional theories of economics deal only with the financial value of goods and services. They do not place an economic value on human activities outside of the marketplace, such as parenting. Because of the prospect of an inadequately prepared workforce in the United States, however, economists are beginning to place a financial value on the human factors in our economy. We no longer can assume that there will be an adequate supply of productive workers.

As the preceding chapters have shown, the quality of the workforce has a direct relationship to the quality of parenting children receive. Because it adversely affects the motivation, the competence, and the availability of workers and because it actually costs society money, incompetent parenting drains the economy. Conversely, competent parenting tangibly benefits the economy by producing competent adults who generate money.

On the average, parents spend $144,000 in rearing a child through high school.[2] This figure offers a basis for estimating the financial value of parenting, but it does not include the resulting economic productivity of the child as an adult. Taking the latter into account, as an adult worker to the age of sixty, the average child will contribute $900,000 to the nation's economy and pay $100,000 in federal income taxes. When these amounts are added to the parental contribution, the total economic value of competently parenting a child exceeds $1 million in 1994 dollars.

This calculation offers a basis for assigning financial value to the time parents spend rearing their children. If we assume that the total value of raising a child is $1 million, an hourly rate for the value of parenting can be calculated. One formula for doing so would be to assume that parenting involves twelve hours a day for four years; eight hours a day for one year; and six hours a day for thirteen years to rear a child. This would total 48,910 hours and yield an hourly rate of $20.45. Of course, this would not take into account rearing more than one child at a time and the wide range of actual hours devoted to childrearing, but it is a start. It begins to recognize the financial value of competent parenting.

As impressive as the financial value of parenting may be, looking only at its financial benefits does not tell the whole story because the quality of life cannot be measured solely in economic terms. The effect of parenting on social outcomes is important as well. Although still not reaching existential elements in the quality of life, the effectiveness of competent parenting can be measured by nonfinancial gains, such as in years of productive life, in reductions in crime, in improved health, and in reductions in the numbers of neglected and abused children.

Establishing the financial and social value of competent parenting can help our materialistic society appreciate the role of competent parenting in determining the quality of the workforce and thereby the health of our economy. At the least, the public must become aware of the devastating financial costs and losses to society caused by incompetent parenting.

Large sums of public moneys are spent on neglected and abused children who eventually become threats to public safety as habitual criminals and drains on the economy as adults dependent on welfare. Moreover, untold losses to the economy result from those who become unemployable adults. In order to illustrate the magnitude of the problem, this chapter is devoted to estimates of these costs to society.

As will be demonstrated, the most incompetent parents cost society $2 million for each child in direct expenditures, in losses of revenue by the government, and in losses of spending in the national economy. We will see that, conservatively estimated, the offspring of a comparatively small number of incompetent parents, who can be readily identified, cost society $1 trillion during their lifetimes. Ironically, much of our current expenditures for social and correctional services provided for these people actually tend to perpetuate rather than to alleviate the intergenerational cycle of parental incompetence.

These costs reflect only a fraction of the total financial losses to society caused by incompetent parenting. They do not take into account the expenses of crime, such as the loss of property, medical costs for the victims, the financial repercussions of the loss of life and work, the expenditures on security and law enforcement, the effect of crime on insurance premiums, and the legal costs of prosecution and defense. *U.S. News and World Report* estimated those costs to be $524 billion in 1993. Even that figure does not take into account a host of other factors, such as the medical costs of premature and handicapped infants.

In order to stimulate interest in more sophisticated and definitive analyses, I have undertaken an estimate of some of the most evident burdens placed upon society by three kinds of social problems resulting from incompetent parenting: habitual criminality, chronic welfare dependency, and the population of abused and neglected children.

The Costs of Habitual Criminals

As described in chapter 4, the juvenile backgrounds of habitual criminals are characterized by disordered families, multiple arrests, and sequential placements in mental health and correctional facilities.

A sophisticated means for determining the costs of criminality has yet to be devised. Until this is achieved, however, useful estimates can be made. To this end, I used a paradigm for calculating the costs of illnesses to estimate the costs of habitual criminality based upon a national and a Wisconsin study of habitual criminals.[3] From these two sources, I devised the models depicted in Tables 1, 2, and 3 in which 47 percent of adult habitual criminals are projected as coming from families with criminal members, 30 percent from single-parent, welfare-supported households, and 23 percent from backgrounds as "children of the state" in multiple foster-care and institutional placements.

The first two types of families in themselves do not necessarily meet the criteria of incompetent parenting in the sense of adjudicated child abuse and neglect. The offspring of those included in this analysis, however, show manifestations in their habitual criminal careers of a lack of earlier affectionate bonding and a lack of exposure to prosocial values.[4] It is likely that the parents of these habitual criminals were incompetent but were not legally identified as such, since the actual prevalence of incompetent parenting exceeds the reported and substantiated cases of child abuse and neglect.

In order to gain an appreciation of the financial costs of habitual criminals to society, I have used the conservative national figure of 535,219 incarcerated habitual criminals, as cited in chapter 4, and estimated their direct costs to government and the indirect costs of the loss of their contributions to the national economy and to income taxes during their years outside of the workforce. While acknowledging that direct costs vary from one state to another, I have based my estimates on expenses in the state of Wisconsin and federal income and tax averages as detailed in the Appendix. Future costs obviously will be greater in less valuable dollars.

My estimate of the numbers of habitual criminals is based upon currently incarcerated individuals. It does not take into account individuals with similar profiles who are not imprisoned. A basis for estimating that population has not been found, but the numbers undoubtedly substantially exceed those who are in prison.

Because of the socioeconomic, gender, and racial biases in crime and its management, this analysis does not address the large, but seldom-detected population of incompetently parented "white collar" habitual criminals.

Reared with Criminal Family Members

In this model the habitual criminals have a background of living at home with four or five siblings and at least one criminal family member. I placed 47 percent of the 535,219 habitual criminals, or 251,553, of the incarcerated population, in this category for the purpose of this analysis.

The direct costs to government, losses in government revenue, and losses to the national economy of members of this group are itemized in Table 1. This model reveals a direct cost of $58,202 during the juvenile years; a direct cost of $896,181 during the adult years to the age of sixty; and a total direct cost of $954,383. The indirect costs are in the loss in federal taxes that totals $100,002 and the loss of spendable income to the economy that totals $821,310. In sum the total cost for each individual to the age of sixty is $1,875,695. Consequently, the aggregate national cost of this population totals $472 billion.

Single-Parent, Welfare-Supported Families

The second model involves 30 percent of the habitual criminals. It consists of those who come from single-parent families that received sustained welfare payments in some form. This category represents 160,565 individuals in this analysis.

The direct cost to government of members of this group during their juvenile years is $157,862 and during adulthood is $896,301; this totals $1,054,163 (see Table 2). The indirect costs in loss in taxes is $100,002 and in loss to the economy is $821,310. The total cost for each individual to the age of sixty is $1,975,475 with an aggregate cost to society for this population of $317 billion.

Early and Multiple Placements

The third model is of "hard-core" habitual criminals who were placed in foster homes early in life followed by sequential placements in mental hospitals, group homes, and juvenile correctional facilities prior to adult penal institutions. Of the 535,219 incarcerated recidivists, 23 percent, or 123,100, are classified as such individuals in this analysis.

Table 1. Financial Cost of a Habitual Criminal from a Family with a Criminal Member

1. Lived at home with parent(s) and 4–5 siblings (from birth to 13 years)		
2. Lived at home with parent(s) and siblings (ages 13 to 15 years):		
Arrests by police (3)	$	648
Court costs (2)		4,622
Detained overnight (1)		108
Social worker services		5,266
3. Juvenile correctional institution (ages 15 to 15¼ years)		
Arrest by police (1)	$	216
Court costs (1)		2,311
Detained overnight (1)		108
Correctional facility		10,572
4. Lived at home with family (ages 15¼ to 17¼ years)		
5. Juvenile correctional institution (ages 17¼ to 18 years)		
Arrest by police (1)	$	216
Court costs (1)		2,311
Detained overnight		108
Correctional facilities		31,716
6. Adult prison (ages 18 to 60 years; 40 years prison and 2 years on probation)		
Arrests by police (3 × $216)	$	648
Court costs (3 × $2,311)		6,933
Detained in jail ($108 × 60)		6,480
Adult prison ($22,056 × 40)		882,120
Total juvenile cost	$	58,202
Total adult cost	$	896,181
Total direct cost for services	$	954,383
Loss of federal income taxes ($21,936 single person: $2381 × 42 years)	$	100,002
Total direct cost to government	$	1,054,385
Loss to national economy ($19,555 × 42 years)	$	821,310
Total monetary loss to society for individual	$	1,875,695
Aggregate loss of this category (47% or 251,553 persons)		$471,836,700,000

Table 2. Financial Cost of a Habitual Criminal from a Single-Parent, Welfare Family

1. Lived at home with single mother (from birth to 13 years)		
AFDC payments	$	60,271
Social services ($2,633 × 13)		34,229
2. Lived at home with parent (ages 13 to 15 years)		
Arrests by police (3)	$	648
Court costs (2)		4,622
Detained overnight (1)		108
Probation services		5,266
3. Juvenile correctional institution (ages 15 to 15¼ years)		
Arrest by police (1)	$	216
Court costs (1)		2,311
Detained overnight (1)		108
Correctional facilities		10,572
4. Lived at home with parent (ages 15¼ to 17¼ years)		
Probation (1 year)	$	2,633
Arrest by police (1)		216
Court costs (1)		2,311
5. Juvenile correctional institution (ages 17¼ to 18 years)		
Arrest by police (1)	$	216
Court costs (1)		2,311
Detained overnight		108
Juvenile facilities		31,716
6. Adult prison (ages 18 to 60 years; 40 years prison & 2 years on probation)		
Court costs (3 × $2,311)	$	6,933
Arrests by police (3 × $216)		648
Jail detention ($108 × 60)		6,480
Adult prison ($22,056 × 40)		882,240
Total juvenile cost	$	157,862
Total adult cost	$	896,301
Total direct cost for services	$	1,054,163
Loss of federal income taxes ($21,936 single person: $2381 × 42)	$	100,002
Total direct cost to government	$	1,154,165
Loss to national economy ($19,555 × 42 years)	$	821,310
Total monetary loss to society for individual	$	1,975,475
Aggregate loss of this category (30% or 160,565 persons)		$317,192,140,000

Table 3. Financial Cost of a Habitual Criminal with Multiple Placements

1. Single mother with one child (unwed teenager; birth to 3 years)		
Social services ($2,633 × 3)	$	7,899
AFDC payments ($5,023 × 3)		15,069
2. Foster home (ages 3 to 10 years)		
Social services ($2,633 × 7)		18,431
Foster home ($3,324 × 7)		23,268
Court costs ($2,311 × 7)		16,177
3. Mental hospital (ages 10 to 11 years)		
Hospital ($396 × 365 days)	$	144,540
Court costs (1)		2,311
4. Child-caring institution (ages 11 to 14 years)		
Social services ($2,633 × 3)	$	7,899
Group home ($30,540 × 3)		91,620
Arrests by police ($216 × 3)		648
5. Juvenile correctional institution (ages 14 to 18 years)		
Correctional cost ($3,524 × 36 months)	$	126,864
Court costs ($2,311 × 4)		9,244
Arrests by police ($216 × 4)		864
Detention ($108 × 60 days)		6,480
6. Adult prison (ages 18–60 years; 40 years prison and 2 years on probation)		
Court costs ($2,311 × 3)	$	6,933
Arrests by police ($216 × 3)		648
Jail ($108 × 60 days)		6,480
Adult prison ($22,056 × 40 years)		882,240
Total juvenile cost	$	481,034
Total adult cost	$	896,301
Total direct cost for services	$	1,377,335
Loss of federal income taxes ($21,936 single person: $2381 × 42)	$	100,002
Total direct cost to government	$	1,477,337
Total loss to national economy ($19,555 × 42 years)	$	821,310
Total monetary loss to society for individual	$	2,298,647
Aggregate loss of this category (23% or 123,100 persons)		$282,963,440,000

Table 3 shows the juvenile direct cost to the government of $481,034; the adult cost of $896,301; and a total direct cost of $1,377,335. Adding the tax loss and the loss to the national economy reveals a total monetary loss to society of $2,298,647 for each individual to the age of sixty and an aggregate cost for this group of $283 billion.

The Costs of Intergenerational Welfare Dependency

A variety of statistics can be used to estimate the costs of inter-generational welfare dependency to our society.

In June, 1992, 4.8 million families in the United States received Aid to the Families of Dependent Children (AFDC).[5] Of the 13.7 million persons who received assistance, 4.4 million were adults, and 9.3 million were children; 10,832 of the mothers were fourteen years old or younger. In addition 81 percent received food stamps, and all were eligible for Medicaid. The average AFDC family of one adult and two children received $418 a month, or $5,022 per year in 1992.

The probability of leaving AFDC support decreases the longer a recipient is on the rolls.[6] About 30 percent of single mothers who ever receive benefits spend no more than two years on welfare. But another 40 percent receive benefits for three to seven years, and another 30 percent receive benefits for eight or more years. Because long-term recipients are more likely to be receiving benefits at any particular time, however, at each point in time they represent a large share of the caseload. Thus, those who receive benefits for eight or more years (the welfare dependent) constitute about 65 percent of the total AFDC caseload in any given month. If those persons were removed from the public assistance roles, according to my estimate the saving in AFDC payments would be over $12 billion annually.

In 1990 over half of the AFDC payments were disbursed to households containing women who bore their first children as teen-agers. This amounted to $9.5 billion of the total payments of $19 billion and did not include administrative costs, food stamps, or Medicaid.[7] When those other costs were added, in 1992 the federal government spent almost $34 billion on all forms of welfare programs for families started by teenagers. That was $12.5 billion higher than in 1988, in part because of an increase in births to teenagers.

The alarms now being sounded about "children having children" are less responses to the increasing adverse consequences of premature births and more responses to the adverse consequences of incompetent childrearing. Neonatal intensive care is expensive, however, and the long-term costs of the care of handicapped babies and children is great as well.

For example, a committee of experts appointed by the New York State Task Force on Life and the Law concluded that two-thirds of the fetuses from twenty-five to twenty-eight weeks gestation can be expected to survive with intensive care that exceeds $200,000 in cost for each fetus; of those survivors 30 percent can be expected to be moderately to severely handicapped throughout their lives.[8] The much greater long-term medical and social costs to maintain their lives remain to be calculated.

THE COSTS OF CHILD ABUSE AND NEGLECT SERVICES

Another example of the financial repercussions of incompetent parenting is the direct cost of interventions in situations of child abuse and neglect. Among those costs are the expenses of the 407,000 children in foster care in 1992.[9]

In 1983 Deborah Daro estimated the financial cost of child abuse and neglect services.[10] If her estimates are translated into 1994 costs for an estimated 690,000 children who actually receive those services, current annual costs can be estimated. Those annual costs are in hospitalization ($31.9 million); rehabilitation and special education ($11.1 million); foster care ($3.2 billion); social service case management ($1.9 billion); and court expenses ($597 million). The costs of the various forms of treatment the children receive range widely from $3,600 to $36,000 per child per year. These services cost public and private service systems between $2.7 and $26.6 billion annually. All of the costs incurred in the management of abused and neglected children add up to from $8.4 billion to $32.3 billion annually, or $12,174 to $46,870 for each child.

These costs are based on the 65 percent of the substantiated cases of child abuse and neglect who actually receive services. It does not include the 35 percent who need services but do not receive them.

More significantly, if all of these services for abused and neglected children successfully reduced the long-term costs associated with their continuing dysfunctioning, the costs of treating abusing and neglecting families would be recouped in higher productivity, less welfare dependency, and, ultimately, less child abuse. The prevailing evidence suggests, however, that these treatment efforts at best are successful with only half of the cases and that the incompetent parents who actually spawn habitual criminality and chronic welfare dependency by neglecting their children are the least likely to achieve successful outcomes.[11]

Given the high cost of treatment services and their limited successes, preventive efforts are far more efficacious alternatives.

LOSSES IN NATIONAL PRODUCTIVITY

Unemployment is often thought to be caused simply by the lack of jobs. Overlooked is the fact that many of the unemployed lack essential work and literacy skills and cannot qualify for available jobs. The surprising number of young adults who are unfit for military service reflects this fact.

In 1980 the Department of Defense commissioned a nationwide assessment of the abilities of current and potential armed forces recruits.[12] Thirty-one percent of all the young males and females (72% for African Americans and 59% for Hispanics) between the ages of sixteen and twenty-three, about 8 million in number, were found to be ineligible, or only conditionally eligible, for military service because of their poor performance on aptitude tests. There is no reason to believe that the situation is any better now.

This finding is supported by other sources. For example, the Committee on Economic Development estimated that 1 million youths leave high school without graduating each year.[13] Moreover, the Committee considered 30 percent of the school population to be educationally disadvantaged and likely to be difficult to employ as adults and to drain the economy in welfare and social service costs. The Committee further estimated that each class of school dropouts costs the nation more than $240 billion in lost earnings and forgone taxes over their lifetimes. This does not include the billions more for crime control, welfare payments, health care, and other social services for those who become habitual criminals and for those who become dependent on welfare.

Projections by the U.S. Census Bureau indicate that by the turn of the century the number of persons from 14 to 24 years of age will decrease from 46 million in 1980 to 40.6 million in the year 2000. The impact of this smaller population of 14- to 24-year-olds can be expected to be widely felt.[14] Colleges will have declining numbers of applicants. The workforce will be dramatically affected because there will be less qualified entry-level employees. At the same time the proportion of high-skilled jobs is likely to increase as those who enter the job market are undereducated and underskilled for the demands of the twenty-first century.

In addition by the year 2000 the proportion of minority children under the age of eighteen will be at least 38 percent, so that by the year 2020 currently defined minority groups will rise to one-third of the U.S. population from 17 percent in 1985.[15] The Center for the Study of Social Policy has projected that by the year 2000 at the present rate 70 percent of African American families will be headed by single women and more than 70 percent of African American men, or some 6 million, will not be employable. At an average annual income of $21,936 in 1994 dollars, that means a loss of at least $132 billion to the national economy annually from that group alone.

Because of the increasing demand for a skilled workforce, the previously mentioned standard of suitability for military service can be applied to suitability for employment. If the 31 percent Defense Department figure is used with the year 2000 workforce, there would be at least 23.7 million marginal or unemployable adults. The loss to the national economy would approximate $520 billion annually in their spendable income alone, without taking into account the value of the goods and services not produced.

Another usually unrecognized drain on the nation's productive capital is business crime. In a materialistic society in which success by any means is adulated, unscrupulous individuals have many opportunities for "white collar" crime. Even before the enormous savings and loan scandal of the 1980s was revealed, an estimated $200 billion a year was lost to this kind of crime.[16]

THE TOTAL COST OF INCOMPETENT PARENTING

Because money is the driving force in our capitalistic nation, I have estimated the monetary losses resulting from incompetent parenting as a concrete means of highlighting the financial value of competent parenting.

We have seen how incompetent parenting is costly in a number of ways, the most prominent being in the financial repercussions of habitual criminality, of chronic welfare dependency, and of child abuse and neglect service expenses (see Table 4). It also contributes to the growing number of unskilled, illiterate adults who erode national productivity.

Although representing a tiny fraction of the population (0.2%), habitual criminals have an inordinate impact on the quality of life in the United States by causing much of the serious crime that necessitates the deployment of massive security, law enforcement, and correctional resources that cost over $78 billion a year.[17] Excluding that cost and the costs of the crimes committed, the total loss to society from habitual criminality, conservatively estimated is $1.072 trillion over the offenders' potentially productive years. That represents an average of $2 million for each individual.

The second product of incompetent parenting is intergenerational welfare dependency. Only a minority (26%) of the parents who ever

Table 4. Estimates of the Cost of Incompetent Parenting in the United States

	Individual		Total population	
	Annual	Over 60 years of life	Annual	Over 60 years of life
Criminal recidivism	$34,166	$2 million	$17.8 billion	$1.1 trillion
Welfare dependency	$ 5,022	$ 301,320	$12.4 billion	$744 billion
Child abuse and neglect services	$12,174	$ 730,440	$ 8.4 billion	$504 billion
Total	$51,362	$3,031,760	$38.6 billion	$2.4 trillion

receive welfare payments are chronically dependent on them. They constitute only 0.4 percent of the population, but they persistently drain public resources and national productivity. The cost of welfare dependency in AFDC payments alone is $12.4 billion annually. Over a sixty-year period that cost totals $744 billion.

The third cost of incompetent parenting is represented by the array of services required to investigate and manage cases of child abuse and neglect. The direct costs of child abuse and neglect services for 0.3 percent of the population are at least $8.4 billion annually, or $12,174 for each child. Over a sixty-year period this totals at least $504 billion.

The aggregate cost of these three categories is $2.37 trillion. All of this expense arises from 0.9 percent of the population of the United States.

The fourth category obviously is the result of more than incompetent parenting, but the association is close enough to warrant including it in our calculations. The loss in national productivity from an estimated 23.7 million unqualified workers in the year 2000 over a forty-two-year period (the adult years used in the preceding calculations) would be 21.8 trillion 1994 dollars, or $520 billion annually.

All of these calculations are based upon conservative estimates for readily identified populations that represent only a fraction of the total costs of incompetent parenting. They do not reflect the improved quality of life of the nation that would result from safe streets and from the availability for other purposes of the money now spent on the products of incompetent parenting. They also do not reflect the future costs of successive generations repeating the same patterns.

I hope that these crude estimates will stimulate the interest of economists in studying more definitively the actual financial consequences of incompetent parenting. Unfortunately, these figures also reveal that a significant segment of our economy depends upon servicing the products of incompetent parenting, just as the manufacturers of armaments depend upon hostilities between nations.[18] For this reason at least subtle resistance to solving the problem can be expected from those quarters.

PRIORITIZING RISKS TO OUR SOCIETY

With the growing interest in preventing the pollution of our environment and preventing illnesses, attention is being devoted to risk reduction. As science progresses and as our ability to detect risks to the quality of our lives improves, our opportunities for reducing those risks have increased as well. To date we have proceeded haphazardly, responding to each risk as it is identified without prioritizing it. For example, the range of unacceptable risks is from 1 in 10,000 for federally regulated drugs to 3 in 100 for factory-work injuries to 1 in 10 for lung cancer for smokers.[19] In this perspective the risk of damage to children by incompetent parenting is at least 1 in 3. In this light, the risk created by incompetent parenting to society is the greatest hazard of all, yet it is unrecognized.

There is no question that competent parenting has financial value for society. In contrast with the $2 million cost to society of each child who is grossly incompetently parented, competent parents contribute $1 million in gain for society for each child they raise. In social cost terms the more important benefits of fostering competent parenting are reductions in crime, child abuse and neglect, and welfare dependency and increased employment for the nation. Beyond these measurable benefits are incalculable gains in personal fulfillment and happiness. These facts must be recognized in our social policies and workplaces.

We have the choice of continuing to ineffectively react to the devastating consequences of incompetent parenting or to proactively prevent this tragic waste of human and economic resources by ensuring competent parenting for all of our children. But there are formidable obstacles to dealing with incompetent parenting. Among them are prevalent social values in the United States that undermine the responsibilities of parents and children to each other. In this way our society both actively and passively contributes to incompetent parenting.

Chapter 6

The Tolerance of Incompetent Parenting

Not only does democracy make men forget their ancestors, but it also clouds their view of their descendants and isolates them from their contemporaries. Each man is forever thrown back on himself alone, and there is danger that he may be shut up in the solitude of his own personal interests.

ALEXIS DE TOCQUEVILLE, *Democracy in America* (1840)[1]

One of the most illuminating commentaries on the history of this country is the writing of the French nobleman Alexis de Toqueville about the fledgling United States in the 1830s.

De Toqueville made a number of prescient observations. One of them was that the self-interest of individuals fostered by a capitalistic democracy enhanced economic prosperity, but it did not create a "serviceable bond" between individuals and their communities. The emphasis on financial gain encouraged people to exchange money rather than personal relationships. As a result, de Toqueville foresaw that Americans would become alienated from each other as each person became immersed in the selfish pursuit of material gain.

De Toqueville's prediction has come true in many ways. Since his time alienation has fragmented families and permeated the fabric of our society. This alienation has been expressed in the form of "individualism" in which the interests of the individual rather than the interests of other people determine one's conduct. This kind of individualism together with vocational specialization and the mobility of our population has reduced the participation of individuals in groups that extend beyond their own immediate interests and in the lives of members of their own families.

As a result, individualistic social values often overshadow our altruistic cultural values that support families and community life.[2] For example, the competitive, individualistic orientation of our society encourages financial success without concern for the welfare of others. Our market economy revolves around buying, selling, and advertising. This environment is fertile soil for self-indulgence and for exploiting others. As a result, the short-term satisfaction of personal desires increasingly has taken priority over long-term commitments to spouses and to parenting.

The challenge of living in the United States always has been defining the line between our freedom to act and our freedom from being acted upon by another person—between freedom and justice. This tension between our freedoms and our responsibilities is clearly brought into focus in family relationships where the freedoms of parents and children contrast with their responsibilities to each other.

In this chapter I will describe reasons why our society tolerates and even encourages incompetent parenting. They are: (1) the influence of individualism on our social values; (2) the impact of individualism on our social structures; (3) the disparagement of parenting; (4) our fragmented reactions to social problems; (5) our crisis–recoil political responses; and (6) the rise in our society's threshold for deviancy.

The Impact of Individualism on Social Values

Individualism has great appeal because it emphasizes our freedom to do as we wish and gives us license to ignore our responsibilities to others. This emphasis has affected our society's values in at least three significant ways. The first is the reluctance to postpone immediate gratification that undermines making unpleasant present-day decisions in order to avoid long-range problems. The second is the emphasis on the freedom to engage in sexual behavior that obscures awareness that sexual behavior can be more harmful than aggressive behavior to other persons. The third is failing to help incompetent and self-defeating persons lead more effective lives and thereby missing opportunities for the prevention of social problems.

The Reluctance to Postpone Gratification

Previous generations of Americans have opened up frontiers, fought wars at home and abroad, and made countless personal sacrifices so that their children would inherit a better world. But this moral commitment to the future was submerged by the radical course of the economy of the United States in the 1980s, according to the economist Benjamin Friedman.[3]

Since 1980, Friedman notes that we have pursued a policy that amounts to living not just in, but just for, the present. In our preoccupation with immediate gratification, we have seemed to be living well by running up our national debt and selling off our national assets. The costs of federal policies that would bankrupt you and me and corporations have lowered the standard of living for most families and children in this country and have reduced the influence of the United States in the global economy.

Our individualistic emphasis on personal and special interests poses a powerful resistance to making long-range decisions that will place our economy on a more secure footing. These same forces stand in the way of making long-range decisions that encourage and support childrearing.

Minimizing the Harm of Sexual Behavior

We can see the exploitation of both sexual and aggressive behavior in the media for commercial purposes. At the same time aggressive behavior is limited by numerous laws because of its obviously damaging effect on other people.

In contrast, sexual behavior is less regulated by society, because it is regarded as a private activity. This obscures the fact that sexual behavior often has more serious and lasting consequences than aggressive behavior, such as the emotional damage of sexual abuse and the physical damage of sexually transmitted diseases, most recently AIDS. Two results of minimizing the damage caused by sexual behavior are that the sexual abuse of 1 in 5 women and the infection of 1 in 4 teenagers and young adults with sexually transmitted diseases are not recognized as epidemics. Moreover, our educational efforts are focused on the responsibility of children to protect themselves from molesters rather than on the responsibility of adults to restrain themselves from so exploiting children.

Even more generally, the tendency to regard sexually transmitted diseases and pregnancy as the only undesirable consequences of sexual behavior leads to overlooking the psychological, moral, and emotional consequences of sexual behavior in the form of guilt and low self-esteem. By encouraging "recreational" and exploitative sexual activity, elements of our society ignore the psychological and emotional hazards of sexual behavior for individuals and for society. Out-of-wedlock pregnancy is regarded as a possible undesirable side effect of sexual intercourse, but it often is not recognized as a physical and developmental hazard for the mother, as a health and developmental hazard for the child, and as an economic hazard for society.

Minimizing the hazards of sexual behavior also is reflected in the assumptions that adolescents will have sexual intercourse and that they can be induced to handle their sexual impulses wisely through education and the availability of contraceptives. Those assumptions ignore the inherent vulnerability of teenagers to serious lapses in judgment as will be elaborated upon in chapter 9. In fact the risk of pregnancy is not realistically managed by many adolescents, particularly those who are the most unstable, even when they have had sex education and have access to contraception.

The United States is rapidly reaching the point at which limits must be set on the freedom of individuals to do as they wish when other people are affected by their aggressive and sexual behavior, particularly when those other people are children. We can no longer presume that childbirth is a completely private matter and ignore its consequences for society.

The Failure to Intervene before Damage Is Done

Michel Crozier, a twentieth-century de Toqueville, sees the deeply embedded belief in the innate goodness of people as an important factor in America's failings.[4] That confidence worked well when people were in short supply and had to cooperate with each other, and when natural resources were abundant. But that confidence in the innate goodness of everyone sours when people compete for limited resources. It is naive when it fails to take into account the fact that there is a small, but highly significant, number of intractably dangerous and irresponsible people.

In the context of the reluctance to forego immediate gratifications, our society permits individuals to harm themselves and to pose problems for others until certain thresholds of imminent or actual damage to others are crossed. The point at which limits are set on aggressive and sexual behavior is strongly influenced by our emphasis on the freedom and autonomy of individuals. We emphasize the innate goodness of people by assuming that everyone is capable of furthering their own interests and acting wisely. When carried to extremes, this well-intentioned and essential protection of the rights of individuals actually encourages self-defeating behavior and the exploitation of vulnerable segments of the population by commercial and criminal interests.

Examples of this failure to protect vulnerable persons, and of actually exploiting them, are seen when we lower the legal drinking age leading to an increase in teenage drinking; when we legalize gambling that absorbs money from the poor and ruins compulsive gamblers; when we are lenient with alcoholic drivers who have repeated accidents; when we fail to control concealable handguns that enable unstable people to commit violent assaults and murders; when we ignore the epidemic of sexually transmitted diseases; and when we permit severely mentally ill persons, including parents, to refuse effective treatment and thereby to remain unable to function in society and unable to parent their children.

Furthermore, the popular belief that anyone can completely change their lives by simply changing their attitudes makes it difficult for many of us to accept the fact that some people are unable to change in spite of their personal beliefs and promises that they will do so.

More specifically, the legal system assumes that all adults are able to handle their own affairs unless they are formally adjudicated to be mentally incompetent. This assumption reflects our vital respect for the autonomy of individuals; however, it is contradicted by the fact that a small but significant segment of the population does not meet the legal definition of mental incompetence but is socially incompetent and cannot live within the law. The actions of those individuals adversely affect society as a whole, but the legal system is unable to act until they commit legally defined crimes. This policy makes it difficult to prevent crime and welfare dependency.

The legal system also implicitly assumes that it is preferable to let the guilty go free than to falsely convict an innocent person. The likelihood that five out of six persons will be the victims of major crimes during their lifetimes seriously challenges that doctrine. Furthermore, the victims of crimes find that the criminal justice system is not oriented toward considering their interests. They often are subjected to stressful experiences in legal proceedings that can be more traumatic for them than the injuries or property losses they sustained in the first place.

Another essential principle in our legal system is that a person is innocent until proved guilty of a crime. That concept has been extended to the presumption that all persons are law-abiding until they are convicted of breaking laws. This means that our society generally does not act to regulate behavior until proved damage has been done. The line is drawn between acceptable and unacceptable behavior only at the point at which a person harms others or when there is a clear and present danger of doing so. The definitions of harm to others include physical, social, psychological, and emotional damage. Our society tolerates those kinds of harm to oneself short of suicide but does draw the line on inflicting the same kind of harm on others, as when public slander occurs or a psychotherapist engages in sexual behavior with a client.

In this context, arguments for the government's role in protecting individuals from harming themselves are regarded as offensive paternalism by "liberals" and as offensive invasions of privacy by "conservatives." The resulting emphasis on the freedom of individuals to be irresponsible and to fail means that there are continual tugs to loosen societal restraints on irresponsible behavior. This tendency makes it extremely difficult for our society to take preventive actions.

A commonly accepted canon of civilized society, however, is that privacy can be compromised when the public interests are threatened. When the predominating public sentiment so dictates, restrictions of individual freedom can be justified by inordinate repercussions of that freedom. A dramatic example is the recent regulation of smoking because of its health hazards to nonsmokers.[5] This reveals that it is possible to limit behavior before it actually cause harm to other people. There clearly are circumstances under which interventions on the freedom and privacy of individuals can be made without sacrificing our cherished values. Still the fact that children can be seriously harmed by their own parents frequently is overlooked with unappreciated devastating consequences for our society.

Because of our society's failure to respond to the abuse and neglect of children before it happens, its failure to respond to welfare dependency before it becomes chronic, and its failure to respond to habitual criminals prior to the commission of crimes, a small fraction of the population freely engages in behavior that ultimately impairs the quality of life of our entire society to the point where the personal safety of everyone in our nation has deteriorated to unacceptable levels.

Fortunately, the courts have drawn a line between a parent's prerogative to be personally irresponsible and a parent's prerogative to behave irresponsibly toward one's child, as we will see in chapter 8. It is with children that the delicate balance between our freedom as individuals to act and our responsibilities to others can be most clearly distinguished. If we build on this foundation, we can do much to ensure the competent parenting of children and thereby prevent social problems.

The dominance of these expressions of individualism over common interests has made it difficult for our society to recognize and deal with incompetent parenting. The effects of individualism on social values are evident in the United States, but their ultimate impact on a society's structures can be most clearly illustrated by the consequences of similar trends in Sweden, a small and relatively homogeneous country without an underclass as we know it. This comparison is especially appropriate because Sweden often has been regarded as a model society. Actually Sweden's experience illustrates the societal fragmentation that results from individualism. It may well foreshadow what will happen in the United States beyond the creation of our underclass, the most obvious marker of breakdown in our society.

The Impact of Individualism on Social Structures

The sociologist, David Popenoe, used Sweden as a prototype of the kind of society that emerges when individualistic values predominate over altruistic values in families and in communities.[6] As will be seen, there are similarities, as well as critical differences, between the situations in Sweden and in the United States.

When we look at Sweden, the contemporary decline of the influence of families there appears to be related to that society's emphasis on individualism in recent decades, in part as a reaction against family dominance in the form of paternalism. In the past families posed a powerful constraint on individualism in Sweden.

The extent of control over individuals in the family-oriented cultures of Scandinavia was vividly described by the Englishman T. R. Malthus after his visit to Norway in 1799.[7] Then every Norwegian male had to serve in the armed forces, and, once drafted, "the man could not marry without producing a certificate signed by the minister of his parish that he had substance enough to support a wife and family, and even then it was at the will of the officer to let him marry or not."

Against this Scandinavian background of family-state control of individual lives, Sweden gradually shifted toward the liberation of individuals from the influences of their families.

The "Postnuclear" Family

During the 1960s the growing affluence of Sweden, in part related to public benefits, permitted individuals to become more self-sufficient. Premarital sexual intercourse became increasingly common, and contraceptives prevented unwanted children and forced marriages. Later marriages and postponed first births were accelerated by the movement of women into the labor force, as the norm became the full-time employment of parents away from home.

There also was a rapid decline in marriages, because young people decided to delay marriage until children were on the way. Divorce also occurred earlier, as legal restrictions on divorce were eased. Nonmarital cohabitation became widely accepted, and why one needed to marry just to have children no longer was obvious. The decrease in legal marriages led to a large increase in out-of-wedlock births as a result of nonmarital cohabitation, designated by Popenoe as the "postnuclear" family. As unmarried couples moved apart and as married couples divorced, the chances of a child living through childhood with both biological parents diminished markedly.

At the same time, more family functions were performed by persons or agencies outside of the family, especially education, child care, and meal service. There also was a rapid increase in single-person, "nonfamily," and single-parent households.

The trend toward "postnuclear" families with unmarried parents has been accompanied by many positive developments for individuals in Sweden. Few women would want to return to legalized patriarchy, when divorce was next to impossible. Few of the elderly want to depend upon the care of unwilling children. Few mothers want to be excluded from the possibility of joining the workforce. And no one wants to face the prospect of poverty without public assistance.

At the same time, there are undesirable aspects of the "postnuclear" family from the point of view of children and thus of society's next generation. Even if actual behavior might suggest otherwise, Western cultural values hold that children need the continuing love and support of parents in lasting marriages based on a commitment to childrearing. The decline of the marriage-based family strikes at the very root of this ideal.

Although parents no longer need children in their lives for economic reasons, children still need parents as much as they ever did. They need not just adults, but parents with whom they can form affectionate attachment bonds. The time, patience, and love of caring parents have no substitutes in paid employees or technological efficiency. In short, children need committed parents, and they need dependable environments. In Sweden, as in the United States, it has become increasingly likely that they will have neither one in postnuclear families.

The Demise of the Family as a Mediating Social Structure

Because we think of our own families in highly personalized terms, we usually do not think of families as vital structures of society—

certainly not as social institutions. It is only when families are not formed or when they break down that we realize how important families are to society. The most clear-cut example is when a child is without a family, and one must be found or created for that child.

Families actually are "mediating structures" that stand between individuals and their societies.[8] Families that incorporate cultural values are mediating structures between individuals, their society, and their culture. As an example of the mediating function of families, the social psychological evidence reveals that parent–child relationships are the most effective means of protecting individuals from the confusing demands of modern societies. At the same time friendship and community networks are needed to connect families with society.

Neighborhoods, religious groups, and voluntary organizations are mediating structures between families and society. On the one hand, these mediating structures protect individuals from incursions of society's impersonal "megastructures," such as educational, law-enforcement, and corporate bureaucracies. They also insulate the young from the influences of antisocial peer groups. On the other hand, these mediating structures enable society's megastructures to reach individuals with a personalized face. Most importantly for society, when joined together in local communities, regional entities, and national groups, these mediating structures also can hold the megastructures of society accountable.

The institution of the family has been seriously buffeted by the recent tide of events in Sweden. The emergence of the uncommitted postnuclear family has weakened parent–child ties. These unstable relationships also do not function as mediating structures in society because their integrity depends on the current state of adult relationships rather than on the commitment of adults to cultural childrearing objectives.

The Swedish experience provides no reason to be sanguine about the family's immediate future in the United States. While the mating impulse may be as robust as ever, the extension of that impulse into committed parent–child relationships clearly has weakened in Sweden. The reduction of committed family ties results in the lessened commitment of individuals to other mediating structures in their own communities and ultimately in less participation of individuals in their own governance.

The Deterioration of Community Mediating Structures

The empirical evidence about the negative social implications of the decline of family influences in Sweden is not completely convincing. But there is no question that the decline in committed family relationships has been accompanied by a diminished commitment of people to community mediating structures. It is the loss of community mediating structures, which follows the loss of families as mediating structures, that threatens the integrity of a society.

Sweden's health care system, work productivity, and employment level are exemplary compared to the United States, but community mediating structures have deteriorated.[9] For example, local religious organizations have almost disappeared; voluntary health, educational, and welfare associations are less evident; and urban neighborhoods have lost their social functions. Individuals increasingly live in social isolation in a fragmented society. The popular attitude is that society is to blame for poverty, delinquency, and other social ills. The sense of individual responsibility and the participation of individuals in their own governance have eroded.

Centralized political megastructures, unchecked by mediating structures of politically active citizens can drift in the direction of social control. Such tendencies raise the specter of a mass society, consisting of relatively unattached individuals without shared ideals, on the one hand, and powerful megastructures filling the mediating structure vacuum, on the other hand.

The highly centralized megastructures of Sweden show the signs of such a mass society in the sense that the state has assumed family functions that further undermine the integrity of families. Whether one agrees with this interpretation or not, the potential for the social control of individual lives cannot be discounted when socially isolated persons feel little obligation to each other and when the government is not held accountable by mediating structures.

One result of the decline in mediating structures in Sweden is an increase in delinquency. Precisely because they are impersonal, the megastructures of law enforcement and social services are inadequate replacements for parents, relatives, neighbors, and pastors. This situation now exists in the United States as well.

Although the Swedish socialist state has shown concern about certain rights of children, such as by restricting the traditional right of parents to discipline children as they see fit by outlawing spanking, Sweden has not taken into account the impact of postnuclear families on its children.

Obviously, a government cannot regulate or promote affectionate bonds between parents and children. There is much to be said, however, for the state signaling in various ways that the stability of family relationships is extremely important to children and to society as a whole.

The Relevance of Sweden's Experience to the United States

The Swedish experience with the postnuclear family bears on the situation in the United States, which is now what U.S. Senator Daniel Patrick Moynihan called a "postmarital" society.[10]

The two-parent married family in which American socialization has taken place is losing ground.[11] There is an emphasis on adapting to family dysfunctions rather than on emulating functional families. No-fault divorce laws make it easy to end marriages and do not take into account the consequences of divorce, especially for the affected children.

The Swedish lesson is that a reduction of committed family ties results in a reduction in the commitment of individuals to the mediating structures of their own communities and ultimately in a reduction in the participation of individuals in their own governance. The general loss of mediating structures in our society would further weaken the accountability of our government to the people, as already is starkly seen in the situation of the underclass in the United States.

The absence of mediating structures in the American underclass is a direct result of postmarital families in which many parents also are incompetent. When they do not value civility and respect for others, individuals create unsafe neighborhoods that resemble war zones. Growing up in such surroundings with access to guns, drugs, and alcohol conveys the message that violence is normal. This has led the United States to a situation that replicates that of the rich and the poor in Victorian England, as described by Benjamin Disraeli:[12] "Two nations, between whom there is no intercourse and no sympathy; who are as ignorant of each other's habits, thoughts, and feelings, as if they were dwellers in different zones, or inhabitants of different planets."

In the United States, "two nations" of African American and

Caucasian people have emerged as predicted by Alexis de Tocqueville, who grimly noted:[13]

> The most formidable of all the ills that threaten the future of the Union arises from the presence of a black population on its territory. The abolition of slavery will, in the common course of things, increase the repugnance of the white population for the blacks. You may set the Negro free, but you cannot make him otherwise than an alien to those of European origin.

The political scientist Andrew Hacker points out that although legal slavery may be in the past, segregation and subordination of the African American population persists so that, even today, a stigma is imposed on many African American children at birth.[14] One result is self-inflicted genocide in the ghettos by young men who waste their lives and the lives of others because they are alienated from the disenfranchising society in which they live. There are no mediating structures between them and society. In that context incompetent parenting does not attract attention.

Popenoe poses the vital question: should we wait for further social science research before making moral judgments about such an important social trend as toward the postnuclear uncommitted family? More to the point, can the social sciences answer such questions? Many of the immediate effects of the decline in committed family relationships cannot be measured by the empirical methods of the social sciences. They have more to do with the inner states of people that ultimately result in crime, welfare dependency, and unemployability.

Popenoe concludes that the social sciences can help, but they never can determine the goals and the customs of our culture. Those goals and customs lie within the realm of moral ideals, especially the hopes of our culture and of our society for our children. The realization of those hopes depends upon the status of parenting in our society.

THE DISPARAGEMENT OF PARENTING

In addition to the erosion of family life, following the trend in Sweden, the disparagement of parenting in the United States is another manifestation of the domination of individualistic values over values that support parenting.

Parenting Lacks Financial Value

In the capitalistic model, parenting generally is regarded as a private activity outside of the realm of public concern. In contrast, in the socialistic model the rearing of children is regarded as a primary concern of the state.

As a capitalistic society with socialistic qualities, the United States has viewed childrearing as a private matter unless it is terminated by parental death or abandonment or unless it is deemed to have damaged a child. Otherwise our society has limited its role in childrearing to publicly supported education, unless parents choose to provide education for their children themselves privately.

More to the point, in our capitalistic economy parenting is not regarded as having economic value. The traditional markers of economic status and progress do not take into account activities that are unremunerated. Even when child care is purchased, its financial value is low. In this context parents are seen as more useful to society in the workforce where their productivity can be valued in monetary terms. In capitalistic terms, hiring nonparents to care for children has appeal, because remunerated jobs that increase the Gross Domestic Product are created by delegating child care. Only then does child care have economic value by creating jobs.

In addition to favoring the creation of a child care industry as a capitalistic supplement to parenting, our society is imbued with materialistic values that encourage parents to seek alternatives to caring for their own children. The belief is widely held that both parents should be employed away from home on a full-time basis in order to generate enough income to pay others to care for their children and to purchase luxury goods and services for their families.

For many parents following commercially fostered trends is important in maintaining images of success and sophistication. Those parents are attracted to the expertise of professionals and to new and novel technologies that free them from what they regard as the menial chores of childrearing.

All of these factors operate to disparage parenting as an important and useful activity. When you can pay someone else to do an unvalued job better, why do it yourself? Even when childrearing is appealing to adults, the lack of social support of parenting, which is regarded as "caretaking" or "caregiving" rather than as a growth process for both children and parents, creates doubt about the value of parenting.

Why not create a society in which professionals care for children, and parents are free to pursue their own interests and careers? It sounds ideal now as it did to Plato and to countless social reformers since his time. It is the trend in the United States, as it has been in Sweden, but for capitalistic rather than for socialistic reasons.

The Lack of Commitment to Child–Parent Relationships

In recent decades public policies in the United States have shied away from the idea that certain family forms are more desirable than others. Instead there has been subtle encouragement of alternative families in the same spirit that has recognized the legitimacy of alternative life styles for individuals. There has been little emphasis on the social benefits of marriage or on the social and economic contributions made by parents who devote themselves to childrearing. There has been no public effort to promote childbearing in the context of marriage. Until recently, public policies have discouraged marriage.

The message seems to be that there is no reason to prefer one life style over another for childrearing, as revealed in the sentiment expressed by Nobel Laureate Toni Morrison in a *Time* magazine interview:[15] "The little nuclear family is a paradigm that just doesn't work. It doesn't work for white or black people. Why we are hanging on to it, I don't know."

Even in ancient Greece, Plato's conception of the ideal republic was one in which children would be raised more efficiently by the state than by parents, who then would be free to pursue their own careers. The wealthy always have hired others to care for their children. This motif runs through contemporary attitudes toward adult careers and toward parenting in the United States.

Yet the institutionalization of the care of young children was not realized in ancient Greece, and it has failed in all subsequent social experiments from those in the People's Republic of China to the Israeli kibbutzim.[16] The wealthy who have purchased child care have not enjoyed close family relationships. These failures have occurred because the fact that parenting is a fulfilling career in itself has been overlooked.

Although childrearing involves personal sacrifices for parents and for children alike, it actually can be a creative, fulfilling life style for both. For example, as Jim Henson, the creator of the Muppets, pointed out, children give parents license to express the childish, "crazy" parts of themselves.

The rewards of parenthood are easily obscured for contemporary parents who pursue the goals of consumers trying to "have it all now" in a material sense and who do not appreciate the personal rewards of childrearing. As with any career, parenting has its burdens and satisfactions. Unlike other careers, it involves affectionate attachment bonds between people. The fact that many individuals have not found family relationships to be rewarding does not detract from the importance of parent–child relationships for individuals and for society. It is through the committed parenting they receive that children become the committed citizens essential for a democratic society. For this reason, the ways in which children are parented affect everyone.

Both childhood and parenthood are complementary developmental stages in the life cycle. They are essential to the survival of societies and to the survival of the human race. In the light of its current disparagement in the United States, the vital importance of parenting needs to be recognized. As the source of our society's human resources, parenting is more important than oil fields and forests. It is both a fulfilling career for adults and an essential institution of society.

The need for greater visibility of societal concern for parents and children in general is illustrated by the following statement of James Garbarino, President of the Erikson Institute for Advanced Study in Child Development:[17]

> When I moved to Illinois a couple of years ago, I brought into the state a three-year-old automobile and a three-year-old child. The community said to me, "Look, we're very concerned about that automobile. We want you to get it registered. We want it inspected periodically to insure that you're taking adequate care of it and that it works well. You also have to have a license to operate that vehicle, because we know that not just anyone can do that."
>
> My three-year-old child, on the other hand, was completely invisible. There was no notion that the community needed or wanted to know that I had brought a child into it, what the status of the child was, or whether I was prepared to care for the child. Only

if I were to seriously neglect or mistreat the child would the community notice, and even then it would be a very grudging notice. I believe that the larger community must set some minimum standards of care in a positive way, not simply when there is mistreatment, and intervention is needed.

As this anecdote suggests, in order to ensure that children have the opportunity to develop affectionate attachment bonds with their parents statutory statements of society's expectations of parents are needed.

Expanding the Definition of Family

Broadening the definition of family to include households without children creates additional problems for parents. They already are beleaguered in the workplace and in communities by competition with adults who do not have children. Moreover, people who live together increasingly define themselves as families. Allowing the concept of the family to be blurred by those who do not have childrearing responsibilities but desire family benefits intended for parents with children dilutes support for parenting even more. For this reason, the support of *parenting* is a more appropriate focus for public policies than the support of ambiguous *families* that include people without childrearing responsibilities.

The basic structure of our society depends on competent parents and on committed relationships that facilitate parenting. This highlights the importance of distinguishing between household units that include parents and children and those that do not, rather than regarding them as equivalent. Other intimate living arrangements can be recognized as domestic partnerships without confusing them with childrearing families that deserve special consideration because of their importance in rearing society's children. A distinction should be made between dependents who are children and those who are not.

In the face of these trends, unless our society devotes special efforts to protecting and supporting children and their parents, competing adult interests inevitably will take precedence. This will happen simply because parents who are raising children constitute only 26 percent of the population in the United States, and their families occupy only 37 percent of the households.[18]

Because children and their families constitute a minority of the population in the United States, we need public policies that enhance rather than undermine parenting, as they now do. For example, the annual federal income tax deduction for a dependent child would be over $6000 now if it simply had kept up with inflation over the years.

SOCIETY'S FRAGMENTED REACTIONS TO SOCIAL PROBLEMS

Beyond the fragmenting effect of individualism on the social values and the mediating structures of our society and beyond the disparagement of parenting, additional factors contribute to the tolerance of incompetent parenting in the United States and dilute efforts to address the underlying causes of social problems.

The fear of tyranny of the Revolutionary War period biased our political and legal systems toward protecting individual freedoms even at the expense of community interests. The checks and balances in our constitutional democracy favor the protection of individuals and minority interests from collective actions over the formation of consensus around common interests. Consequently, our political and legal systems make it easier for special interest groups to block action than to join together to take action for the common good.

The Competition between Special Interests

Just as higher education and science have become divided into separate specialties, our political approaches to social problems are piecemeal and unconnected. They focus on special rather than collective interests by pitting interest groups against each other rather than by fostering cooperation. Because they do not address underlying causes, the consequent partial remedies devised often contribute to the very problems they seek to solve.

For example, the handling of social problems, such as poverty, child abuse, alcoholism, drug abuse, and crime, customarily involves separating each problem as an entity unto itself, as if each one reflected a different problem requiring a different solution. Each problem area then competes with the others for attention and resources. Consequently, the helping professionals concentrate on treating the victims of each societal problem, rather than addressing the underlying causes, and the status quo is inadvertently maintained. The results are costly expenditures for remedial services, and prevention is ignored.

In the professional approach to separate social problems, the mediating structures of families and neighborhoods are replaced by megastructures in the form of service industries for each category of problems. This further weakens the mediating structures. It replaces personal relationships with professional services. Among providers of these services with limited scopes, "It's not my job" is a frequently heard response.

Because it also emphasizes the technical skills of experts, the separation of social problems tends to shift the responsibility for change from the recipients to the providers of services. This results in the increased dependency of individuals on professionals to care for them and to intervene in their lives. It fosters the idea that professionals can raise and care for children better than can parents. Accordingly, the avoidance of parents' responsibilities for their own actions is fostered.

The Institutional Abuse of Children

There are other adverse consequences when the management of personal lives is turned over to impersonal megastructures. For example, the institutional abuse of children and youth usually is thought of in the narrow sense as physical or sexual abuse occurring in group care settings. In a broader sense, however, it occurs as an intrinsic element in the operation of governmental and social institutions that affect young people.[19]

A subtle form of the institutional abuse of children is illustrated by the fact that child welfare, mental health, and legal agencies now occupy an established place in the American economy and are as dependent upon their clients as their clients are upon them. This does not mean that professionals in these agencies wish to promote the continuation of the problems they are supposed to solve. It does mean that the policies and procedures in their uncoordinated, institutionalized systems limit their activities to servicing, instead of preventing and solving, the fragmented problems they confront.[20] When that happens the potential for individuals and families to help themselves is obscured and lost.

Juvenile court judge Justine Polier called attention to a singular example of the institutional abuse of young people by the juvenile court system.[21] Born of charitable impulses, juvenile courts were flawed from the outset. They never were able to become the envisioned guardians of troubled children. Because they were too closely modeled on charity that granted only what could be spared, they never had the resources or community support required to help families in difficulty. In addition, the extent to which the legal system can fail to resolve child custody and visitation contests and actually act against the interests of children is illustrated by the *Morgan v. Foretich* case, in which interminable litigation led to the jailing of a mother, the hiding of a child, and the relocation of mother and child in another country without resolution of the allegation of sexual abuse by the father.

As a consequence of the failures of the juvenile justice system, in the *In re Gault* ruling in 1967 the U.S. Supreme Court found it necessary to protect children from the abuses of the very institution that had been established to help them by insisting that the due process of law be followed in juvenile court proceedings.[22] The unintended result of that action was further distancing of the children from help, as procedural due process became the main concern of the courts. Confronted with heavier caseloads without the benefit of adequate resources, juvenile courts now are unable to help incompetent parents adequately and fail to make a significant impact on the most serious juvenile offenders.

THE POLITICAL CRISIS–RECOIL RESPONSE

There is another societal obstacle to intervening with incompetent parents. It is the crisis–recoil nature of our society's political system.[23] When the mediating structures of families and neighborhoods break down, the crisis–recoil response leads to public overreaction to the resulting crises followed by recoiling from their causes.

The crisis–recoil response is seen in the tendency to deal with individual children by removing them from crises in their families and placing them in foster homes rather than helping their families.[24] Later, the inevitable crisis in the availability of foster homes is dealt with by seeking more foster homes, rather than by addressing the family problems that necessitated so many foster homes in the first place. Beneath these practices lies the failure of public policies to recognize that a child is at the minimum a part of a two-person unit that is dependent on the integrity of the mediating structures of a family, a neighborhood, a school, and a community. As a result, services that focus on individual children and fragment families have been overdeveloped, and services and programs that support parenting and community building have not been sufficiently developed.

Another more obvious example of the crisis–recoil response is our typical response to and punishment of criminal behavior.[25] This approach leads to police intervention after crimes have been committed and to building more prisons in the belief that the greater infusion of money into the penal system will solve the social problem of crime. The punishment of crime then becomes a reality-avoidance mechanism that recoils from facing the underlying causes of crime. The punishment of a culprit permits the public to relax with the illusion that the crisis created by a crime has been resolved.

The crisis–recoil phenomenon is illustrated further by regulations that mandate medical treatment for every newborn who is not born dead.[26] The response to the crisis at birth is to save the life of the child. Because of recoil from the cause of the newborn's crisis and its repercussions, however, there is no assessment of the impact of preserving life and no provision for the treatment of the child after leaving the intensive-care neonatal unit. As a result the child remains dependent on expensive technology simply to maintain physical life often with the consequent financial ruin and disruption of the child's family.

Finally, because children do not vote and because families with children constitute a minority of the population, it is difficult for our political system to address their fundamental problems. The gradual erosion of our quality of life also makes it possible to preserve an illusion of prosperity, because the full impact of our policies, as seen from any moment, always lies in the future and does not demand an immediate response from our crisis-oriented political machinery—unless we open our eyes to the current plight of our children.

Fortunately, public concern can be aroused when there are visible problems. The continual reexamination of institutional megastructures does occur in the United States. The military forces, the post office, the public schools, and welfare programs all wax and wane in the spotlight of public interest. Now the social institution of the family as a cultural mediating structure is being accorded attention.

Often taken for granted in the past, the importance of family ties is highlighted in divorce custody and visitation matters. Then parents find that the lack of access to their children makes them aware of how important their children are to them. In a similar way, large numbers of men and women who desire children and encounter fertility problems know the distress of not having children in their lives. The significance of children is evident—when they are not available. Even more widespread is the ambivalence and guilt parents employed away from home experience when they have difficulty finding satisfactory day care for their children.

There is growing awareness that rhetorical statements about the rights and interests of children have little implementation in political and legal actions. There is an emerging awareness that individuals without connections with their families and with their communities often harm themselves and others.

We cannot rely on the crisis–recoil nature of our political system to solve our social problems. We need to strengthen the mediating structures that can solve those problems by more clearly articulating our underlying, shared, cultural values that support family and community relationships, the theme of chapter 10.

THE ELEVATED THRESHOLD OF DEVIANCY

Finally the products of incompetent parenting have so permeated our society that we have become inured to them.

Senator Daniel Patrick Moynihan points out that societies under stress, much like individuals, turn to pain killers of various kinds to cover up distressing social problems.[27] He notes that the amount of deviant behavior in our society has increased beyond the levels that we can easily afford to recognize. Accordingly, we have been redefining deviancy so as to exempt much of the conduct that we previously deplored. Prime examples are the degrees of violence, homelessness, and crime that now exist and that several decades ago would have been considered intolerable.

This numbing tendency represents a kind of conditioning process that reflects the human tendency to adapt to stressful circumstances over which we perceive ourselves as having no control. A common metaphor for this phenomenon is the failure of a frog to jump from water that is gradually heated to the point of extinguishing the frog's life.

It also appears that our violence-prone society needs its delinquents and criminals who act out the hidden impulses of the rest of us and whom we then subject to indignant censure.[28] In this sense, the "badness" of delinquents and of criminals is an externalization of our own impulses to be "bad." By punishing others who are "bad," we avoid facing our own "badness." Thus, our society's fascination with and provocation of antisocial behavior mingle with demands for punishment in prisons that permit us to avoid looking into our own contributions to crime.

This antisocial undertow in our society predominates in our present social climate that lacks a commitment to expecting and supporting competent parenting as the antidote to antisocial behavior. Furthermore, we have expected the schools and governmental agencies to correct our social problems, as if parents had nothing to do with the outcomes of their children's lives.

We cannot expect to have prospering children when our society does not model, and actually undermines, the development of character. The good life is portrayed as gaining power, pleasure, and property, sometimes by any means. There is little emphasis on the strength of character we need to control our impulses, to tolerate frustration, and to postpone gratification—the essential qualities for life in a civilized society. Our children are not born with these qualities. They learn them from adults who model them. They learn them, or do not learn them, most indelibly from their parents who are supported by a social environment that sets acceptable limits for behavior.

As the nation's largest permanent minority, children encounter special obstacles to achieving recognition and representation in social policies because they are unable to speak for themselves. Unlike other minorities, their special interests are underrepresented in the political process. Therefore, the developmental needs of children and the importance of parenting will not be accorded appropriate attention until our society's contributions to incompetent parenting are addressed. Unfortunately, the prejudice and discrimination against children arising from juvenile ageism stands in the way.

Chapter 7

Juvenile Ageism

Youth is a wonderful thing.
What a crime to waste it on children!

—GEORGE BERNARD SHAW

We can appreciate the humor in George Bernard Shaw's comment. Even children might smile. But if the words *Jews, blacks,* or *gays* were substituted for the word *children,* prejudice would be instantly apparent—and resented.

The fact that we do not recognize this slur against children illustrates the ingrained nature of juvenile ageism. Even when I point this out, you may still discount its importance—after all we are just referring to children, and they are not protesting.

We are well acquainted with racism and sexism, and we are beginning to acknowledged ageism against the elderly. But the other form of ageism—juvenile ageism—is virtually unknown. It is concealed by our rhetoric that idealizes children as we largely ignore their interests in the affairs of the adult world. It is expressed when we view childhood and parenting solely through the eyes of adults.

The prejudice of juvenile ageism, which is as virulent as racism and as pervasive as sexism, is the greatest barrier to recognizing the interests of children in our political processes, in child caring systems, and in households. The most glaring forms of discrimination based on juvenile ageism are violations of abused and neglected children's civil rights that would be recognized in the United States as rejection, oppression, torture, enslavement, and murder if they took place with an adult of any race or of either sex.

Our lack of awareness of juvenile ageism is understandable. First of all, it is eclipsed by our concern about racism and sexism. Second, we all are juvenile ageists to some degree. Third, we all have difficulty recognizing our own prejudices, even when they are pointed out to us. This is the natural result of the fact that we all hold preconceived ideas that guide our attitudes and choices. As much as we might like to believe otherwise, all of our judgments are biased, or prejudiced, by our past experiences and by our current emotional states. Furthermore, we are inclined to reject contradictions of our own judgments.

The writer Jean-François Revel called attention to the way in which we frequently reject genuine knowledge and prefer to base our ideas and our actions on false information, even when doing so may be contrary to our own interests.[1] Revel pointed out that we tend to use our intellectual faculties to protect the beliefs that are especially dear to us.

It is not surprising then that convincing us that we are prejudiced is not an easy task. This is particularly the case with juvenile ageism. In some ways, to speak of ageism against the young in the 1990s resembles speaking of racism in Atlanta, Georgia, in the 1850s. Then the economic interests and the latent guilt of plantation owners precluded recognizing the racism involved in slavery. Today, the economic interests and the latent guilt of many adults preclude recognizing juvenile ageism that overrides the interests of children in our society and in our families.

There is another reason why juvenile ageism and other prejudices are easily obscured. It is that prejudice can be expressed in benevolent as well as malevolent ways. We can recognize prejudice as an attitude and discrimination as resulting behavior when they are expressed in obviously malevolent ways, even without conscious intent. For example, when children are oppressed, abused, and neglected, it is easier to entertain the existence of juvenile ageism than it is when we believe that we are helping them.

Yet prejudice and discrimination can be expressed in benevolent and idealizing ways. As an illustration, before racism was generally accepted as a social problem, many people benevolently believed that slaves were content and needed direction. Before sexism was openly revealed, many people believed that women were naturally dependent and were satisfied with subservient occupations. The idealization of motherhood still makes it possible for men to avoid their responsibilities in childrearing.

Now many of us under the influence of benevolent ageism believe that the elderly are better off with special care away from their families and that children are better off in supervised environments away from their families. Many of us believe that all of the material wishes of our children should be gratified or that our children should have better lives than we did during our childhoods. In each of these instances we do not recognize that overly protective and indulgent attitudes can harm our children by preventing them from learning how to handle life's challenges and to take advantage of life's opportunities themselves, just as overly protective and indulgent attitudes harm racial minorities, women, and the elderly. The harmful effects of overprotection and of overindulgence are the least evident with children because the important opportunities and challenges they will not learn how to access or handle lie in the future.

Because children really are dependent, the guise of protecting and indulging them can readily conceal juvenile ageism. The inherent dependency of children positions them to be the victims of prejudice and discrimination.

THE DYNAMICS OF PREJUDICE AND DISCRIMINATION

The critical importance of the natural dependency of children in juvenile ageism becomes evident when we consider the dynamics of prejudice.

Destructive prejudice in either its malevolent or benevolent forms is a defensive reaction to frustration based on an attitude of superiority over the other person evoked by competition for space, materials, or time in order to give the prejudiced person superior access to those resources.[2] It is facilitated by differences in appearance, interests, and sophistication between the prejudiced and the victims. It persists because it serves adaptive purposes for the prejudiced and for the victims. It is reinforced by the compliance of victims who thereby validate the prejudice. It also is reinforced by the rebellious reactions of the victims, who then are blamed for the frustrations and guilt they cause the prejudiced.

The dependency of children and their natural inclinations to challenge authority make them prime targets for prejudice and discrimination when they place competitive demands upon adults for space, for material and emotional resources, and for time, or when they arouse anxiety in adults.

More specific psychological factors foster the prejudice of ageism. An important determinant of both elder and juvenile ageism in the United States is the high priority we place on the image of being carefree and independent. In conflict with this image is the fact that both the elderly and the young pose concerns for us and restrict our independence. They also remind us that we are vulnerable and dependent ourselves. The elderly remind us that we will age and die. The young remind us that we have childlike, dependent parts of ourselves. In an effort to ward off the anxieties created by these psychological factors, we tend to avoid the elderly and to turn away from our children by expecting both to be independent and to care for themselves.

At a deeper level, those of us who are parents naturally harbor ambivalent feelings toward our children because they necessitate sacrifices of our own interests.[3] This ambivalence is accentuated by conflicts between the demands of our careers and the responsibilities of childrearing. Moreover, many of us harbor remnants of the frightened, hurt, or angry children we once were. This blocks empathy with the needs of our own children and results in either excessive anger toward them or overprotection of them.

Most importantly, our society has become detached from cultural values that support committed parent–child relationships in the context of family life, as I will discuss more fully in chapter 10.

For all of these reasons, ageism was defined as a prejudice and identified as discrimination toward the elderly before it was seen as applying to the young as well.

ELDER AGEISM

In 1969 the physician Robert Butler described "ageism" as a prejudice and as a form of institutional discrimination against the elderly in housing, employment, and health care.[4] In 1970 the Gray Panthers organization was created as an advocacy group to combat ageism. The next year in his address to the White House Conference on Aging, President Nixon condemned "ageism."

In addition to these kinds of institutional ageism, elder ageism at the individual level was pointed out by the Group for the Advancement of Psychiatry when the younger avoid the older in a society: "that regards death as a personal affront and that values the action, vigor, and skills of youth over the contemplation, experience, and wisdom of old age."[5]

The Select Committee on Aging of the U.S. House of Representatives estimated that 5 percent of the nation's elderly, or more than 1.5 million persons, are the victims of abuse and neglect.[6] Intriguingly, the abuse and the neglect of the elderly have been readily identified as reflecting ageism, whereas the abuse and the neglect of children have not been so recognized.

THE FORMS OF JUVENILE AGEISM

In contrast with the elderly who are readily seen as victims of ageism, it is difficult for many people to believe that children also can be the victims of prejudice and discrimination because of their age.

One reason for this is that most of us do not encounter egregious forms of juvenile ageism in our own lives. Although children have been bought, sold, and murdered with impunity in the past, whenever historians have focused on a specific time period and used reliable sources of information, most children have been found to be as valued and as well treated as they are today.[7] Still the merciless exploitation of child labor in the United States was a major social issue until the enactment of federal anti-child-labor legislation in 1916.

The existence of juvenile ageism was suggested early in this century by Maria Montessori when she called attention to the "universal prejudices" against children.[8] She saw prejudice in the attitude that adults always know "what is best for children." More specifically, she cited as prejudices the false assumptions that children must be taught to learn, overlooking their innate thirst for learning; that children's minds are empty, overlooking their rich imaginations; and that young children do not work, overlooking the growth-producing nature of their play.

It was not until the 1970s that prejudice and discrimination against children were described as expressions of ageism by Chester Pierce, another child psychiatrist, and by myself.[9] In 1980 Michael Rothenberg, a pediatrician, suggested the existence of an unconscious national conspiracy against children because of the vast discrepancy between prochildren rhetoric and actions at the federal level.

In addition to the abuse and neglect that also characterize elder ageism, juvenile ageism is expressed more broadly by interferences with the opportunities for children to fulfill their potentials in life. In order to demonstrate these facets of juvenile ageism, I will describe the ways in which it occurs in both institutional and individual forms.

Institutional Juvenile Ageism

The facts that children seldom have been included in descriptions of ageism and that even the recognition of juvenile ageism tends to be resisted are prima facie manifestations of institutional juvenile ageism. Even references to the young in the literature on ageism have concerned young adults. Strikingly, the educational literature for children has referred to ageism only as it affects the elderly.[10] In itself simply this exclusion of children whose status is defined by age from thinking about age-based prejudice and discrimination is the ultimate institutional expression of juvenile ageism.

More specific examples of institutional juvenile ageism I will describe are when children are ignored as inherent members of society with developmental needs that are as important as the needs and desires of adults; when children are unnecessarily segregated from public places and public media; when parenting is disparaged; when children are treated as adults; when child-caring systems do not serve the interests of children; and when child-development research is biased against children.

Ageism That Ignores the Interests of Children in Our Society.   The fact that one can debate whether or not children are full-fledged citizens of the United States is a reflection of juvenile ageism. When that question is raised, the issue really is not their citizenship but the rights of children and the responsibilities of adults to them.

Still, whenever the interests of adults and children conflict in our society, the interests of adults usually prevail as if children were not citizens of equal standing. The resulting plight of children in the United States was summarized in the 1989 Report of the Select Committee on Children, Youth, and Families of the U.S. House of Representatives, and it is epitomized by the fact that one in four preschool children now lives in poverty.[11] Two years later in 1991, the National Commission on Children appointed by Congress and by President Bush, pointed out "that the most prosperous nation in the world seems to be failing its children."

The generally low priority of federal, state, and county funding for children, especially those who are at risk for developmental problems, is the most glaring example of institutional ageism. In general federal expenditures for each child are less than one tenth the expenditure for each elderly person.[12] More specifically between 1980 and 1990 $40 billion was cut from federal programs that affected neglected children, while $1.9 trillion was spent on military items.

An example of the low funding priority of abused and neglected children was described by the associate director of the Milwaukee Department of Human Services.[13] He pointed out that it is easier to get money for a penguin exhibit in the zoo than for child protection, because there are "friends" of museums and "friends" of zoos at budget appropriation hearings, but there are no "friends" of abused and neglected children. The following expenditures from each $10.00 of Milwaukee County property taxes illustrate this point: Park System, $2.01; Museum, $0.36; Zoo, $0.15; Performing Arts Center, $0.12; Symphony, $0.07; Child Protection, $0.04.

Another kind of institutional ageism can be found in the way that children are ignored in adult affairs that directly affect them. This is seen in the ways in which the interests of children are not taken into account sufficiently in divorce matters.[14] One result is that many children are the victims of inadequate and unpaid child support. Even though the typical child support award provides less than half the cost of raising a child, from 60 to 80 percent of noncustodial parents do not pay it. Furthermore, child support obligations often are treated in the same way as unpaid credit card debts, ignoring the moral and legal obligation of parents to financially support their children as a greater responsibility than a commercial debt. The lack of enforcement of child support obligations amounts to societal de facto support of child neglect.

Ageism also is reflected in the current judicial practice of interpreting divorce rules governing the equal division of property as applying only to adults in a family and thereby as requiring the sale of the family home in order to divide assets between the parents. This ignores the financial stake of children in the capital assets of the family and the fact that the family dwelling is the home of the children as well as the home of the parents. The interests of children in preserving their home, neighborhood, and school district often are not taken into account in divorce settlements.

Ageism That Segregates Children.   The most pervasive form of institutional juvenile ageism is the exclusion of children from public aspects of our society.

Because of the necessity to protect children from unsafe public places and from the undesirable influences of movies, television programs, and magazines, certain public aspects of our society are "off limits" to children. The emphasis is on excluding children from harmful public influences rather than on creating a society in which children can freely participate. When we define the limits of our tolerance of public behavior, we act as though children are not members of the public. We set limits of tolerance according to the lowest adult standards as if children were not present.

It is true that children and adults live in different worlds. The world of a child is defined by the child's parents and by the limited range of the child's environment. For this reason, it is possible to conceptualize a private adult world to which children can be denied access. For example, parents may restrict access to the parental bedroom. Society also may do this by designating certain private places as accessible only to adults. But it does not follow that children should be denied access to places or to media that are designated as public and thereby should be accessible to all regardless of race, creed, or age.

The exclusion of children from our thinking about what constitute public places and media is illustrated by the fact that children are denied the right to free access to public places, public information, and public entertainment so that adults can have free access to activities that are regarded as harmful to children and to many adults for that matter. The constitutional right to free expression by adults often is pitted successfully against the need to protect children from pornography and violence in the media, as if children did not also have rights as members of the public as well. Instead of designating private places and media for adults, we try to segregate children from public places and media and, in effect, create a private world for them.

Our society has abandoned its role in protecting children so that children and their parents are expected to protect themselves from dangerous influences and environments. Children have lost the freedom of movement and the freedom of association provided by neighborhoods in which they can freely play.[15] Neighborhoods have been disrupted not only by crime and drugs and less dramatically by suburban shopping malls but also by social engineering. The main thrust of our social policies has been to transfer the care of children from informal home and neighborhood settings to institutions designed for custodial and educational purposes throughout the daytime hours.

One such social policy is expressed in the movement for day care, often justified on the undeniable grounds that parents employed away from home need it but also on the grounds that day-care centers are superior to parent care because they can take advantage of the latest innovations in education and in child psychology. Among other things, this policy of segregating children under professional supervision deprives children of learning first hand that people take responsibility for each other without being paid to do so simply because they live in the same communities. Jane Jacobs, the author, suggested an attitude underlying this outcome in the *Death and Life of Great American Cities* :[16] "The myth that playgrounds and grass and hired guards or supervisors are innately wholesome for children and that the city streets filled with ordinary people, are innately evil for children, boils down to a deep contempt for ordinary people (and for children)."

The obvious facts that many public aspects of our society and its environments are not fit for children usually is minimized because the interests of children are not considered important enough in the United States to influence our social conduct. Rather than our society creating a suitable public atmosphere and environment for children, parents are expected to protect and to segregate their children. Our societal, community, and media standards would be quite different if all adults took seriously, as do most parents, the fact that they are modeling values and behavior for the young members of our society.

The expectation that parents should segregate their children from unsafe public places and undesirable public media exposures is based upon the same principle of segregation that has been used to deny public accesses to ethnic minorities and women. For example, the same rationalization that children should be segregated from the undesirable influences of our society rather than accommodating society to children also has been used to segregate women from the undesirable influences of the freewheeling "man's world." Fortunately, the harassment of women in the armed forces and in workplaces is no longer publicly tolerated. Our armed forces and our workplaces are now expected to respectfully accommodate the presence of women. The same result could be accomplished for children in our communities.

Because it is difficult to recognize the segregation of children for their own protection as a form of benevolent discrimination, that segregation can be better appreciated by comparing it to the same form of discrimination against adults. How would you react to promoting publicly sanctioned information, entertainment, and events that were offensive or harmful to African Americans, to women, or to the handicapped, and then restricting the access of those groups to those materials and events? I doubt that you would publicly tolerate influences that are recognized as offensive and harmful to any of those minority groups. Yet in the United States we tolerate and even condone events and materials that are offensive and harmful to children, who comprise one-quarter of our population.

There is no escaping the conclusion that children are being treated as inferior beings, rather than as equal citizens of our society. The most obvious consequence of this form of juvenile ageism is the struggle parents encounter in the United States against the violent and sexually stimulating influences to which their children are continually exposed. They are expected to protect their children from those influences. They also are expected to gird their children against the dangers of public places.

If our society respected its immature members, it would ensure the safety of children in the neighborhoods in which they live. It also would support parents' efforts to foster the development of their children rather than accepting, and even promoting, influences that are inimical to the development of children.

Ageism That Disparages Parenting.   Because children are the raison d'être of parenting, anything that undermines parents discriminates against the developmental needs of children. Consequently, both the obvious and the subtle disparagement of parenting in the United States adversely affects children.

For example, parenting generally is not accorded economic status in the United States. Unlike other Western nations, the United States does not recognize parenting as having economic value to society. Many parents are diverted from rearing their children to financially remunerative employment. Child care is regarded as a custodial or as an educational function that can be marketed rather than as a fulfilling developmental experience for both adults and children.

In many circles parenthood has come to be regarded as an optional accessory rather than as a developmental stage in the life cycle of both men and women. The consequences of this trend in the United States are reflected in a 1990 Gallup survey that found that the employment of parents away from home made it easier for women to lead personally satisfying lives, but made it more difficult for them to raise children and to have successful marriages when men do not value parenting and homemaking responsibilities.

The disparagement of parenting is felt particularly strongly by women and men who place a higher priority on parenting than on employment away from home during their children's early lives.[17] This disparagement is revealed in the general use of "working" women and men to refer to those who are employed away from home with the implication that homemaking is not work or is less important than remunerated employment.

Ageism That Treats Children as Adults.   Perhaps surprisingly, juvenile ageism is expressed when children are treated as adults. When adult responsibilities are placed prematurely on children, they are expected to be independent at the cost of fulfilling their own developmental needs. This occurs when children are expected to completely adjust to adults' personal problems, work schedules, and life-styles. It also occurs when children are expected to perform like adults in school and in athletics at ever earlier ages.

This form of juvenile ageism is combined with racism and sexism when adolescent girls of minority groups are encouraged to become, and are supported as, premature parents. In the process, those adolescents are treated like adults, and their own developmental needs are ignored and compromised.

Children are subtly treated as independent adults in other ways as well. A child is a dependent part of a parent–child unit and is not an independent person. Yet systems that serve children often treat them as free-standing persons, and interventions intended to help them actually harm them.

The anthropologist Margaret Mead eloquently called attention to the institutional response to children as if they are independent persons.[18] This occurs when the fact that children are the dependent parts of two-person parent–child units is ignored. Since most crisis interventions occur after rather than before damage to children occurs, children are the victims of crisis–recoil processes that lead to overreaction to crises in their lives followed by recoiling from the causes of the crises. This is seen in the policies and practices that remove children from their homes at times of crisis, as if they were independent persons, rather than recognizing their inherent dependency on their parents and focusing instead on helping their families.

The failures of the juvenile justice system illustrate the ways in which systems designed to protect and help children have the opposite effect when they ignore the dependency of children on their parents.[19] In the *In re Gault* ruling in 1967, the U.S. Supreme Court found it necessary to protect children from inappropriate placements away from home by the courts that were established to help them. As is true with many institutional interventions presumed to help children, however, even that decision in itself aggravated the situation by focusing the attention of courts on procedural due process for minors, as if they were adults, and by further distancing the affected children and their parents from appropriate help.

Another example of institutional juvenile ageism was reflected by a lawyer from the Los Angeles Chapter of the organization Victims of Child Abuse Legislation when he said: "They're always trying to throw away the Bill of Rights to protect children." [20] This statement was made in opposition to legislation that would recognize that children are not adults and are at a disadvantage in an adult courtroom and need special consideration. The obvious implications were that children and adults should be treated in the same way in courtrooms and that the Bill of Rights does not apply to children.

Ageism in Child Caring Systems.   When the responsibility for managing the lives of children is turned over to impersonal institutions, adverse consequences for the children can result because institutions have their own interests that may or may not correspond with the interests of the children they serve.

Social service, correctional, legal, and mental health institutions now occupy established places in the economy and are as dependent on their clients as their clients are upon them. This does not mean that professionals in those agencies wish to promote the continuation of the problems they are supposed to solve. It does mean that institutional factors, such as the lack of interagency coordination and collaboration and the protection of budgetary "turfs," can preclude professionals from doing anything other than servicing, as opposed to solving, the economic, social, and family problems they confront.[21]

A prominent example of inadvertent ageism expressed through policies and practices that harm children is the way in which the war against child abuse has in some respects become a war against children.[22] This occurs when either one of two blanket policies override considering the needs of a particular cases. The first blanket policy is that children should be protected from abusive parents, and the second is that the integrity of families should be preserved. When the child protection policy dominates, children can be removed from their homes and placed in foster care without remedying the conditions in their families that led to the removal, and with the sequel of multiple foster-home placements as they become increasingly disruptive. In contrast, because of the shortage of effective services and the failure to follow child abuse and neglect statutory requirements and timetables, the family preservation policy can lead to keeping children in families that continue to damage their children. Instead of adhering to blanket policies, the needs of each child and family should be taken into account in interventions intended to help them.

There is a long history of using the schools for achieving sociopolitical aims, such as crime prevention, poverty amelioration, and racial integration.[23] Each of these aims may be laudable in its own right, but each also can deflect attention from the developmental needs of children and from the more important roles of parent–child relationships in those social problems.

Services advertised as benefits for children can serve the interests of those who provide them rather than the interests of the affected children. For example, the day-care industry can serve the needs of adults who delegate child care and those who provide it, rather than the needs of the children themselves.

In another vein, modern forms of artificial insemination and childbearing are colored by the juvenile ageist assumption that children are commodities.[24] Embryos and fetuses are referred to as the "products of conception," and many "workers" labor in an industry that produces and markets this commodity, including laboratory technicians, doctors, lawyers, and surrogate mothers.

The production of a baby through in vitro fertilization can involve five separate persons: the female genitor, the male genitor, the female carrier, the social mother, and the social father. Each person brings new rights and duties to an enterprise in which the interests of the potential children are seldom considered. Accordingly, the Warnock Report in England recommended that a statutory licensing authority be established to regulate both infertility research and services in order to deal with the ethical questions involved.[25] The Supreme Court of France outlawed surrogate motherhood entirely, holding that it violates a woman's body and improperly undermines the practice of adoption.

Another example of interventions in the health care system based on considerations other than those of children and their families can be seen in federal regulations that mandate treatment for every newborn not born dead. This is done without regard for the consequences for the newborn's quality of life and for the newborn's family. No financial provisions are made for these severely handicapped, technologically dependent children once they leave neonatal intensive care.[26] Their families are frequently stressed financially and psychologically thereafter, and the quality of life of both the affected children and their families is impaired.

Ageism in Child Development Research.   Ironically, the way questions are framed in contemporary child development research can reflect an ageist bias against children.

Research on child abuse and neglect usually asks whether or not abuse and neglect harm children, rather than whether abuse and neglect are in the developmental interests of children. Instead of assuming that children need competent parenting, the assumption is that children are not harmed by abuse and neglect unless damage to them can be proved. As a result, the research focus is on the damage to, or the resilience of, abused and neglected children rather than on the children's developmental interests in the quality of the parenting they receive.

In a similar vein, research on the effects of the institutional day care of children usually takes for granted the unavailability of parents employed away from home and assesses whether or not this is harmful to children, rather than asking how much nonparental care is in the developmental interests of either the children or their parents.

In both of these examples the developmental needs of children for parenting and the developmental needs of parents to parent are not taken into account; rather the emphasis is on assessing the harm children experience from incompetent parenting and from separation from their parents.

Individual Juvenile Ageism

Ageism as a prejudice against an individual child is an expression of disregard for that child as a person with developmental needs and with moral and legal rights. This form of juvenile ageism is most commonly seen when children are regarded as the property of their parents.

The most extreme form of individual ageism is seen in the belief that parents own their children as chattel. This assumption draws upon the deeply ingrained assumption that biological parents have natural affection for their offspring and that parenthood is their biological right. It is supported by the legal assumption that others can interfere with parental authority only in extreme situations when parents damage their children by abuse or neglect.

Ironically, in spite of the pervasive contemporary emphasis on individual freedom and of the progress made in recognizing the moral and legal rights of children, the view persists that children are the property of their parents, as indicated in the following examples.

Killing a Child Is Not Murder.   Homicide has become the leading cause of death by injury for infants in the United States. In 1991, 1383 children were reported to have died at the hands of abusers, a 54 percent increase in six years.[27] That figure actually is low since the deaths of children from inflicted injuries often are mistakenly attributed to accidents or illnesses.

Juvenile ageism was clearly revealed in two cases in which a parent's killing of a child was not regarded as murder.[28] In Indiana, murder charges against Melody Baldwin were dropped when she pleaded guilty to child abuse by giving her four-year-old son a fatal dose of a drug. In another case in Wisconsin, a judge remarked that the death by beating of her twenty-month-old son by a twenty-six-year-old prostitute "may well have been a benevolent grace for the child" because of the child's sordid life circumstances.

A more subtle, but revealing, sign of unintentional juvenile ageism is a New York City Child Fatality Report that noted the deaths of premature newborns caused by their mothers' drug abuse as "death from natural causes."[29]

The Fetus Is the Property of the Mother.   There has been a long-standing legal tendency to regard the unborn child solely as a part of the mother's body and, therefore, as the property of the mother.[30] This was modified in 1973 when the U.S. Supreme Court in *Roe v. Wade* recognized the rights of a woman over the rights of the fetus during the first trimester, of the fetus over the mother in the second and third trimesters, and of the physician throughout pregnancy to make decisions regarding the termination of the pregnancy.

The specification of maternal and fetal rights during pregnancy has given rise to the abortion controversy that the U.S. Supreme Court returned to the state legislatures in *Webster v. Reproductive Health Services* in 1989.[31] In this process the definition of what actually constitutes ageism against a fetus remains to be clarified as our society struggles to define its stand on this matter. In the medical community the trend is toward recognizing a dyadic model in which both the mother and the fetus are regarded as patients.

Fetal Damage Is Not the Responsibility of the Parent.   In most states whether or not a pregnant woman's drug abuse constitutes child abuse is an open question. Some prosecutors, judges, and child-protection workers say they have an obligation to protect fetuses.[32] For example, the district attorney of California's Butte County vowed to seek jail terms for pregnant women who refuse to obtain treatment for drug abuse. Others say that such action would be creating rights for the fetus that have no foundation in law. In this vein in 1991, the Michigan Court of Appeals ruled that Kimberly Hardy, a twenty-four-year-old factory worker, should not stand trial on child abuse charges for using crack hours before her son's birth because the statutes did not apply to fetuses.

Still, in Westchester County, New York, a drug-abusing woman known as Deborah B lost custody of her baby at birth after a judge ruled while she was pregnant that the child was likely to be neglected after birth. [33]

In another case in Washington, DC, twenty-nine-year-old Brenda Vaughn pleaded guilty to forgery. [34] Because she was pregnant and tests showed that she had used cocaine, the Superior Court in the District of Columbia sent her to jail until the date the baby was due in order to protect the fetus from drug abuse. That case kindled heated debate about the use of both child abuse and drug laws to prosecute women who take illegal drugs while pregnant and to place their newborn babies in foster care.

Efforts to incarcerate pregnant drug addicts to prevent fetal damage have been criticized because, if a women can be arrested for endangering a fetus with cocaine, she might be arrested for drinking alcohol or smoking as well. [35] This overly generalizing attitude and the failure to relate damage to a fetus to that child's disabilities after birth both are manifestations of juvenile ageism.

Removal of a Child from Adoptive Parents.   Ageism exists when the interests of children are disregarded by removing them from their psychological parents and returning them to incompetent biological parents simply because of technical legal errors in the adoptive process. In these instances the child is treated as an object that can be readily moved from one place to another rather than as a human being with developmental interests and needs.

The case of *In the Interests of J.-L.-W.* in Wisconsin in 1981 is an example. [36] In that instance, a five-month-old boy was abandoned by his mother. When he was eighteen months old, the parental rights of his mother were terminated so that he could be adopted by his aunt and uncle who, in fact, were his psychological parents. At the age of two and one-half the Wisconsin Supreme Court precipitously returned him to his biological mother because of a technical error in the court adoption action, rather than ordering a new trial that would take into account the child's present circumstances and developmental interests. The legal solution, in this case, treated the child as a commodity held in storage and ignored the fact that he was taken away from the only parents he knew.

In New Haven, Connecticut, in 1992 a Superior Court judge returned a one-year-old girl to her nineteen-year-old mother who had abandoned her at birth and whose parental rights had been terminated.[37] Five months after the termination of her parental rights her mother changed her mind and asked to have her child returned. After the ensuing legal action, the child was returned to her biological mother at the age of one year without taking into account the attachment bonds she had formed with her adoptive parents—the only known parents to her. A similar result occurred in 1993 when Jessica DeBoer was removed from her adoptive parents in Michigan and returned to her biological parents in Iowa at the age of two and one-half on technical legal grounds.

On the other hand, when the legal issue at stake hinges on the biological versus the psychological relationship between parent and child, the psychological relationship has been construed to be paramount. For example, in 1983 in *Lehr v. Robertson* the U.S. Supreme Court held that the emotional attachment between parent and child rather than their biological relationship defines the family.[38]

Retrieval of "Switched" Baby. The belief that a child is the property of the biological parents also is illustrated by the usual response to "baby switching" at birth. An example is the effort of a Sarasota, Florida, couple to determine, after she died, if their nine-year-old daughter had been mistakenly switched at birth with another nine-year-old girl without considering the adverse effect of such a pursuit on the living child.[39] This led to the highly publicized "divorce" of Kimberly Mays from those biological parents after they obtained visiting rights with her and her later choice to live with them.

Parental Abduction of Children. The kidnapping of children by their own parents is another example of the way in which children are regarded as the possessions of their parents.

One facet of the parental abduction phenomenon is family violence. In some instances the abductors are the violent ones and in other instances the abductors are fleeing violence. In still other instances parents attempt to ease their own emotional pain by abducting their children irrespective of the pain caused the other parent and the confusion and upset experienced by the children.

Although there probably are times when the interests of children are served by parental abduction, the most common theme is one of parents retaliating against or hurting each other without considering the impact of kidnapping on their children.[40]

Corporal Punishment. Confusion over the legitimacy of corporal punishment is illustrated by the fact that it is prohibited in public schools by statute in many states but has not been regarded by the U.S. Supreme Court as cruel and unusual in the sense of the Eighth or the Fourteenth Amendments to the Constitution.[41]

There are those who advocate corporal punishment as consistent with Biblical teachings. There also are those who see any form of physical intervention with children as constituting child abuse and as promoting violence in society.

Those who advocate the corporal punishment of children can use their beliefs to disguise child abuse. Those who oppose corporal punishment can use their beliefs to deprive children of learning the realistic consequences of their behavior. Juvenile ageism is evidenced in both instances when the realistic developmental interests of children are not taken into account as adults base their behavior on abstract beliefs about the advantages and disadvantages of physical interventions rather than on the circumstances in which physical interventions are appropriate.

AREAS OF PROGRESS

In spite of the foregoing evidence that juvenile ageism permeates our society, gradual progress has been made over the years in rectifying the oppression and exploitation of children. This trend has been aided by the articulation of children's legal rights. At the same time, there is recent evidence of slippage in these gains.

Child-Labor Laws

Child-labor laws began to appear in the 1850s to protect children from commercial exploitation.[42] The passage of the federal Keating-Owen Act in 1916 finally established a national anti-child-labor policy.

The exploitation of child labor is no longer a major issue; however, since 1985 child-labor violations have more than doubled, and states are passing new legislation to limit minors' working hours.[43]

Public Education

Compulsory school-attendance laws were enacted in the United States in the 1870s; however, they were not extended to the age of sixteen until 1909 in New York.[44] Today, state constitutions mandate public education, and states aspire to provide high school and advanced education for everyone.

Still, the indications are that the quality of public education has deteriorated across the nation as indicated in chapter 1.

Child Abuse and Neglect Legislation

The New York Society for the Prevention of Cruelty to Children was formed in 1874 as an outgrowth of the New York Society for the Prevention of Cruelty to Animals.[45] Ironically, even today the maltreatment of animals evokes a greater public reaction than the maltreatment of children.

Public child protection agencies began to appear in the 1910s and 1920s as a result of the activities of national and state humane societies. Ultimately the federal Child Abuse Prevention and Treatment Act of 1974 required states to institute child-abuse reporting.

Today child abuse and neglect are national issues; however, effective interventions remain in short supply, and even the national collection of data was curtailed for a time in the recent past.[46]

Health Care

The rights of minors have been identified and acted upon by the courts in the health care of children.[47] As an example, in *Prince v. Commonwealth of Massachusetts* in 1944, the U.S. Supreme Court held: "Parents may be free to become martyrs themselves, but it does not follow that they are free, in identical circumstances, to make martyrs of their children."

Another example is *Walker v. Superior Court* in 1988 in which the California Supreme Court held that the welfare of children is paramount when parents exercise their beliefs in spiritual healing contrary to the medical interests of their children.

Many state laws also facilitate the medical care of adolescents by allowing certain minors to consent to treatment for specific problems, such as venereal disease, drug and alcohol abuse, and organ donation. The Childhood Immunization Initiative of 1993 has increased the immunization of young children.

In spite of these gains, many children currently do not receive adequate health care, many young children lack adequate immunizations, and levels of sexually transmitted diseases have reached epidemic proportions among adolescents.[48]

"Illegitimate" Children

A child born out of wedlock has been legally defined as "illegitimate," a stark reflection of ageism in which innocent children bear the stigma of their parents' behavior.[49] At the same time, the U.S. Supreme Court has upheld the right of "illegitimate" children to be supported by their fathers and has gone far toward eliminating the distinctions that once made them actual second-class citizens.

Still, a child's right to knowledge of one's parenthood and a child's interpretation of the distinction between biological and "real," or psychological, parenthood often are obscured by ageism. The use of "real" or "natural" to designate biological rather than psychological parents callously ignores the painful and confusing impact of these emotionally charged words on adopted children whose adoptive parents in fact are their real and natural parents. They certainly are not unreal or unnatural parents.

The Sexual Exploitation of Children

Children are protected from sexual exploitation by adults through statutes that brand such activity as criminal. That protection was further extended when in 1990 the U.S. Supreme Court in *Osborne v. Ohio* held that pornography depicting children was qualitatively different from that depicting adults.[50] The Court ruled that those who possess as well as those who sell child pornography are not protected by the freedoms of expression and privacy. The Court also upheld state statutes that outlaw the possession of child pornography.

Although the Johnson and Meese Commissions on Pornography in the United States and the Williams Commission on Pornography in England all agreed that children constitute a special case in the governmental regulation of pornography, the focus of those commissions was on minors as the subjects but not as the consumers of pornography.[51] This means that, although the use of children as the subjects of pornography has been regarded as repugnant, the exposure of children to pornography has been sidestepped as a significant social issue until recently.

In 1990 the Federal Communications Commission developed regulations to ban "indecent" broadcast programming to protect children as consumers.[52] It based this ban on the compelling government interest to protect children by a narrowly tailored regulation that would not infringe on the First Amendment rights of broadcasting. Also in 1990 the U.S. Congress passed the Children's Television Act which requires broadcasters to "serve the educational and informational needs of children."

The courts continue to have difficulty balancing the First Amendment rights of adults and the compelling interests of society in protecting children from offensive material. At the same time the sexual abuse of children is receiving unprecedented levels of attention as a major problem in the United States. Even as our society recoils from child molestation, we offer children's bodies as spectacles in the media and in advertising, giving children the very erotic attention we say we want to avoid.[53]

Protection from Damaged Conception

The extent to which the protection of children can be carried is illustrated by legal developments around the concept of damage to germinal cells when women are exposed to toxins and radiation in the workplace.

In a controversial 1989 decision in *United Auto Workers v. Johnson Controls* by the U.S. Court of Appeals for the 7th Circuit, fertile women were barred from jobs that posed potential risks for unconceived and unborn children.[54] In that instance, the motive for protecting children appeared to be based upon the commercial interest of avoiding lawsuits. That decision was reversed by the U.S. Supreme Court in 1991 because it infringed on the right of women to equal opportunities for employment. Again the financial interests of adults were placed above the developmental interests of the unborn. The outcome might have been different if the equally relevant germinal tissue of men had been the subject of the litigation as well.

As it now stands, the employment rights of adults stand above the rights of unborn and unconceived children. In addition the protection of both sexes from toxins and radiation that are hazardous to germinal tissue in the workplace remains an unexamined issue.

AN ANTIDOTE TO JUVENILE AGEISM: CHILDREN'S CIVIL RIGHTS

Fortunately, the United States provides a climate in which destructive prejudice and discrimination can be addressed. Inroads already have been made against racism, sexism, and elder ageism by the political advocacy of the civil rights of racial minorities, women, and the elderly. This could be extended to advocacy for the civil rights of children as well.

Our society has made progress in combating racism, sexism, and elder ageism by focusing on the civil rights of adults. In a similar way, the identification and the promotion of the civil rights of children and youth by calling attention to their victimization may well be the most effective and enduring means for overcoming juvenile ageism in the United States. Unlike racism and sexism, juvenile ageism is not directly based on competition for employment. Therefore, a broad base of humanitarian support might be tapped to counteract it.

The civil rights most relevant to children include freedom from racial and gender discrimination; the right to life, liberty, and personal security; freedom from slavery and involuntary servitude; freedom from torture and from cruel or degrading treatment and punishment; freedom from interference with privacy; freedom of thought and conscience; and freedom to express opinions.

When cast simply in terms of civil rights, children now are being victimized in the United States. There are a diminishing number of public places in which children are safe. Moreover, the cruel and degrading treatment that violates basic civil rights certainly applies to millions of physically and sexually abused children in this country. When juvenile ageism is combined with racism and sexism, as with adolescent African American and Hispanic mothers, the effects of multiple prejudices and discriminations are particularly egregious.

In addition, children have been acknowledged by virtually all "bills of rights" for children to have the rights to nurturant parenting, to education, and to guidance by benign authority. Millions of neglected children are denied these rights to competent parenting.

The civil rights approach to child advocacy helps to distinguish it from "advocacy" for children which is motivated by other interests and actually conflicts with the interests of the affected children. Those forms of advocacy seek services for children based on the needs of adults rather than the needs of children.

AUTHENTIC CHILD ADVOCACY

Since the welfare of children depends upon the welfare of their parents, the first concern in child advocacy is to ensure that parenting is supported by our society and that parents are helped to be competent. This means that anything in our society that undermines parenting needs to be redressed. More specifically, incompetent parents need training, treatment, and parenting support. When those measures are not effective, the affected children need to have competent parenting provided for them through the termination of parental rights and adoption.

Individual professional case advocacy also is needed to guide specific children through the maze of fragmented and discontinuous social, mental health, educational, and legal services in order to ensure that they are not harmed by the very efforts that are intended to help them.[55]

At the same time, the facts that children do not vote and that families with children constitute a minority of the population make authentic child advocacy an uphill struggle. Although the political power of the elderly has begun to reverse elder ageism, the lack of political representation of the young sets the stage for their continued victimization. This is reflected in the fact that, while the poverty of the politically represented elderly has decreased over the last decade, the poverty of politically unrepresented children has increased.

The increasing involvement of the elderly with the young, as reflected in the over 100 organizations that sponsor Washington-based Generations United, may well enable grandparents in particular to devote time and energy to addressing juvenile ageism.[56] In this way, the politically represented segment of the population subjected to ageism could speak for the politically unrepresented children who also are the victims of ageism. When it incorporates the interests of women who are mothers, feminist activism also can benefit children.

We like to think of ourselves as nurturant and protective of children. This attitude obscures the fact that victimization of the young regularly occurs because of institutional and individual juvenile ageism. For this reason, the welfare of the next generation depends upon juvenile ageism receiving the attention now accorded to racism and sexism. From our society's point of view, juvenile ageism is an even more serious problem than elder ageism, because the future of our society depends upon the welfare of our children.

Some fear that short-term sacrifices by adults for the long-term gain of children would be politically unpopular in a society devoted to immediate gratification. Yet, the direct benefits to adults of a society in which children can thrive are reductions in crime, safe streets, integrity in commerce and politics, and wholesome environments for everyone. Counteracting juvenile ageism would benefit adults as well as the next generation and could be the theme around which improving our entire society can be organized.

The immediate question is whether our emphasis should be upon continuing to train children to cope with the stressors our society imposes upon them or upon minimizing the avoidable stressors to which they are exposed. The former course is an ageist emphasis on the responsibility of children to cope with adult failings and inaction, while the latter course emphasizes society's responsibility to protect and nurture its children.

If juvenile ageism in our society is not addressed, the next generation is in peril. The emphasis will continue to fall on children to protect themselves from the hostile, exploitative elements of our society, rather than on creating a benevolent society that protects its young.

Chapter 8

A Child's Right to Competent Parenting

We are always too busy for our children. We never give them the time nor interest they deserve. We lavish gifts upon them; but the most precious gift—our personal association, which means so much to them—we give grudgingly and throw it away on those who care for it so little.

MARK TWAIN[1]

You may well have mixed feelings about how children are faring in the United States today. You probably can think of many children who are better off today than we were at their ages, but those children are likely to be your own and those of your friends. Without much effort, however, you also can think of more children who are worse off. Certainly in my work that is the rule, not the exception.

Too many children in the United States suffer today, not only because they are neglected and abused, but because efforts to help them are misplaced and often harm them. Moreover, in recent decades the political emphasis on the equal treatment of all citizens has tended to obscure the fact that children, adolescents, and their parents have needs that merit special consideration.

There is no doubt that children have come a long way from past oppression to their present state of protection, even adulation, in the United States. From earlier centuries in which children were barely recognized as more than miniature adults, we have come to appreciate childhood and adolescence as stages of development during which personalities and skills are shaped. Because of the efforts of "child savers" of the last century to free children and adolescents from oppressive labor, we now have reached a time in which we can contemplate ways of assuring them fulfilling lives. We also can begin to appreciate the contributions parents make to society.

The advancement of the status of children is reflected in the growing interest in the rights of children. More specifically, the moral rights of children to have competent parenting and to not live in foster care or institutions have been proposed.[2] This focus on the moral rights of children fits into the broader advancement of the moral rights of human beings in the form of human rights and civil rights.

For adults these human and civil rights have become legal rights in the United States. We now are poised for the first time in history to actually make these same human rights and civil rights available to children.

THE CIVIL RIGHTS OF CHILDREN

Before considering the rights of children, I would like to focus on their basis in human rights in general. Respect for those human rights has been achieved by adults only through great effort and vigilance. Even more effort and vigilance will be required to apply human rights to children.

History and the contemporary world situation repeatedly demonstrate that powerful forces inevitably conspire to limit our freedoms.[3] Prior to the founding of the United Nations in 1945, the "natural rights of man" that grew out of the Enlightenment were not understood in many parts of the world to include women, as still is the case. For this reason Eleanor Roosevelt suggested that "human rights" replace "the rights of man."

The fundamental human rights have been defined by a number of philosophers and politicians.[4] They specify the minimum standards of civilized behavior and include civil, political, economic, social, and cultural rights; of these, the civil rights are the most relevant to children.

The basic civil rights as they now are identified derive from the seventeenth and eighteenth century reformist theories that supported the English, American, and French revolutions. Those that apply to children include freedom from racial and equivalent forms of discrimination; the right to life and personal security; freedom from slavery and involuntary servitude; freedom from torture and from cruel, inhuman, or degrading treatment and punishment; freedom from interference with privacy; freedom of thought, conscience, and religion; and freedom of opinion and expression.

The obligation of adults to recognize the civil rights of children was raised in 1922 in England by Eglantyne Jebb, founder of the Save the Children Fund, in the *Charter of the Rights of the Child*.[5] That idealistic charter spelled out the entitlement of all children to be protected from exploitation; to be given the chance for full physical, mental, and moral development; and to be taught to live a life of service to their fellow men and women. That charter was adopted by the League of Nations in 1924 as the *Geneva Declaration of the Rights of the Child*. It became the first international instrument whereby "men and women of all nations" accepted the belief that "the child must be given the means requisite for its normal development, both materially and spiritually."

The specific civil rights of children have been enumerated subsequently in a variety of organizational creeds, bills of rights for children, and White House Conferences on Children in the United States, in addition to declarations of the United Nations.[6] For example, the 1930 White House Conference on Child Health and Protection specifically referred to the emotionally disturbed child:

> Who has a right: (1) to growing up in a world which does not set him apart, which looks at him not with scorn or pity or ridicule— but which welcomes him, exactly as it welcomes every child . . . and (2) to a life in which his handicap casts no shadow, but which is full day by day with those things that make it worthwhile, with comradeship, love, work, play, laughter, and tears—a life in which these things bring continually increasing growth, richness, release of energies, and joy in achievement.

Similar hopes have been held for children by the United Nations. The *United Nations Declaration of Human Rights* in 1948 was extended to the *Declaration of the Rights of the Child* in 1959. The latter document stated:

> The child shall enjoy special protection, and shall be given oppor-
> tunities and facilities, by law and by other means, to enable him to
> develop physically, mentally, morally, spiritually, and socially in a
> healthy and normal manner and in conditions of freedom and
> dignity. In the enactment of laws for this purpose the best interests
> of the child shall be the paramount consideration.

This declaration also affirmed the obligation of adults to ensure the realization of the civil rights of children.

More recently, the *United Nations Convention on the Rights of the Child* adopted by the General Assembly in 1989 recognized the importance of parenting in the development of children by stating "that the child, for the full and harmonious development of his or her personality, should grow up in a family environment in an atmosphere of happiness, love and understanding."[7]

Although the principal responsibility for children in societies lies with their families, the *United Nations Convention on the Rights of the Child* acknowledges that many children are unable to depend upon either their parents or the state for protection. It recognizes that the maltreatment of children takes many forms: poverty, abandonment, exploitation for their labor or sexuality, abuse by traffic or sale, as civilians or combatants in wars, and by violence perpetrated by the state. The *Convention* says:

> States parties shall take all appropriate legislative, administrative,
> social and educational measures to protect the child from all forms
> of physical or mental violence, injury or abuse, neglect or negligent
> treatment, maltreatment or exploitation including sexual abuse,
> while in the care of parent(s), legal guardian(s) or any other person
> who has the care of the child.

Implicit in these statements about the civil rights of children are two types of developmental civil rights beyond those held for adults. The first is the right to competent parenting and to education. The second is the right to be guided by benign authority that protects children from acting in ways that we, as adults, would wish to be restrained from acting if we were children. The emphasis of the *United Nations Convention* clearly is preventive and is on protecting children from abuse and neglect rather than on intervening after abuse and neglect have occurred.

Most people also would agree that children have vested interests in their own moral development. The interest of a child in developing a character that will enable that child to become a competent citizen is as important to that child as the child's interest in not being abused or neglected. If given a choice, no child would choose to suffer the consequences of a damaged character.

The *United Nations Convention* clearly declares that the state has a role in childrearing. Because the consent of children is not required for the exercise of parental power, it is in the privacy of their homes that their civil rights are the least assured.[8] The comment of one delinquent youth captures the essence of the way in which children can be oppressed in their families: "It was the intensity of my father's and brother's abuse of me, the physical pain and the concentration camp atmosphere, that eventually put calluses on my good feelings."

Because of the abuse and neglect of children in their families, much of the current debate about children's rights is over the degree to which their civil rights should become legal rights. Along this line, Judge Charles Gill, co-convener of the National Task Force for Children's Constitutional Rights, advocates an amendment to the U.S. Constitution to legally guarantee children's basic civil rights.

As all of these declarations demonstrate, whenever adults publicly express their hopes for children, they conclude that children have a moral right to competent parenting. In fact, certain moral civil rights of children have become legal rights in the United States.

THE LEGAL RIGHTS OF CHILDREN

The gradual emergence of children's legal rights in the United States began by treating them differently than adults in criminal law through the establishment of juvenile courts. More recently their legal rights have been extended under the *parens patriae* doctrine, which justifies state intervention on parental authority. Under this doctrine the state can assume the ultimate power of terminating parental rights.

The *parens patriae* doctrine is based on three assumptions:[9] (1) that childhood is a period of dependency and risk in which supervision is essential; (2) that the family is of primary importance in the supervision of children, but that the state should play a primary role in the education of children and intervene when the family fails to provide adequate nurturance, moral training, or supervision; and (3) that, when parents disagree or fail, the appropriate authority to decide what is in a child's interests is a public official.

The *parens patriae* doctrine can compel parents and children to act in ways beneficial to society, but it never has presumed that the state could assume parenting functions.

State Interventions on Parental Authority

The courts generally honor parental authority because it is assumed to be based upon wisdom and love for a child. Children's moral rights, however, become legal rights when parents are not sufficiently motivated by moral considerations to avoid harming or neglecting their children. Consequently, the U.S. Supreme Court in *Ginsberg v. New York* recognized society's interest in protecting children from abuses that might prevent their growth into independent citizens:[10] "The state also has an independent interest in the well-being of its youth (and an interest) to protect the welfare of children (and to see that they are) safeguarded from abuses which might prevent their growth into free and independent well-developed . . . citizens."

Our legal system also distinguishes between what parents may do to themselves and what they may do to their children. For example, adults may refuse essential medical treatment for themselves, but parents usually are not allowed to do so for their children. They also are not permitted to physically harm their children or to allow children to physically harm themselves.

Legal sanctions against parents can be used when persuasion and education are insufficient to protect their children. This is consistent with the fact that persuasion and education generally are not sufficient in themselves to control harmful behavior to others, as is evident in the need for laws against crime and exploitative sexual behavior. Just as adult aggressive and sexual behavior can adversely affect others, incompetent parenting also adversely affects others—the children first and society later.

Because some persons cannot be persuaded or educated to behave responsibly as parents, the legal regulation of parenting now takes place through child abuse and neglect statutes.

Balancing the Rights of Parents and Children

When family matters are brought into the legal system, the interests of children, of parents, and of the state need to be carefully identified and balanced against each other in order to determine the appropriate rule of law that governs a specific case.

The legal rights of children are specified as their rights to nurturance, to protection, and to make certain choices.[11] The law recognizes the right of children to food, shelter, clothing, and medical care through statutory definitions of child neglect. It recognizes the right of children to be protected from the harmful acts of others, as defined by child abuse and sexual assault statutes. It also recognizes their right to make choices in "age-grading" statutes that award privileges and responsibilities at certain ages, such as choice in postdivorce custody and visitation matters, eligibility for motor vehicle operating licenses, and eligibility to vote and to marry.

In general the law has shifted away from fully backing parental authority and is moving in the direction of defining the limits of parental power beyond that of proscribing child abuse and neglect. The Juvenile Justice and Delinquency Prevention Act of 1974 removed the "status offenses" of incorrigibility and running away from the category of juvenile delinquency, so that these behaviors now are regarded as resulting from the lack or inappropriate usage of parental authority rather than as resulting solely from the inherent qualities of the affected children and youths.

Because the informal sanctions available to parents for controlling their children and because the disadvantages of misbehavior and running away are so obvious, incorrigibility and running away now are seen as symptoms of family problems that cannot be addressed effectively by state intervention upon the children. The focus has shifted to therapeutic interventions with the families.

The Liability of Parents

The courts now are beginning to consider a child's right to competent parenting in a legal sense by defining the liability of parents and of the state for damage to children. As long ago as 1963, in *Zepeda v.*

Zepeda, a child sued his father for having caused him to be born out of wedlock.[12] Although that suit was unsuccessful, it raised the persisting question of a child's legal right to be wanted, loved, and nurtured—in essence to be competently parented.

Children have successfully sued their parents for negligence, such as for injuries caused by automobile accidents, and have brought actions against third parties, such as when a person alienates one of their parents from the family. Parents also may be held legally responsible if their childrearing decisions harm others.[13] Because children themselves cannot be sued, every state except New Hampshire allows victims to file civil suits against parents for damage caused by their children.

At the same time courts are reluctant to create or aggravate strife between parents and their children. Therefore, the common-law doctrine of parental immunity has maintained that, absent willful and wanton misconduct, children may not sue their parents for mere negligence within the scope of the parental relationship.[14] Yet incest is regarded as a criminal offense outside the purview of parental immunity, and most states have set aside the parental immunity doctrine so that children may now sue their parents under a variety of circumstances. For example, in 1992 in Orlando, Florida, eleven-year-old Gregory Kingsley successfully sued to legally "divorce" his mother so that he could be adopted by his foster parents.

The Liability of the State

In spite of the existence of the *parens patriae* doctrine, the duty of the state to protect children has not been clearly established in case law. On the contrary, there is a presumption that the state cannot be held responsible for its failure to intervene in family matters.

The U.S. Supreme Court in *DeShaney v. Winnebago County Department of Social Services*, ruled in 1989 that the state is not required by the Fourteenth Amendment to protect the life, liberty, or property of its citizens against invasion by private actors.[15] In effect the ruling appeared to hold that children do not have a constitutional right to the protection of the state.

That case involved a lawsuit on behalf of Joshua DeShaney, who suffered brain damage from repeated beatings by his father at the age of four. As a result Joshua was expected to remain institutionalized for life. The U.S. Supreme Court rejected arguments that the state had a duty to protect Joshua because it once placed him in foster care and later because social workers suspected he was being abused by his father but took no action. It held that only "when the state takes a person into its custody and holds him there against his will" does the Fourteenth Amendment due process clause require officials to take responsibility for the individual's safety and well-being. At the same time, the Court did not rule out the possibility that the state acquired a duty under tort law to provide Joshua with protection.

In a similar way, an appellate court in California upheld a local court's dismissal of a suit by a seventeen-year-old boy who alleged that he had been damaged by the state's mismanagement of his adoption as a newborn:[16]

> At the age of seventeen, Dennis Smith filed a complaint against the Alameda County Social Services Agency based upon the allegation that the Agency was liable for damages because it negligently failed to carry out its responsibilities to find an adoptive home for him as an infant. Shortly after his birth, Dennis' mother relinquished him to the custody of the Agency for the purpose of adoption. The Agency placed Dennis in a series of foster homes, but no one adopted him.
>
> The thrust of Dennis' legal action was that the Agency negligently or intentionally failed to take reasonable actions to bring about his adoption. The Agency left him with one set of foster parents for many years without asking them whether they wanted to adopt him. The Agency knew or should have known that other foster parents with whom Dennis was placed never intended to adopt him.
>
> As a direct consequence of the Agency's failures, Dennis never was adopted, but spent his entire childhood in a series of foster and group homes. Therefore, he was deprived of proper and effective parental care and guidance and a secure family environment. Dennis alleged that this caused him mental and emotional damage and grave interference with his development.

The dismissal of Dennis' complaint was upheld in appellate court on a number of grounds, including the difficulty in directly linking damage to Dennis to the Alameda County Social Services Department's failure to arrange for his adoption. Significant other grounds were that the proposed liability would not reduce future harm to others and more likely would impede the proper functioning of adoption agencies that operate under budgetary constraints.

Another point made by the court was that, since Dennis had become a "hard-to-place" child, the Department did not have a mandatory duty to place him or protect him from the injury of not being adopted. It apparently did not recognize that the Department's conduct had resulted in his becoming hard to place.

Furthermore, in response to an additional complaint of educational malpractice in the management of Dennis's education, the appellate court held that seeking damages for educational malpractice was precluded by the difficulties of assessing the wrongs and injuries involved and the incalculable burden that would be imposed on our public school systems by such successful actions.

The Smith case highlights the reluctance of courts to make decisions that impose practical burdens on social agencies and public schools. It also implies that liability could result if there were convincing linkage of early life experience and later outcome. It now is possible to make such linkages in specific cases. The liability of agencies and schools would be even more likely if the civil right of children to competent parenting and the legal right of children to an education were vigorously pursued.

In contrast with Dennis Smith's case, Cook County, Illinois, settled out of court a claim by an eighteen-year-old boy that he had been damaged by the negligence and incompetence of county social workers. In this case the linkage between professional practices and damage to Billy Nichols apparently was made effectively:[17]

> In December of 1981, attorneys for the State of Illinois and Cook County paid $150,000 in an out-of-court settlement as a result of a suit of a former dependent child, Billy Nichols, who had been entrusted to the public child welfare system and later as an adult sued the county social service agency for ruining his life. The allegation was that the prolonged negligence and incompetence of social workers kept Billy dependent and unfit to live in society. His records were nearly two feet high and spanned twenty years.
>
> On September 19, 1960, Billy and his seven-month-old sister were abandoned by their mother and found eating garbage behind a skid-row mission in Chicago. Billy's age (approximately five) was

a mystery, and his speech was unintelligible. He was sent to an institution for the retarded in Michigan for four years. After a subsequent stormy foster-home placement, he was placed in Cook County's juvenile security prison for nearly three years, although the superintendent repeatedly petitioned the court to remove him.

In 1969 a legal aid lawyer, Pat Murphy, filed a class-action suit to release dependent and neglected children from prison on behalf of Billy. At the age of fourteen Billy was transferred to Elgin State Hospital, where he ran away ten times and ultimately was committed to the Illinois Security Hospital at Chester at the age of eighteen. Three years later Attorney Murphy intervened again, and Nichols was enrolled in a psychiatric program for two years, until he was jailed for car theft. His suit against the state was instituted in 1978.*

As these cases illustrate, the law has favored the privacy of the family and has protected parents and the state from suits by children. There is a growing trend though to use legal class action suits to force improvements in child welfare services.[18] Such class action suits have been successful in obtaining specialized educational services for children, and they could have similar effects in obtaining child welfare services.

The increasing ability to link damage to a child directly to the behavior of parents and to the actions or inactions of the state is moving the law in the direction of legally recognizing the moral right of children to competent parenting and of regulating parenting.

Cultural Expectations of Parents and Children

Although it may seem as though there are none at times, there actually are cultural expectations of parents and children in the United States. These expectations have evolved over the years and become evident when children are brought into courts, where the concept that the rights to conceive and to give birth to a child also accord parental ownership of that child is no longer tenable.

There even is a biological basis for the legal position that we do not own our children. The genes we give to our children are not our own. In

---

*©Copyrighted December 14, 1981, Chicago Tribune Company. All rights reserved. Used with permission.

the process of reproduction our genes are mixed with another assortment. But our genes are not really ours; they are only a part of the species' store. They have a life of their own beyond our control extending back through previous generations and into successive generations. We are only temporary hosts to our own genes and to our children.

When family matters are adjudicated in courts, there are a variety of case and common law precedents that determine expectations of parents in legal decision making.[19] These expectations also are articulated in laws that define child abuse and neglect and in the common law judicial oversight of parent–child relationships in child abuse and neglect and divorce custody matters.

In general in our courts parents are expected:

1. To provide a place of residence that legitimizes a child's identity in a community.
2. To provide sufficient income for a child's clothing, shelter, education, health care, and social and recreational activities.
3. To provide the love, security, and emotional support necessary for the emotional development of a child.
4. To foster the intellectual, social, and moral development of a child.
5. To socialize a child by setting limits and encouraging socially acceptable behavior.
6. To protect a child from physical, emotional, and social harm.
7. To maintain family interaction on a stable, satisfying basis through communication, problem solving, and responding to individual needs.

On the other hand, in our courts children are expected to reciprocate these parental responsibilities. Children are expected to learn how to respond to benign authority in order to be able to interact comfortably and effectively with others. Without this ability, they remain self-centered and insensitive to others.

Children are expected:

1. To learn the appropriate attitudes and values of their cultures and to act in accordance with them.
2. To accept parental authority and to behave in ways acceptable to the community.

3. To meet the appropriate emotional needs of parents by responding affectionately to them, confiding in them, and respecting them.
4. To cooperate with their parents in protecting themselves from danger and in meeting their own physical, emotional, and educational needs.
5. To help maintain family unity and reduce family tensions by cooperating and sharing with other members of the family and by showing loyalty to the family group.
6. To perform appropriate tasks and to care for the material things provided for them.

These implicit cultural expectations of parents and children are expressions of the moral and civil right of children to competent parenting and of the reciprocal obligations of children to respect and cooperate with their parents. Competent parenting is a legal right in the negative sense that incompetent parenting is a cause for state intervention and the possible termination of parental rights. Because we are paying an ever larger share of the cost of rearing, educating, and treating them, our society also has a financial stake in the welfare of our children. Therefore, public decision making for children needs to take into account the interests of children, to acknowledge that parents usually protect those interests best, but, when they do not, to intervene in compliance with existing statutes to ensure that children receive competent parenting.

Children prick our consciences. They can painfully remind us that we are their flawed models, but they also can evoke our highest ideals. Although inevitable conflicts exist between the interests of older and younger generations, it seems clear that the American cultural will is to promote the competent parenting of its children, as it is for the United Nations. We need to find feasible ways to do so. Some of those ways are revealed when we recognize that each parent has a right to be competent if possible.

Chapter 9

A Parent's Right to Be Competent

Does anyone understand that the jobless father often destroys himself, his family, and his community? Does anyone understand the frustration of the mother who knows that her children will need the best education possible, but she can't afford it and the national community won't help pay for it? Does anyone understand that the young men who make city streets dangerous and destroy themselves with drugs could have been proud, productive citizens? Does anybody understand that these problems can destroy this country? (p. xv)

—RICHARD GORDON HATCHER, Mayor, Gary, Indiana, 1971[1]

Because most of my clinical work is with parents who are foundering, I try to emphasize their strengths and to avoid adding to their feelings of failure and guilt. At the same time I need to help them acknowledge their problems so that they can better manage their personal and family affairs. This experience has made me aware of the fact that the work of parents is not sufficiently appreciated by our society. We do not fully realize how stressful parenting is and how important it is to all of us that each parent be as competent as possible.

To say that a parent has a right to be competent may well seem to stretch the notion of rights too far. If we give the matter careful thought, however, the logic for regarding competent parenting as a right in our society is compelling.

First of all, by definition the parent–child unit is irreducible. The

163

other half of a child is a parent and the other half of a parent is a child. This means that the interests of children and the interests of adults in their parenting roles are inseparable. When parents face dangerous environments, poverty, unemployment, illness, and mental incapacities, their children inevitably face the same problems in addition to the risk of incompetent parenting. Therefore, if children's interests are to be pursued, the interests of parents also need to be taken into account. If children have a moral right to be competently parented, then parents have a moral right to be competent if they possibly can be. If this rationale is not enough to establish the moral right of parents to be competent, there are at least two more.

The second rationale is that the integrity of society itself depends upon the competent parenting of its children. Incompetent parenting threatens the very survival of a society. Therefore, competent parenting is an essential function of society and deserves the status of a right.

The third rationale is that human beings have a biological predisposition toward competent parenting which is necessary for the survival of our species. The goal of the human reproductive cycle is parenthood, not just procreation. Conceiving and giving birth to a child are but the beginnings of the reproductive stage of life. They initiate parenthood as the fruition of the developmental stages of childhood, adolescence, and adulthood. In the most personal sense, competent parenting fulfills the role of an adult in the reproductive cycle of the species as a woman or as a man. Therefore, in order to preserve the human species and our society adults need to fulfill their biological potentials if they choose to do so and to pursue their personal development by becoming competent parents.

Although the expression of an adult's reproductive capacity through parenting contributes to fulfillment in life, the lives of adults certainly can be fulfilling without directly participating in the reproductive cycle. U.S. Bureau of the Census statistics reveal that one in five adults do not marry, and many who do marry do not have an interest in parenting.[2] Fortunately, neither the survival of the species nor the fulfillment of individuals depends upon each adult becoming a parent. As members of society, however, it is not unreasonable to expect that adults who are not parents have a moral responsibility to support the parenting of the next generation.

The preceding line of thinking reveals two vital aspects of parenthood that are commonly overlooked. The first is that parenthood itself is a developmental stage in the life cycle. The maturing and emotionally satisfying elements of parenthood are fundamental, if not explicit, motivations to become a parent. These benefits of parenting are more readily appreciated by parents who had self-fulfilling childhood relationships with their own parents than by those who did not.

The second overlooked aspect of parenthood is that the readiness for parenthood follows completion of the adolescent stage of life. Achieving the capacity to assume responsibility for one's own life as an adult is the essential foundation of competent parenting. Achieving that capacity is a prerequisite for assuming responsibility for the life of another person. Conversely, the premature assumption of parenting responsibilities by an adolescent interferes with the developmental progression of that teenager's adolescence.

In the past preparation for the developmental aspects of parenthood took place largely through families. With the loosening of family ties and the prevalence of family strife in the United States, information about parenting now often must come from educational and clinical sources. Thus, family education has entered high school curricula, and parent training has become an integral part of protective services for children and supportive services for families. There also is increasing pressure for schools to assume greater responsibilities for parenting children.

Preceding chapters of this book have brought out the powerful reasons why society's most appropriate and cost-effective role is to support and promote competent parenting, rather than to have its schools and child-caring services take over parenting functions. This means that parents need support to be competent whenever possible.

In addition we need to respect adolescence as an essential developmental stage in life that precedes parenthood and that is compromised by premature childbearing and childrearing.

PARENTHOOD AS A DEVELOPMENTAL PROCESS

A survey of U.S. college graduates revealed that most of them place a high value on childrearing.[3] At the same time they held values that limit childbirth and that detach childrearing from marriage. They approved the use of contraceptives, vasectomy, and abortion to prevent births. They also endorsed easy divorces, extramarital cohabitation, and marriages without children. Most significantly they were aware that becoming a parent dramatically changes one's life style.

Yet our society appears to regard parenthood as consisting simply of the custodial care of a child without special responsibility for the child's development and without growth-producing possibilities for parents themselves. In fact parenthood is an important adult developmental stage in the life cycle. It parallels the development of children. It involves furthering the interests and the needs of both parents and children.

Adults who do become parents know that parenthood is an absorbing role in life. They more or less consciously discover that parenthood is a growth process in which they revive and work through related past experiences in their own lives.[4] Those parents who successfully meet the developmental challenges of parenthood achieve a new level of psychological and emotional maturity. Just as children can grow and experience changes in their relationships with their parents, so parents can grow and experience changes in their relationships with their children.

There are a series of predictable challenges that can be maturing experiences for parents. First they learn to adapt their lives to the cues of babies. Then they learn to accept and limit toddlers' behavior as they and their toddlers learn to separate from each other. Later they learn to deal with the provocations of school-age children and to accept the emerging independence of adolescents. These experiences stimulate parents' development of their own coping skills, their own self-esteem, and their own altruism.

Many adults need help in learning how to experience parenthood as a developmental phase in their own lives. They need help in learning how to grow with their children. Some need education and clinical treatment in order to be able to function as competent parents. An even smaller but critical number are unable to function as competent parents at all. Many of those are children themselves.

THE DEVELOPMENTAL READINESS FOR PARENTHOOD

In spite of the rhetoric inveighing against teenage pregnancies, our society actually places little emphasis on readiness to assume the responsibilities of parenthood. Childbirths from unplanned or impulsively initiated pregnancies generally are accepted simply as facts of life, even for young adolescents.

Our society's acceptance and support of adolescent childbirth glosses over the fact that it is the most obvious challenge to a child's right to competent parenting and to a parent's right to be competent. In the context of the predatory sexual behavior of both males and females, this attitude makes adolescence a particularly difficult stage of development in our society.

In order to understand the situation of contemporary adolescents, let us take a close look at the special qualities of adolescence.

The Earlier Onset of Puberty

Over the last century, young people have found their entry into adulthood delayed by the increasing complexity of modern societies, while they have been entering puberty at earlier ages. The initiation of coitus now occurs earlier as the age of marriage occurs later. Consequently, extramarital coitus has become a common means of coping with the increasing delay in forming families.

The earlier onset of menstruation has made pregnancy possible at younger ages, although the capacity for conception may not occur for one to three years after its onset.[5] In Northern Europe from 1900 to 1970, the average onset of menstruation dropped from the age of 15.5 to 13.5. In the United States it shifted from the age of 14 to 12.5 over the same time span.

The biological pressure to engage in sexual activity now begins during the middle or junior high school years. As one thirteen-year-old girl put it: "It's cool to have sex. Everybody does it." This attitude is reflected in the earlier onset and greater prevalence of adolescent sexual intercourse. For eighteen-year-olds in the United States in 1991, 56 percent of Caucasian females and 70 percent of Caucasian males and 67 percent of African American females and 85 percent of African American males had had sexual intercourse.[6] By the age of twenty 68 percent of females and 86 percent of males of all races were "sexually active."

Although the onset of menstruation is generally thought to be the hallmark of puberty in girls, it is just one milestone in a complex developmental process involving physical growth and psychological changes that result from maturing hormonal stimulation and brain development.[7] For example, the uterus usually does not reach full adult size until the completion of physical growth. More importantly, the maturation of the parts of the brain that control the sexual drives is not completed until eighteen to twenty years of age. Thus, mature sexual hormones activate drives controlled by immature teenage brains.

Although good health and nutrition play roles in the earlier onset of puberty, the controversial theory also has been advanced that children who grow up under dangerous conditions are primed genetically to increase the chances of having their genes survive into the next generation by attraction to earlier sex, to earlier parenthood, and to having large numbers of children.[8] The theory holds that, because of their dangerous life circumstances, evolution primes those persons to have earlier puberties in order to boost their chances of early procreation and of having large numbers of offspring in order to enhance the chances of survival of their genes in the next generation. Whether or not the theory is correct, the phenomenon exists.

The Developmental Stages of Adolescence

From the cultural and societal points of view, adolescence is a distinct and vital stage of human development in both indigenous and modern societies. During adolescence for the first time boys and girls learn to accommodate the emotional and physical realities of social living for themselves. Because adolescence is such a personal experience, adolescents tend to "reinvent the wheel" in their attitudes and behavior in each of their own lives.

Each young person also progresses through adolescence at a unique rate so that there are wide individual variations in physical, emotional, and social maturity. Some thirteen-year-olds are more mature in one or more of these aspects than are some eighteen-year-olds.

In both nonindustrialized and industrialized societies, adolescence is a period of semiautonomy. In indigenous societies most adolescents have two rites of passage.[9] The first is around puberty and marks the individual's readiness to enter training for adulthood. The second is during late adolescence and marks the individual's formal entrance into adult status. Ironically, indigenous societies do not equate puberty and adulthood, whereas the current trend in the United States is to equate them, as reflected in references to adolescent girls as women and adolescent boys as men.

In Western nations adolescence has not always been recognized as an extension of childhood. Even children have been treated as adults and exploited in the labor market. The recognition of adolescence as an immature phase in life came through three historical innovations that defined adolescence as the stage of development preceding adulthood.[10] The first was child labor legislation in the late nineteenth century that began to specify hours and conditions under which persons under eighteen, sixteen, and fourteen could work. The second was compulsory education which was introduced later for children between six and eighteen, typically to the age of sixteen. The third was the establishment early in the twentieth century of special juvenile codes and courts for persons under the age of eighteen.

Whether it be from the biological, psychological, or social point of view, adolescence is an inevitable and perpetual developmental stage in the life cycle. It cannot be bypassed or eliminated by wish, education, childbirth, parenthood, or legislation.

The developmental stage of adolescence has early, middle, and late phases. These phases deal with such developmental tasks as revising the body image, learning intellectual skills, adding peer to parental attachments, consolidating gender and social roles, attaining a mature value system, and forming an autonomous identity as a valued person as a basis for intimate relationships as an adult.

During *early adolescence* between twelve and fifteen, young persons are preoccupied with accommodating bodily changes and learning how to cope with newly acquired sensations and skills. They turn to others for mirroring and acceptance that provides them with self-validation. They are highly sensitive to criticism and to blandishments that foster risk-taking behavior.

During *middle adolescence* from fifteen to seventeen, teenagers are preoccupied with exploring intimate relationships with other people. At the same time, instinctual urges toward sexual activity encouraged by contemporary social values thrust boys and girls into sexual encounters before they have had the opportunity to become fully familiar with their own bodies, their own feelings, and their cultural values. As a result many middle adolescents assume pseudoadult facades and engage in adult behaviors in efforts to quickly shed the trappings of childhood. They are vulnerable to seduction, exploitation, and betrayal. This especially is the case for middle adolescents who are temperamentally inclined to form intense relationships.

Late adolescence flowers during the senior year of high school and a variable number of succeeding years. The central issue then is settling on one's identity in realistic social roles and in choosing a life style and a career. During this time access to opportunities for education and for employment is vital.

From the point of view of decision-making skills, there is a clear distinction between teenagers under and over fifteen years of age. Awareness of the importance of the future consequences of one's actions and seeking appropriate advice progressively increases after the age of fifteen. A study of high school twelfth graders, however, found that only half regarded future consequences and obtaining advice as important in their decision making.[11]

Adolescents themselves usually acknowledge that they are unprepared for parenthood, as illustrated by Project Alive, a Chicago Youth Centers program designed to help teenagers become aware of the realities of parenthood:[12]

> Pairs of boys and girls were asked to care for a five-pound bag of flour constantly, as if it were their baby. When asked to recount their "parenting" experiences, most of the students found it filled with "constant headaches," and "hardly any fun." Another said, "Me and my girl, neither one of us have time for a baby. We don't have any money. We need to be trying to get an education and be somebody. We're just kids ourselves. What do we look like having a baby now?"

The Adolescent's Need for Parenting

Adolescents need to be able to act experimentally without suffering long-range consequences. Unfortunately, their actions can have consequences that foreclose their options in life: accidents can kill and disable, delinquency can become criminality, and sexual behavior can result in pregnancy and childbirth. Unlike their affluent counterparts, poor adolescents who experiment in risky behaviors often close doors that can never be opened again. Those who grow up in poverty are given very little margin for error in negotiating the developmental tasks of adolescence.

All adolescents need help in preventing and minimizing the consequences of their impulsive actions. The most important motivation for adolescents to restrain their immediate urges is the prospect that if they do so, there will be later benefits. Adolescents who are convinced that success in school, avoiding pregnancy, and preparing for attractive jobs will benefit them behave differently than those who do not have such hope for the future.

When adolescents get into trouble, it is not simply because their environments have offered few realistic alternatives for them, although this may well be the case. It is not just because the institutions of the community are insensitive or unresponsive to their needs, although they often are. Certainly these are real obstacles for many adolescents, but there are opportunities to prevent their difficulties that go unheeded and unused as well.

Hope for the future for adolescents comes not only from their communities since adolescent alienation occurs in affluent as well as disadvantaged neighborhoods. It comes more fundamentally from the modeling of responsible behavior and from limit setting by their parents. It is the investment of their parents in their welfare that helps adolescents avoid the consequences of serious errors in judgment. "My parents wouldn't like it" is the most frequently heard reason adolescents use for "staying out of trouble."

Unfortunately, surveys carried out by the Department of Child and Family Studies at the University of Wisconsin indicate that even in families with two parents only half of the adolescents surveyed talked with their mothers and only one-quarter talked with their fathers about their concerns.[13] Because of this lack of communication between adolescents and parents, the pressure on societal institutions to assume parental functions is increasing. For example, school-based health clinics that bypass the roles of parents in securing health care for their teenagers are growing in popularity.

When parental guidance is not available, the sense of invulnerability ("it can't happen to me") inherent in adolescence can lead an adolescent to engage in risky behavior that has life-altering consequences. Without the sense that "I have parents who care about what I do," adolescents are highly susceptible to peer pressures that can be contrary to their interests.

The lack of a specific developmental opportunity exists for many adolescents who grow up without a supportive father. It is not just that a child misses a father, rather it is the lack of consistent experiences with an older male in a caring, protective role that counts. For a girl having a father means having a significant love object as a foil for one's femininity and having an early sense of value as a female person. Through a relationship with her father a girl acquires her attitudes about men and herself in relation to them. For a boy a positive relationship with a father provides a role model for emulation.

Because adolescent development depends upon caring relationships with parents or parent figures, educational and clinical efforts in themselves cannot replace competent parenting in protecting adolescents from their own risk-taking behavior. Adolescents need competent parenting as much as do younger children.

In our confusing and seductive social climate, it is evident that adolescents need the support of parents who personally care about the way their sons and daughters lead their lives and whose motives are not to exploit them.

The Lack of Opportunities for Adolescents

As a part of their development as adolescents, teenagers need a variety of absorbing experiences that harmonize their hopes, thoughts, emotions, and activities without life-altering consequences. They also need to develop personal goals and to have opportunities for achieving them.

A growing number of youths feel that the future holds little promise for them. Those adolescents do not see themselves as gaining from completing high school. They become alienated from a society that does not provide opportunities for a promising future for them. They become hedonistic because they cannot imagine achieving long-range goals by present-day self-restraint.

Adolescents who grow up in environments with few material assets and few world-expanding experiences have little reason to aspire to opportunities that seem to lie beyond their reach. Poverty in itself contributes to a lack of future orientation in people and to unrestrained sexual behavior.[14] The possession of money and property can create an awareness of one's personal stake in the future consequences of present actions, an awareness that is lacking for people without those assets.

The lack of opportunities for social and economic advancement was recognized as contributing to unrestricted procreation long ago. For example, during the early 1800s, the English economist and demographer T. R. Malthus attributed the rapid increase in the population of Ireland to the English subjugation of Irish Catholics, who, seeing no escape from their lowly condition, "spent their lives proliferating."[15] He pointed out then that no people could plan for the future unless "they believed that their industrious exertion would benefit them."

In the United States today many adolescents live under circumstances that limit their opportunities in life and that foster early childbirth. When they become parents, the responsibilities of childrearing further limit their opportunities to complete their educations and to find fulfilling careers, thus creating a vicious circle. Those responsibilities also interfere with the personal maturation that flows from living through all of the stages of adolescence as preparation for the commitments involved in intimate adult relationships and in caring for children.

In contrast adolescents who grow up in supportive family and school environments are much more likely to have hope for their futures. Because their developmental courses are not interrupted by parenthood, they have opportunities to experiment, to learn from their mistakes, and to build solid foundations of self-esteem for later independent living.

The Attainment of Adulthood

Although adulthood is achieved in our society overnight on one's eighteenth birthday from most legal points of view, there actually is a gradual transition from childhood to adulthood. For this reason, in certain ways adolescent girls can legitimately refer to themselves as women and adolescent boys can refer to themselves as men.

In legal language the transition from childhood to adulthood is described in rather unflattering terms. Adulthood is achieved by the removal of the "disabilities of infancy"! Laws define the transition from childhood to adulthood by establishing a sequence of ages after which "the disabilities of infancy" are removed and special liberties, entitlements, and responsibilities are conferred on children and youth.[16] As the grading of rights by age in these laws reflects, the attainment of adulthood, or the "age of majority," is not sharply defined but occurs in stages.

Most importantly, the attainment of adulthood by legal "emancipation" from childhood is not clear-cut. Traditionally minors have gained emancipation by marriage, by entry into a military service, or by leaving home and becoming self-supporting. Thus marriage is considered to be an emancipating act. At the same time, it usually cannot be consummated by a minor without parental consent, as is true for enlistment in the military services as well.

A minor can be legally emancipated from one's parents and can assume the rights and obligations of adulthood before reaching the legal age of majority. When that happens, however, it means paying the full price for one's misdeeds and for one's own support. The issue of attaining adulthood is raised most commonly when an adolescent becomes pregnant.

THE DILEMMA OF ADOLESCENT PREGNANCY

Adolescence is a time for trying out different social roles. Egocentricity, impulsiveness, exploitativeness, and immediate gratification are at their peak even in well-integrated teenagers. These developmental imperatives often are ignored in educational and clinical efforts that assume that given information and contraceptives adolescents will use both wisely.

Preventing Adolescent Pregnancy

Although there is little question that adolescents need to know the facts about sexual behavior and contraception, this is not enough to curtail adolescent pregnancies. In the absence of societal, familial, and peer support to exercise restraint and in the presence of media and peer encouragement to be "sexually active," adolescents cannot be expected to establish control over their emerging reproductive capacities.

The societal encouragement of teenage sexual intercourse is reflected in the common usage of the phrase "sexually active." This implies that exercising self-restraint is being "sexually inactive or passive," a negatively valued state in our achievement-oriented society. Referring to adolescent girls as "women" and adolescent boys as "men" also fosters a premature sense of having attained adulthood. This is reflected in the attitudes of high school students who are offended when they are referred to as boys and girls.

In this context, 1 in 4 females becomes pregnant by the age of 18 in the United States; 1 in 6 gives birth prior to the age of 19.[17] Teenagers who become pregnant often are vulnerable adolescents at the outset. There is a relationship between sexual activity and the anxiety, low self-esteem, and antisocial values that underlie teenage smoking and alcohol and drug usage. Teenagers who use tobacco, alcohol, and other drugs are much more likely to start having sexual intercourse at an early age and are more likely to initiate pregnancy than those who do not. Without the support of attitudes and values that realistically place sexuality in the context of enduring human relationships, sexual activity may well be a means for gaining peer acceptance. Common examples for girls are engaging in sex in emulation of an admired peer or as a means of pleasing a boy friend. For boys, sexual intercourse and impregnation may well be sought simply to demonstrate sexual prowess and the achievement of manhood.

Much of the failure to use contraceptives lies not in the lack of knowledge or availability, but in the ambivalence adolescents harbor about contraception and its inconvenience.[18] For example, a national survey conducted in 1988 revealed that in spite of the availability of educational and health promotion programs only 58 percent of the boys reported condom use. Even more strikingly, among the 9 percent of high-risk teenagers who used intravenous drugs, frequented prostitutes, or had sexually transmitted diseases, only one in five used condoms. Another study revealed that 63 percent of teenagers placed on contraceptive programs did not use them continuously. One reason for this omission was the sense of invulnerability to danger and death that led the adolescents to believe that they were immune to the consequences of their actions. With this attitude, pregnancy as the result of sexual intercourse was regarded as "happening to others, not me." Similarly, an adolescent's naive view of parenthood can fail to take into account the realities involved in childrearing.

Both boys and girls who engage in casual or "recreational" sexual intercourse do not initiate sexual activity in the context of enduring personal relationships. For them sexual intercourse usually is an impulsive sensual experience. For this reason, they may not learn to integrate sensual pleasure with the intimacy and commitment involved in mature sexuality.[19] At least 1 in 4 contract sexually transmitted diseases. And, especially for girls, casual sexual activity can result in a loss of self-esteem and a distorted concept of their own feminine worth as well.

Furthermore, the predatory behavior of boys is encouraged by the prevalent sexist attitude that the responsibilities for the control of sexual intercourse and for the use of contraceptives lie with girls. Boys also may disdain the use of contraceptives that interfere with their own pleasure and convenience.

The prevention of teenage pregnancy also must take into account the fact that significant segments of the adolescent population are not inclined to avoid it and may actually seek pregnancy. In one study one-fifth of the girls described their pregnancies as planned, and over one-half desired to give birth once they became pregnant.[20]

Most importantly, the confusion of adolescents about sexual behavior mirrors that of many adults who deny that values restraining sexual activity are an appropriate component of childrearing at all. In his book *The Modernization of Sex,* Paul Robinson described sexual activity simply as a physical act, like eating or riding a bicycle, and denied that values, other than good manners, apply to sexual activity.[21] This attitude underlies much of the commercial advertising and entertainment directed at teenagers.

Because of all of these psychological and social pressures, sex education and contraceptive availability are insufficient in themselves to prevent adolescent pregnancies, which occur in the context of the pervasive lack of foresight and planning inherent in the lives of many adolescents. Ironically, those adolescents who are the most likely to become pregnant are those who are the least likely to profit from preventive education and services. For this reason, teenage pregnancy is resistant to most health and educational preventive efforts.

All of these factors point to the conclusion that reducing teenage births will depend upon more than just the availability of health-care and educational interventions. By their very nature adolescents always will be immature and dependent upon the influence of adult values and upon adult limit setting for the development of self-esteem, self-control, and prosocial values. They also always will be susceptible to impulsive, self-defeating behavior because of their inherent adolescent sense of invulnerability. They need encouragement to exercise self-restraint and sound judgment by their parents and by society.

When Adolescents Become Pregnant

Adolescent pregnancy highlights the dilemmas involved in determining the attainment of adulthood. For example, in the United States there is a strong emphasis on the reproductive freedom of women.[22] In this view when a girl becomes a woman is a critical issue in determining if, when, and how she will bear children.

The pregnant adolescent dramatically poses the difficult task of defining when an adolescent becomes an adult. For especially mature teenagers, pregnancy and childbirth can accelerate the attainment of adulthood. For most, however, pregnancy places adult responsibilities on adolescents who are not yet prepared to enter adulthood.

More specifically, the literature on teenage pregnancy and contraception reveals that adolescents who become pregnant have difficulty envisioning alternatives and reasoning about the consequences of childbirth. This point is illustrated by the following conversation I had in my office with a fifteen-year-old Caucasian girl from a middle-class family:

DOCTOR: I'm told that the test results show that you are pregnant.
PATIENT: My boyfriend and I knew it because the condom broke one time.
DOCTOR: What do you plan to do?

PATIENT: I'm going to have my baby and keep it. My boyfriend will drop out of school to support us.
DOCTOR: Do you think that you are old enough to raise a child?
PATIENT: No. I certainly wouldn't try to get pregnant.
DOCTOR: Then how is it that you plan to raise this baby?
PATIENT: Oh, it was an accident. Besides I don't like school, and I can get $425 a month. I know a lot of women who are doing it.

The dilemma of adolescent pregnancy is clearly revealed by the arguments against and for parental notification of a teenager's pregnancy.[23]

The intensity of the debate over a condition that cannot be concealed for long reveals its emotional and irrational elements. The main arguments against parental notification of an adolescent's pregnancy are that (1) minors have the same constitutional right to privacy on sexual matters and to control over their bodies as do adults; (2) parents might pressure an adolescent into a decision to have an abortion or to continue the pregnancy that would not be hers; (3) the fear of parental notification might keep a pregnant adolescent from obtaining an abortion or prenatal care; (4) parents might lose control of their reactions and harm the adolescent; and (5) if a minor wishes to terminate her pregnancy, she should be able to do so without her parents' permission because it is difficult to think of a circumstance in which her interests would be served by bearing a child she does not want under parental pressure to do so.

The case for parental notification rests on concerns that (1) if a pregnant adolescent does not inform her parents, she cannot truly give "informed consent" to have an abortion or to continue the pregnancy without realistic knowledge of her own capacities to be a parent and her family's ability and willingness to help her; (2) parents themselves have legitimate interests in being informed about circumstances that affect them, particularly since 80 percent of teenage girls live with their parents after childbirth; and (3) because parents are expected to be responsible for the care and nurturance of their dependent teenagers and in some states for their teenagers' children, they have a right to guide their behavior. This viewpoint includes making provisions for exceptional situations in which minors need court protection from parental abuse or are considered to be legally emancipated.

Underlying the attitudes toward notifying parents of their children's pregnancies is the dependent–independent nature of parent–adolescent relationships, which even under optimal circumstances are ambivalent. In practice the question of adolescent pregnancy often arises when those relationships are strained, adding to the complexity of the matter. Unfortunately, the usual reaction of professionals and other adults to adolescent pregnancy is to take an adolescent's often distorted perceptions of unworkable family relationships at face value, rather than to focus on improving those family relationships.

In spite of its obvious importance, the impact of an adolescent's pregnancy on her family is seldom taken into account when she becomes pregnant.[24] The adolescent's parents, siblings, and grandparents experience anger, disappointment, hurt, and even joy, as they struggle to cope with the crisis of adolescent pregnancy.

Against this background, in 1975 the U.S. Supreme Court held in *Poe v. Gerstein* that minors have a constitutional right to choose whether or not to bear a child.[25] The court pointed out that, where fundamental rights are involved, their limitation could only be justified when there is a "compelling state interest" in doing so. This compelling interest was recognized in 1990 in *Hodgson et al. v. Minnesota et al.* and subsequently affirmed in *Ohio v. Akron Center for Reproductive Health et al.* when the U.S. Supreme Court held that states may require parental consent before a minor can end her pregnancy provided that the option of a judge's approval in lieu of parental approval is available. Along this line, the Council on Ethical and Judicial Affairs of the American Medical Association adopted a middle-of-the-road position and concluded that, while minors should be strongly encouraged to discuss their pregnancies with their parents and other adults, minors should not be required to involve their parents before deciding whether to undergo an abortion.

The argument against parental notification of their adolescents' pregnancies presumes an irrational parental response and treats adolescents as adults. The argument for parental notification presumes a rational parental response to their adolescent's situation, but provides for recourse from an irrational response through the courts if it occurs. The varying stances of state laws related to this issue provide opportunities for research on the relative merits of each position.

The ambiguity in defining adulthood becomes even more evident when adolescents become parents.

The Dilemma of Adolescent Parenthood

For the first time in almost two decades, the birth rate among teenagers in the United States is rising, while it has been decreasing in Europe.[26] One million teenagers become pregnant each year, and half a million give birth.

According to the U.S. Bureau of the Census, in 1992 13 percent of all births and 24 percent of all first births were to teenagers (for teenagers below the age of eighteen the figures were 5% and 9% respectively).[27] Of all first births, 21 percent of Caucasian babies and 43 percent of African American babies were to teenagers. Furthermore, the rate of childbearing for girls between the ages of ten and fourteen increased 15 percent between 1980 and 1990. Of all teenage mothers in 1989, 67 percent were unmarried.

All of these statistics reveal that teenage childbirth is a major national issue. The U.S. General Accounting Office estimated that the public costs of teenage childbearing in the year 1992 alone was $34 billion.[28]

Society's Response to Adolescent Parenthood

Although most adults agree that adolescents are too young to become parents, the response of our society actually is to give financial and educational support to adolescent mothers.

Existing public policies in the United States offer parenthood as an accepted and viable choice to adolescent girls. Public financial assistance and publicly supported education for adolescent parents are indisputable evidence that society supports adolescent parenthood. Although intended as crisis-oriented interventions, without clear statements of this intent and of society's expectation that the children of teenage parents should receive competent parenting, both public assistance policies and teenage parent education programs clearly condone childrearing by adolescents.

Through the act of childbirth adolescent mothers are treated as if they are adults without consideration of the fact that so doing can be harmful to their own development as well as to that of their children. Although sometimes uniting and stabilizing families, the arrival of an adolescent's baby often causes conflicts in families. Yet public programs usually focus on the individual adolescent mother outside of her family context as if she were an independent adult.

There also are financial and peer-based incentives to have and keep babies. In some states teenage girls learn that with babies they can become eligible for Aid to the Families of Dependent Children benefits that initially seem substantial and independence-awarding. If they decide to place their babies for adoption, they lose access to those benefits and additionally suffer the pain of loss of their babies and possible criticism by their peers. Consequently, adoption is an unpopular choice for many childbearing adolescents.

The humanitarian impulse to support an adolescent mother and her child overrides considering other alternatives for her and for her child. This is understandable because adolescent mothers do include good students as well as school dropouts, conscientious family planners as well as those who have one baby after another, the socially skilled as well as those who have difficulty relating to others, and hard workers as well as those who are unemployable.

The crisis-filled nature of teenage childbirth draws society's attention to supporting the adolescent girl as a mother rather than to her own and to her child's developmental needs. As a result, the fact that there are two young persons with developmental needs usually is ignored. Also overlooked is the likelihood that teenage mothers are girls with complicated problems who find an identity for themselves through motherhood and who see pregnancy as more appealing than finishing school or getting a job. Unfortunately, our public policies seem to consider focusing on these issues as intruding on an adolescent's privacy and decision-making rights.

The Impact of Childbirth on Adolescents and Their Families

When adolescents give birth, the emotional reactions stirred up in their parents, in other adults, and in the adolescents themselves create dilemmas that are not easily resolved.

It is likely that mature teenagers with adequate financial and educational resources elect to terminate their pregnancies or to place their babies for adoption. This is the case with thoughtful older parents who are aware of their temporary or permanent inabilities to parent their newborns as well. Since the availability of abortion, of babies born to unwed mothers fifteen to forty-four years of age in 1982, only 6 percent were placed for adoption; that number reflected 12 percent of Caucasian and 0.4 percent of African American mothers who placed their babies for adoption.[29] This seems to apply today as well.

There is no question that most teenagers can learn to care for children; however, the judgment, skill, and knowledge required to rear children in unsupportive environments usually is beyond their developmental capacities.[30] It is one thing to be a babysitter and another thing to be a parent. As adolescent parents act like children themselves, they are prone to periodically neglect parenting tasks, even though they may well take delight and pride in their children.

The girl who becomes a mother and the boy who becomes a father are deprived prematurely of opportunities to socialize freely with male and female peers, to develop skills and hobbies, and to make career choices.[31] The girl in particular is deprived of developing a complete sense of her own body image because the bodily changes induced by childbearing are imposed on her before her own body has completely matured.

Adolescent childbirth also encumbers girls with psychological burdens and limits their options in life. This is particularly the case for the socioeconomically disadvantaged. Since a substantial majority of disadvantaged infants suffer from the multiple effects of both biological and environmental risks, and since the majority of children of adolescent mothers are disadvantaged, the babies make more than the ordinary demands on their already underprepared and possibly overwhelmed mothers. The fact that babies require care twenty-four hours a day for seven days a week and are not always cute, happy, and playful is not in line with the expectations of adolescents. In addition, the fluctuating moods and interests of adolescents add to their frustrations with childrearing.

Still, anthropological studies reveal that adolescent childbearing need not preclude experiencing aspects of adolescent development. Under optimal circumstances an adolescent mother's role as a parent may not exclude her from other roles, such as student, worker, girl friend, wife, and daughter.[32] She may successfully negotiate both supportive and unsupportive systems in order to rear her child. Especially when she can turn over her infant to kin to rear, an adolescent can be a biological mother and remain an adolescent in social terms. Even then, however, her adolescent development is truncated.

Although adolescent girls are strongly influenced by their peers and the media, their families are their primary sources of long-term support when they actually do give birth.[33] At least 80 percent of unmarried teenage mothers live with their families. This means that their basic family unit usually is teenage mother, grandparent(s), and infant. This unit can provide caregiving for the infant, but it also can foster a teenager's regression to former levels of dependency on her mother.

In our society some grandparents become parents for their children's offspring as they continue to be parents for their own children. Many are willing to fill this role because their interests and skills lie in childrearing, and they are young enough to have the energy to do so. When this is the case, adolescent childbearing can have advantages.[34] The benefits are not only from public assistance but, when her infant is esteemed by family members, the adolescent mother can attain an elevated position within her family. Public support for relatives who raise adolescents' children is available in some areas. For example, in New York City alone the number of grandmothers and other relatives who receive public aid in the kinship foster care program skyrocketed from 150 in 1985 to 21,734 in 1991.

But this life style depends upon the willingness of the adolescent's mother or other kin to continue to parent the adolescent daughter as they assume additional childrearing responsibilities themselves. Often this is not the case. For example, in San Francisco, Chicago, and New York, increasing numbers of grandmothers have been forced into childrearing by their own daughters who are drug addicts.[35] Some rear their grandchildren because they are afraid of being injured or killed if they file child abuse or neglect charges against their own daughters.

Contemporary grandmothers are becoming less willing to accept parenting roles. Although in the past grandmothers have played an important role in rearing children in disadvantaged areas, many now resent being forced into parenting again because they have their own lives to lead. As one grandmother who was the third of four living generations of teenage parents told me: "Something has to be done about this terrible epidemic of teenage pregnancies. My mother and I got by because there weren't so many drugs around and life was simpler then, but I want my grandchildren to go somewhere in this world and not be left behind like me and their mothers."

When the responsibilities of childrearing are assumed before adolescents are developmentally ready for parenthood, the courses of their lives are dramatically altered as their freedom to develop as adolescents is curtailed. The enjoyment of the emerging independence of their own lives is sacrificed because of the bodily effects of pregnancy and childbirth and because of the responsibilities of childrearing. Many girls are trapped victims of abuse, disappointing love affairs, poverty, and powerlessness. As a result they lack the self-esteem, the dignity, and the self-respect that could motivate them to care enough about themselves to hope for different lives.

For all of these reasons, a look at the actual profiles of teenage mothers is in order.

Profiles of Adolescent Mothers

I have drawn upon the work of the psychologist Herbert Quay in describing four common types of adolescent mothers.[36]

The first group is composed of those who are gratified by attention and affection from males and who fail to use birth control because of the lack of knowledge, personal disorganization, or an unwillingness to prepare for the sexual act. When they give birth, the possession of a baby creates meaning in life for them. When everything in their lives seems up in the air in environments that offer little chance to explore a range of options and that offer few other models, motherhood promises these girls a path to personhood. Having a baby gives them an identity—they are mothers. When this occurs, the babies are valued for the needs they gratify in their mothers, but later they can be neglected or resented because they also have needs of their own that must be met. This was reflected in the statement of a nineteen-year-old mother referred to our clinic because she had neglected her three-year-old daughter:

> Damion and me knew I could get pregnant, and he had condoms, and I had those pills, but you know how it is, we were young and so much in love that we didn't use them. We talked about getting married, but he couldn't get a job, and he started drinking more.

> My baby was so cute, and I felt so important because I had her, but
> she cried a lot, and then she had to have her own way all the time. It
> was just too much for me so I started using and drinking too.

Members of the second group seek a sense of belonging and being
loved by having a baby. They may be reinforced by their subculture's
implicit sanctioning of sexual intercourse and pregnancy. A twenty-
year follow-up study of African American girls disclosed that those
who suffered from depression and low self-esteem were more likely to
become parents than those who did not.[37] Their babies were seen as
sources of love rather than as growing persons who require committed
nurturance. Because their own parenting was inadequate, these girls
were not prepared to form solid affectionate bonds with their own
babies. Later in childhood many of their babies were expected to
become caretakers of younger children themselves. As a sixteen-year-
old girl told me after she gave birth to a baby boy:

> When I got pregnant nobody was really mad at me, but my mother
> and grandmother wanted me to have an abortion. But they had
> babies when they were kids too so I don't listen to them. I decided
> to have my baby because I feel so lonely. You have somebody to
> love, somebody to love you, and somebody to talk to. This is my
> child, and nobody can ever take him away from me.

The third group of girls seek pregnancies for the purpose of
precipitating marriages as means of escaping from their own families.
Studies comparing teenage mothers who chose to place their children
for adoption and those who did not have revealed that those who chose
to keep their babies were troubled girls who fled into pregnancies
because their lives were hectic and difficult.[38] They often were repeating
cycles of family conflict. As a result, troubled teenagers with strained
family relationships are more inclined to be in the position of having and
keeping babies than those who might actually be competent parents. A
twenty-year-old mother described what happened in her life to me:

> I hated my stepfather. He sexually abused me, and my mother did
> nothing to stop him. She said it couldn't be true and blamed me for
> making up lies. I had to get out of there. I never told anyone before,
> but I left off the pill for a while without telling my boyfriend
> hoping that I would get pregnant, and then he would marry me. I
> did but he didn't. As soon as he found out, he didn't want to have

anything more to do with me. They finally got him for child support, and me and my two-year-old get along OK on AFDC.

The fourth group is composed of girls with long-term relationships with males in which unintentional pregnancy occurs and marriage accompanies childbirth. Those marriages are more likely to end in divorce than later ones because they are precipitated rather than planned, and because they occur at young ages.[39] At best one recent study disclosed that three-fourths of Caucasian and one-half of African American teenage marriages to legitimatize a premarital conception before birth were intact after ten years. More typically, studies report that younger marriages are more vulnerable than later ones and that three-fourths of teenage marriages eventually break up.

Cultural Factors in Adolescent Parenthood

There are a variety of subcultural differences in responses to teenage pregnancy and childbirth. This fact has led to bitter controversies over whether or not adolescent parenthood should be accepted as an expression of a legitimate cultural life style.

Caucasian girls have been inclined to resort to abortion and to place babies for adoption. These practices tend to be frowned upon by African Americans for a variety of reasons ranging from cultural tradition to the conviction that one's masculinity or femininity needs to be validated through fecundity.

Currently African Americans are two times more likely to have a child before marriage than Caucasians if their incomes are below the poverty level and, perhaps surprisingly, five times more likely if they are comparatively affluent.[40] The proportion of African American unmarried mothers has increased rapidly, both because of a rise in separation and divorce and because of an increase in the percentage of never-married girls and women. The rise in female-headed families among African Americans is related to declining marriage rates that result in part from the lack of employment of African American males. Even if a young woman desired marriage, she would be unlikely to marry a young man who is likely to be unemployed, to go to jail, or to be killed. As long as there are limited employment opportunities, no amount of remedial education, training, wage subsidies, or other embellishments will make members of the underclass able to sustain marriages and to be as attractive to prospective employers as experienced workers.

Another factor in African American subcultures is that children may be cared for to a significant extent by relatives.[41] For example, the desire to have a baby to demonstrate a boyfriend's masculinity may lead to pregnancy with the expectation that the adolescent girl's mother or grandmother will care for the baby after birth. For this and a variety of other reasons, most African American children live with one parent. This pattern has been interpreted as reflecting the style of African American sexual and reproductive behavior. It also has been seen as adaptive for economically and racially subordinate groups. According to the historian Linda Gordon:

> The Children's Bureau experts knew that southern African Americans had higher rates of out-of-wedlock births from at least the 1920s, but this phenomenon was then seen as a contained, rural, regional pattern, and thus unthreatening, so it remained a very marginal discourse until the "great migration" brought thousands of blacks to the north. In mid-century social workers began to name black reproductive behavior as a problem.

U.S. Bureau of the Census data reveals that before 1950 young African American women were more likely to be married than were Caucasian women. In every census from 1890 to 1960 the percentage of African American households with two parents remained essentially unchanged at about 80 percent.[42] In 1970 it was down to 64 percent, and in 1992 it plummeted to less than 40 percent. This data contradicts the assumption that unwed parenthood is a cultural tradition for African Americans.

Yet whether in the rural South or in the urban North, teenage childbirth and single parenthood is seen by some as the cultural norm for African Americans. For reasons such as this, efforts to reduce minority groups' teenage births are regarded by some as "genocide" and the placement of their children for adoption as "anticultural." These beliefs probably will continue as long as opportunities for demonstrating one's worth other than by childbearing are unavailable or are not pursued by those young people.

The journalist Leon Dash interviewed African American adolescents in Washington, DC, and found that they knew about sex, birth control, and their reproductive abilities as young as the age of eleven.[43] But the poor academic preparation that began in elementary school, the poverty that surrounded them, and their isolation from mainstream American life all contributed to their giving birth to children. For many of the girls, babies were tangible achievements in the face of otherwise dreary futures. Having a baby was a way of announcing: "I am a woman." For many of the boys, the birth of a baby represented a similar rite of passage. Dash concluded that the successful students strove for high school diplomas and the unsuccessful students achieved recognition by having babies.

The African American anthropologist John Ogbu provided an historical perspective on African American attitudes.[44] He suggested that voluntary minorities come to the United States expecting to improve their lives. In contrast, involuntary African American minorities have been less successful because they were incorporated into our society against their will and originally had no expectation of improving their lives. They also may reject academic aspirations that would mean "acting white" and losing the support of their own groups while still not being accepted by Caucasians.

Psychologist Richard Majors and sociologist Janet Mancini Billson vividly described the behavior of some African American males in the United States in their book *Cool Pose*.[45] They point out that the stoic, unflinching self-assuredness of "cool" behavior has its origins in African tribal expressions of masculinity and was historically reinforced by the experience of slavery. They portray it as an adaptive attitude under the adverse circumstances of poverty and racial discrimination. Being "cool" can instill confidence in one's masculinity; however, it also can contribute to crime, violence, and volatile relationships with women.

The African American child psychiatrist James Comer noted long ago that the motivations for teenage parenthood accompany limited life goals for individuals living in modern society and actually tend to perpetuate disadvantage and both sexist and racist discrimination.[46] As evidence of this fact, parenthood rapidly loses its appeal when teenagers in minority groups have opportunities to experience adolescence as a developmental stage and to have hope for the future.

There are significant differences in the ways in which Mexican Americans approach marriage when compared to African Americans and Puerto Ricans living under the same socioeconomic circumstances.[47] Mexican Americans are much more likely to marry after the birth of the first child. Although extramarital affairs for men are tolerated, there often is great anguish when an unmarried woman becomes pregnant. In contrast, Puerto Ricans who live in the continental United States are much more severely afflicted than Mexican Americans and even African Americans by family breakups and by poverty.

When there is unemployment, inadequate education, and low social status, motherhood also can be attractive to Hispanic teenagers who live in a cultural context in which the role of mother has high social value.[48] Thus, pregnancy cannot always be viewed as an interruption in the education and career plans of adolescents. They may regard pregnancy as the only way to assume an adult role and regard childbearing as a sign of maturity and parenthood as a lifetime career in itself. This attitude has influenced the behavior of women and men in a number of cultures as they have been introduced into the United States in the past. This attitude conflicts with contemporary American cultural ideals that stress equal opportunities for self-development for both sexes and has not endured when those opportunities have been available.

The history of our society validates this point. Until recent decades, early motherhood was the career of choice for Caucasian blue-collar families, in part because of stereotypes about the roles of women.[49] Then early marriages strengthened girls' identifications with their mothers and provided boys with socially sanctioned sexual gratification. The inroads made by feminists on sexism have altered that pattern, however. Still, the sexist sexual exploitation of females by males and the sexist restriction of females to childbearing roles strongly operates in some minority groups in the United States today.

All in all regardless of cultural background, early childbearers experience more difficulties, more unhappiness, and as a group end up less well off than teenagers who delay childbearing until adulthood.[50] To ignore the developmental needs of adolescent girls who bear children is a manifestation of sexism and ageism, and for those in minority groups of racism as well. From the feminist point of view, the author Rickie Solinger pointed out how their reproductive capacity has contributed to the oppression of women, particularly when African American and Hispanic females are regarded as only suited for childbearing and for childrearing.

The Children of Adolescent Mothers

The typical result of teenage childrearing is not favorable because single adolescent parenthood and socioeconomic disadvantage go hand in hand. Children born to mothers who began childbearing as teenagers are three times more likely to be poor than children born to mothers who are older.[51]

Most single parents raise their children successfully; however, unwed mothers tend to be more immature and impulsive than those who are married.[52] In addition, the children of single mothers are 72 percent more likely to show "at-risk" behaviors than the children of two-parent families. The rates of abusive violence also are higher among young single mothers than among young two-parent families or older single parents.

A twenty-year follow-up study of 300 low-income Baltimore families documented the consequences of the personal and situational stresses of adolescent childbearing.[53] The preoccupations of those adolescent mothers with their own developmental struggles during their children's formative years bore immense costs for their children. Long-term outcomes were poorest for those whose own parents had a low level of education or a history of welfare dependency and for those who had two or more additional children within five years of the first child. The offspring were at greater risk of developing problems in late adolescence and early adulthood than the children of mothers who did not give birth as teenagers. Although two-thirds of the offspring did not bear children as teenagers themselves, one-third did, and then had bleaker educational and financial prospects than did their own mothers and were less likely to marry. This trend suggests that today's teenage parents are less likely than their own mothers to overcome the handicaps of early childbearing.

Another factor associated with single parenthood in general, and characteristic of adolescent parenthood in particular, is the effect of father absence.[54] A third of the nation's children now live apart from their biological fathers. Growing up without a father and the lack of two parental figures supporting each other are significant contributing factors to delinquency and drug abuse.

In spite of all of these negative factors, the majority of the children of teenage mothers and fathers ultimately do become self-supporting adults, although they never know what their lives would have been if their parents had not assumed the responsibilities of parenthood prematurely in our modern society. But at least one in three are trapped by the interwoven strands of men without jobs; women without husbands; children without fathers; and families without money, hope, skills, opportunities, or effective services that might help them escape from poverty.

In their thorough analysis of the situation, the sociologist–journalist team, Lisbeth and Daniel Schorr, concluded that when a baby is born to a mother who has not yet grown up herself, both mother and baby are likely to have limited futures and to place substantial burdens on society.[55] They are the prototypical sources of habitual criminals, of the long-term welfare dependent, of the unemployable, and of parents who continue the grim cycle.

Social Policy and Teenage Parents

The late 1960s and the early 1970s witnessed the first perception of teenage pregnancy as a major social problem in the United States. That public concern actually was not because of increases in adolescent childbirth, which dropped 45 percent between 1957 and 1983, largely because of the widespread availability of contraception and abortion. It was because of a cluster of volatile issues involving sexuality, abortion, family values, and welfare policies.

At the present time, the rising rate of adolescent childbirth is the driving public issue. About half of all children born in the United States now are destined to live in one-parent families, primarily female-headed, at some point during their lives. More than half of those will live in poverty at least for a time. They are prone to repeat the experiences of their parents, creating a new cycle of family disadvantage. The prospect of a large proportion of the next generation being raised by teenagers poses fundamental questions about the ability of that generation to cope with an ever more demanding and competitive society.

In 1987 the Committee on Child Development Research and Public Policy of the National Research Council concluded that the lack of a coherent policy in the United States toward adolescent pregnancy and childbearing has contributed to the magnitude and the seriousness of the problem.[56] The Committee found that teenage parenthood is a handicap for adolescents because it interferes with the teenager's development and opportunities. It expressed the conviction that the primary goal of policy makers, professionals, parents, and teenagers themselves should be to reduce teenage pregnancies. The Committee emphasized postponing the initiation of sexual intercourse until both males and females are capable of making wise and responsible decisions regarding their personal lives and the formation of families.

Solutions to the problem of adolescent pregnancy have been stymied, however, because of the characteristics of adolescence itself and the desire of many teenagers to have babies. For these reasons, the prevention of adolescent childbearing is a formidable, if not seemingly impossible, task in a democratic republic that prizes personal privacy and individual freedom and that broadly interprets the freedom of speech of the media. In this climate teenage girls and boys are not allowed to operate motor vehicles without being prepared to do so, yet they often are both tacitly and openly encouraged to parent children without any expectations being placed upon them.

American teenagers are exposed to the most self-defeating of all possible messages about sex through our unrestrained media.[57] Sexual intercourse often is depicted as a goal in itself with little reference to its risks and responsibilities. The media tell them that nonmarital sex is exciting and present a romanticized view of sexuality, marriage, and parenthood. Little that they take seriously informs teenagers about the consequences of sexual activity and about the realities of marriage. Moreover, they see premarital sex and cohabitation among the adults they know; and their own parents or their parents' friends may be involved in multiple sexual relationships.

In addition, a flagrant blind spot exists in our view of sexual relations between minors. We prosecute an adult who has sexual relations with a child and ignore the equal, if not greater, hazards of adolescent boys and girls having sexual intercourse with each other. In most states, for an eighteen-year-old man sexual intercourse with a fourteen-year-old is a crime, but for a seventeen-year-old boy it is not. This illogical situation is a typical result of the confused thinking that applies to teenage sexuality, pregnancies, and childbirth.

At the same time teenage girls are told that "good girls should say no" with no such expectation expressed for boys. Few if any other societies exhibit a more confusing combination of permissiveness and prudishness in their treatment of sexual issues. The mixed messages teenagers receive lead to an ambivalence about sex and marriage that stifles communication and results in a pregnancy rate that is twice that of comparable nations.

As it now stands, biological and societal pressures in the United States encourage rather than discourage adolescent pregnancy. The capacity to procreate is present long before an individual possesses the cognitive, emotional, and social maturity to assume responsibility for parenting a child since the maturation of the brain is not complete until the end of the second decade of life. The earlier onset of puberty, the earlier initiation of coitus, and the intense social and peer pressures for sexual activity abetted by the commercial exploitation of sexuality are powerful forces that encourage teenage pregnancies.

Adolescents have been deprived of the guidance of cultural values conveyed by interactive face-to-face communities as our mobile society has witnessed the breakdown of extended families in urban centers that lack a sense of community responsibility. In this context the teenagers who are the most likely to become pregnant are seldom exposed to values and experiences that effectively call their attention to the disadvantages of teenage childbirth. And even with that kind of information a substantial number of adolescents can be expected to ignore it.

Our usual approach to teenage pregnancy is to direct solutions at the teenagers themselves as if they were adults and to advocate sex education, the availability of contraceptives, supportive education, welfare payments, and expanded health care. None of these measures makes an impact on the premature foreclosures of personal, educational, occupational, and developmental opportunities that occur when teenagers deliberately choose to become parents.[58] We cannot reasonably expect family-life education, school-based health clinics, and "increased life options" programs to change sexual behaviors and attitudes acquired through developmentally inappropriate sexual socialization and even sexual abuse.

Our society's failure to deal with the problem of teenage pregnancy actually constitutes a form of sexism against females, ageism against adolescents, and racism against those in minority groups. The combined force of these forms of discrimination is seen most poignantly in the African American adolescent whose disadvantaged status is perpetuated by being impregnated to prove a boy's fecundity (sexism), by being deprived of the opportunity to complete her adolescent development (ageism), and by being regarded as expressing her cultural heritage (racism). With the opposite outcome, other forms of sexism and ageism are evident in societies that openly disparage females and encourage early marriages. For example, some parents in Moslem countries arrange a daughter's marriage before her first menstruation and thereby avoid out-of-wedlock pregnancies but perpetuate a subservient role for women.[59]

If we truly wish to prevent adolescent pregnancies and childbirth, we need to recognize the fact that the developmental characteristics of adolescence and the influences, or the lack thereof, of parents are more important causes of teenage pregnancy than are ignorance and socioeconomic disadvantage. Antipoverty measures alone do not address the key parent–child problems.[60] Ronald Mincy and Susan Weiner of the Urban Institute found that poverty actually is less important than the behavior of her own parents in influencing an adolescent girl's chances of becoming pregnant.

Because of their stage in life and the lack of mediating parental influences, many adolescents are wishful thinkers who lack a future orientation because of their sense of invulnerability and their attraction to risks. They are easily swayed by the belief "it can't happen to me." This omniscient and omnipotent flavoring of adolescence underlies the teenage attitude "I don't care about that now" in spite of knowledge that cigarettes, drugs, noise, and steroids produce disease, addiction, deafness, and a shortened life span. Even more importantly, infants and young children need protection from these characteristics of adolescent parents. These developmental factors in teenage pregnancy are inherent in adolescent immaturity and cannot be eliminated solely by persuasion or education. They can be constructively modified, however, by the influences of competent parenting and by the societal support of self-restraint.

The focus also needs to extend beyond girls to boys and to young men. As long as boys fail to postpone fatherhood until they have steady employment, and as long as men do not support their children, mothers and children will remain trapped in poor neighborhoods where social problems incubate and human resources are wasted. The 1988 Family

Support Act actually widened the gaps in educational and employment advantages that already separate males from their female counterparts by helping young unmarried mothers prepare for jobs without any provisions to help unmarried fathers.

Unfortunately, efforts to solve the social problem of adolescent pregnancy encounter resistant beliefs. One is the belief that public attitudes toward irresponsible sexual behavior cannot be changed. Therefore, when pregnancy occurs, the focus is on abortion or on supporting the teenage mother through pregnancy to adoption or in raising the child herself. Heated arguments revolve around the notification of parents of an adolescent's pregnancy and around the option of abortion. Seldom is the question raised of the competence of adolescents to make life-course-altering decisions or their competence to rear their children. Another resistance arises from an emphasis on a fetus's right to life that does not address that fetus's right to competent parenting after birth.

The possibility of influencing public attitudes toward teenage pregnancy and childbirth actually is greater than many people believe it to be. All that is needed is to mobilize cultural values and civil rights that support competent parenting. Then society's vested interest in each pregnant adolescent becomes apparent. That interest is not primarily in funding and educating the adolescent. It is primarily in insuring that the baby and the adolescent are competently parented. The U.S. Supreme Court already is willing to assume that the Constitution does not bar the state regulation of the sexual behavior of minors.[61] In *Carey v. Population Services International*, the Court noted "that with or without access to contraceptives, the incidence of sexual activity among minors is high, and the consequences of such activity are frequently devastating . . ."

In fact, articulating cultural values that place a high value on parenting and that discourage premature coitus can play a dramatic role in changing teenage behavior, as was demonstrated in this country in the early twentieth century and is evident in other countries today. This could be done through an aggressive public health campaign that highlights the disadvantages of teenage coitus and pregnancy, such as has been mounted against smoking, drug abuse, and driving while drinking. Civic groups, churches, and celebrities also can be enlisted to articulate standards for sexual behavior and parenting, as has been done to promote the immunization of young children.

In 1983 Marie Winn called attention to the many children who are growing up today without childhoods.[62] One symptom of our society's ablation of childhood is regarding teenagers as ready for parenthood after the attainment of biological puberty. When this happens, adolescence is ignored as a crucial developmental stage of life and as necessary preparation for adulthood, especially in our increasingly complicated world.

Our complex society must realize that it cannot afford to shorten the period of nurture and protection of its immature members by allowing them to assume adult responsibilities prematurely. Strikingly, indigenous societies appreciate the immaturity of adolescents and protect them more than we do currently in the United States. If we recognize and act upon the importance of adolescence as a developmental stage, and if we define parenting as an adult responsibility, perhaps we can restore childhood for the children of coming generations. We need an intellectual and moral climate that embodies a commitment to protect and nurture all of our young people—including our adolescents.

For all of these reasons, assuming the responsibilities of childrearing prior to the recognized attainment of adulthood is contrary to the interests of adolescents whose entire life courses are prematurely and permanently altered by bearing and rearing children. This is particularly devastating for economically disadvantaged girls who belong to minority groups and are subjected to the triple prejudices and discriminations of racism, sexism, and ageism.

SOCIAL POLICY AND PARENTING

In our society adults do not have a moral right to succeed. More to the point, they have the right to fail. For parents, however, this principle flies in the face of the moral right of children to competent parenting. Accordingly, there is an exception to an adult's freedom to fail when that adult is in the role of a parent. Few would defend a parent's right to be incompetent and to damage a child.

Because children have a moral right to competent parenting and a legal right to be protected from incompetent parenting, the logical inference is that parents have the moral right to be, and to become, competent parents whenever possible. This also implies that persons need protection from being incompetent parents. Adolescent parents need double protection from the incompetence of their own parents and from being incompetent parents themselves. In addition their children may well need protection from them.

Our society must recognize that even not all adults who conceive and give birth to children are capable of competently parenting them. When they are overwhelmed by the responsibilities of parenthood, help should be available for them. Accordingly, identifying incompetent parenting needs to be a high priority for our society. The moral right to be a competent parent means those who are not deserve help to become so, and those who cannot be competent parents need relief from the responsibilities of parenting by terminating their parental rights. The inescapable conclusions are that our society has a compelling interest in ensuring that children receive, and that their parents are capable of providing, competent parenting.

We need a new way of thinking about children if we are to ensure that they receive the competent parenting they need in order to become competent citizens.

Chapter 10

A New Way of Thinking about Children

As children decline as a proportion of the American population, their lives become more precious, and our responsibility to them even greater. The test now is whether we are motivated to promote policies that we know can reverse these alarming trends in the 1990s, or whether we will enter the 21st century besieged by the worst effects of our failure.

—U.S. House of Representatives Select Committee on Children, Youth, and Families, 1989[1]

I am attracted to working with children because much can be done to help them during their formative years. It is rewarding to see young-sters shift from being seen as a problems in the lives of adults to being sources of satisfaction and pleasure. Those of us who work with children frequently see that kind of result. It keeps us going. All too often, however, we feel helpless when the world in which children live undermines our efforts to help them. We know that the way our society views children and parenting must change.

If we ever are to solve our nation's critical social problems, we need a new way of thinking about children. We must overcome the lack of interest in the welfare of others inherent in individualism and the crisis–

recoil responses of our political processes. These divisive factors make it possible for us to act as though the way in which our children are raised has nothing to do with our social problems. These factors underlie the tolerance of incompetent parenting that continues to erode the quality of life in the United States.

The fate of our nation will not be determined by our emotionally driven reactions to the social crises of the day. It depends on using our collective wisdom to think through ways to prevent our social problems. Without preventive strategies that are coordinated at the federal, state, and local levels, enormous expenditures on remedies for each social crisis will continue with increasingly adverse consequences for our society. Those piecemeal remedies are ineffective because they do not address the underlying causes shared by each social problem. They amount to placing buckets under each leak rather than repairing the roof.

Identifying the root causes of our nation's problems is the first step toward solving them. In order to do so we must shift away from our traditional single cause and single effect linear thinking.

Thomas Kuhn, the scientific philosopher, captured the essence of problem solving by pointing out the way in which paradigm shifts lead to new answers to perplexing problems.[2] For example, the cause of malaria was discovered when thinking shifted from attributing it simply to "bad air" to attributing it to mosquitoes. Ultimately mosquitoes were found to be carrying an organism that attacked red blood cells in susceptible individuals and created the bodily reactions that caused the symptoms of the disease. This paradigm of multiple interacting factors is far more useful in understanding and solving our social problems than a paradigm in which a single cause is indicted, such as poverty, genetics, unemployment, or family breakdown.

The kind of thinking that stands in the way of solving our social problems is easier to understand if we contrast the paradigm of single-cause, self-centered "little picture" thinking with the paradigm of multiple-causes, group-centered "big picture" thinking.

"LITTLE PICTURE" THINKING

Most of us assume that we are realistic and that we think clearly. Yet unrealistic thinking based upon surface impressions, single causes, oversimplification, and indifference to consequences prevails in our personal and public lives. It leads us to react to troublesome social problems with impulsive and prejudiced responses, usually at either permissive or punitive extremes, such as being "soft" or "hard" on crime.

Unrealistic thinking takes into account only a single perspective and blocks accommodating multiple viewpoints. It is single dimensional, or linear, and presses others to conform to its point of view. It is guided by emotionally tinged stereotypes, such as "conservative" and "liberal." It is "little picture" thinking in response to immediate pressures without a long-range perspective.

In order to solve our social problems, one particular single-cause belief needs to be discarded. It is the eighteenth century economist Adam Smith's contention that human beings are mainly motivated by self-interest. That belief inheres in our thinking about social problems in the United States to this day. That belief minimizes the fact that we often do self-defeating things that are contrary to our own interests when we seek short-term pleasure and when we try to avoid discomfort and anxiety. That belief also does not take into account sufficiently the fact that we often act in altruistic ways. As a result, we have difficulty understanding how in negative ways we can make decisions that are contrary to our own interests, and how in positive ways we can unite in the pursuit of common interests.

We live in a society largely oriented toward avoiding the discomforts of unpleasant realities by "little picture" thinking. Among the many devices we have for avoiding unpleasant realities, the most common is keeping related aspects of an issue mentally separate. When we compartmentalize our thoughts, we can maintain contradictory opinions without being mentally discomforted.

For example, when we want to protect American jobs, we endorse tariffs that protect our industries. But when we want lower prices in our stores, we oppose protective tariffs. We oppose government spending in the abstract but want government spending for purposes we support. As long as our thinking is separated in compartments such as these, we are unable to make consistent decisions on the issues before us.

More specifically, "little picture" thinking divides our social problems into separate, unconnected groups. Each one is seen as having a different cause and a different solution. The remedies devised for each of these problems often contribute to the very problem they seek to solve because they do not address the underlying causes all of the problems share in our economy, our neighborhoods, our communities, our families, and our social values.

For example, the handling of social problems, such as poverty, crime, welfare dependency, alcoholism, drug abuse, and domestic abuse, customarily involves separating each of these problem areas as an entity unto itself, as if each one reflected a different problem requiring a different solution. Each problem area then competes with the others for attention and resources. Consequently, the helping professions concentrate on treating the victims of each societal problem, rather than addressing the common underlying causes. The status quo is inadvertently maintained as we have seen in the many unsuccessful efforts to separately attack each of these problems.

When we turn over each of these separate social problems to professionals to solve, the mediating structures of families and neighborhoods are replaced by megastructures in the form of service industries for each category of problems. This further weakens families and neighborhood communities. Personal relationships are replaced by professional services, and the illusion that professionals will solve our social problems is fostered. This phenomenon was seen in the 1960s during the Great Society War on Poverty. Local institutions, including churches and informal voluntary associations, were displaced by professionals trained in specific areas, such as social work and drug abuse counseling. What had been communities became, for antipoverty purposes, collections of social problems to be solved by services from outside of the communities. No profession addressed what it was like to live in those places. As a result the communities sank more deeply into disorder.

Frequently our compartmentalized thinking is linked to politically tainted code words or phrases to which we respond without looking further into an issue. For example, depending upon our preconceived notions we react emotionally to phrases such as "tax and spend" or "trickle-down economics." Such automatic responses are characteristic of the lowest forms of our brains' reactions to threats and crises.

Although perhaps not very flattering, "little picture" thinking is based on the simplest levels of brain functioning.[3] Those levels are biologically gauged to react to immediate threats to our survival, such as an attacking animal. For our hunter–gatherer ancestors, it worked well to take the familiar at face value and only respond to emotions evoked by immediate dangers or pleasures. In our modern world "little picture" thinking is no longer sufficient to ensure individual, and certainly not group, survival. In particular it stands in the way of identifying the causes of crime and welfare dependency.

Fortunately, the higher centers of our brains permit us to engage in the analytic and synthetic problem solving of "big picture" thinking.

"BIG PICTURE" THINKING

In contrast to unrealistic "little picture" thinking, realistic, or "big picture," thinking looks beneath surface impressions, expects multiple causes, deals with complexity, and evaluates the consequences of actions. "Big picture" thinking is multidimensional, or systems oriented, and gets at the multiple causes of events. It is analytic when it focuses on details, and it is synthetic when it focuses on unifying principles.

Most of us live at the "little picture" level of responding to day-to-day needs without devoting much thought to the meaning and the purpose of our lives. We plan for the future occasionally in terms of life insurance, retirement, and educational costs for our children, but we do not have overall strategies for our lives. In military terms, we live as if we are fighting local battles without awareness of the overall purpose of the war.

The "little picture" military metaphor has profound significance for the United States as we reflect on our experiences during the Korean, Vietnamese, and Persian Gulf Wars. Those wars shared limited "little picture" objectives. Previously the American people were welded together by "big picture" strategic threats to democratic freedom by totalitarian states in World Wars I and II. Those wars ended when the "enemies" were defeated. The tactical "little picture" nature of the wars in Korea and Vietnam was ultimately revealed in their reliance upon body counts rather than on defeating an enemy. The continued power of Sadam Hussein after the Persian Gulf War once again revealed the shortsightedness of a war with the "little picture" objective of restoring the monarchy of Kuwait.

The lack of a moral purpose for the Vietnam War led to its termination and to turmoil in the United States, during which the moral issues raised by that war seeped throughout the fabric of American society. As a result, there has been a search for leadership that articulates moral strategies. For example, public support was gained for the Persian Gulf War by drawing upon a "big picture" campaign against the amoral tyrant Sadam Hussein even though that was not the actual objective.

As a result of our dissatisfaction with "little picture" political solutions that do not work, many of us yearn for "big picture" governance. According to the Kettering Foundation's studies of public opinion, a strong interest in cooperative governance is emerging in the United States.[4] Our interest in political processes is being catalyzed by our increasingly sophisticated awareness of the important issues through the media. This trend counters the usual commercial and political ways of influencing people by creating appealing or frightening images. It is generating a substantive interest in the actual performance of the products we buy and the public officials we elect rather than in the images created about them. We crave the truth, even though many of us avoid the painful aspects of the truth by drawing upon the illusions that material comforts and our prejudices provide.

Daniel Yankelovitch, the public opinion analyst, believes that the key to cooperative governance in the United States is to create a new balance between the public and the experts.[5] He points out that the relationship now is badly skewed toward experts at the expense of the public. This unbalanced condition is the result of a societal trend that elevates the specialized knowledge of experts above the public's capacity for making responsible judgments. As a result the compartmentalization of social problems is reinforced.

In addition the media tends to raise public consciousness of a social problem and then to move on to another crisis, as if arousing public concern was an end in itself. The helplessness that often accompanies consciousness raising can be overcome by identifying what needs to be done. Then a third stage of problem resolution can be pursued. When that occurs, Yankelovitch observes that human wisdom emerges in the form of considered public opinion. Then our fundamental capacity to govern ourselves is revealed.

In the process of problem resolution, we can find common interests between disparate political factions. Those of us who are conservatives wish to conserve traditional institutions, but not those that are unworkable. Those of us who are liberals advocate freedom, but not the freedom to harm others. In "big picture" thinking, conservatism and liberalism complement each other and are not mutually exclusive.

Although still dominated by habits of "little picture" thinking, the American public appears to be gradually moving toward more realistic "big picture" thinking. There appears to be a readiness to see life as a cooperative endeavor with fellow human beings rather than as a contest to be won. Many of us have found that simply consuming material goods is not enough to make our lives self-fulfilling. We are learning that the production of material goods should be guided by our beliefs about what really is needed and about how products should be used. The markers of the quality of life are shifting subtly from status in the eyes of others marked by material possessions to self-fulfillment and self-esteem. We are learning that poverty, crime, welfare dependency, and drug abuse will not be successfully managed until we have a thriving economy, safe neighborhoods, cooperative communities, and healthy families.

We also are learning that we will not have a thriving economy, safe neighborhoods, and cooperative communities unless we have a competent citizenry. We will not have competent citizens unless we have competent parents. More broadly, we all can gain personal fulfillment from humanitarian ventures at the intimate and public levels. On the intimate level one way is through parenting or working with children. Our families provide many opportunities for altruistic satisfactions. At the public level, we can gain satisfaction from promoting the welfare of children because they are helpless in the political arena without our support.

All of this indicates that many of us realize that material and vocational fulfillments have only limited potentials in the long run for bringing us satisfaction and happiness. Lasting personal fulfillment is more likely to be achieved in the pursuit of altruistic goals that involve "big picture" cooperation with others rather than by pursuing "little picture" goals that tend to separate and alienate us from each other.

This leads us to ask how "big picture" thinking can be stimulated in a society dominated by self-centered "little picture" thinking. The answer lies in our culture. Because our culture, like all others, has evolved to foster the advancement and the survival of our pluralistic society and of the human species, "big picture" thinking is reflected in most of our cultural values.

Social Values versus Cultural Values

The paradigms of "little picture" and "big picture" thinking can be profitably applied to social problems by distinguishing between the "little picture" tendencies of the *social values* of our society and the "big picture" nature of the *cultural values* of our culture.

Although the terms *society* and *culture* often are used interchangeably, they are very different and at the same time are interdependent. A basic distinction can be made between society and culture by employing the analogy of a tree. *Society* is like the leaves that carry on essential life processes that change with the seasons, and *culture* is like the trunk and roots that provide the enduring, underlying structure and nourishment.

From the political point of view, the society of the United States is shaped by the legislative and executive branches of government, whereas the American culture is evolving from the principles of the Declaration of Independence and the U.S. Constitution as interpreted by the judicial branch.

In this context a vital distinction can be made between social and cultural values, particularly as they apply to our primary interest in childrearing.

Social and Cultural Childrearing Values

Throughout recorded history there has been a fundamental tension between social values and cultural values. That tension is reflected in the eternal struggle between the lust for riches and glory depicted by Homer on the one hand (social values) and the quest for truth and justice by Socrates on the one hand (cultural values).

Social values are the products of society's contemporary life styles and pertain to individual survival issues of power and passion in day-to-day living within the organizational structures of society. Social values are strongly influenced by technology, because they are concerned with enhancing the comforts and power of individuals. Social values fluctuate with the times. Those that apply to trends in tastes and fashions reflect what is called "pop culture."

The objectives of social values that influence childrearing in the United States are to produce competent, competitive, and productive consumers who also are educated and informed citizens. Thus social values favor the development of independent, ambitious children and adults.

In contrast to social values, which fluctuate and are influenced by the "little picture" perspectives of individuals, cultural values encompass the "big picture" and evolve over generations in order to ensure the survival of the species. Cultural values support harmonious group living through reasoning about the critical issues of human existence. They are biologically based on affectionate parent–child attachment bonds.[6] Because of their origins in innate human proclivities, cultural values are durable and enduring.

The childrearing objectives of American cultural values are producing creative, responsible persons capable of committed attachments to other people and of contributing to the common good. These cultural values that inspired the Declaration of Independence and the U.S. Constitution have evolved from ideas about freedom and justice that accommodate diverse ethnic origins and creeds. Except for a few antisocial subcultures, these cultural values are shared by the variety of subcultures in the United States.

Since the survival of the species actually depends upon the collective fitness of individuals, all individuals do not have to be altruistic. For this reason, individual competition can enhance the survival of the fittest, and thereby the group, as long as most individuals are guided by the values of their culture. The survival and prosperity of our society depends upon a critical mass of adults who are guided by our cultural values and are committed to the goals of the commonwealth. Without an infrastructure of cultural values that emphasizes cooperation between people our society cannot endure.

Social values usually are implemented through governmental and commercial policies. For this reason, they cannot create the infrastructure of human relationships needed to ensure commitment to the common good. That infrastructure of society lies in the mediating structures of cultural institutions—in families, religious groups, and voluntary organizations. Therefore, in order to insure its own survival a society needs social values that reflect its cultural values and that support rather than undermine its cultural institutions of which the family is the centerpiece.

When a social and a cultural value conflict, the integrity of a society depends upon the long-range prevailing of the cultural value, even though there often is short-range dominance of the social value. The history of the United States has demonstrated that self-centered social values dominate the public arena until the excesses they create provoke a gradual but ultimately prevailing counterreaction based on the moral values of our culture. This can be seen in the elimination of slavery in the past and in the indictments of public officials in the present.

In recent decades, social values in the United States have stressed materialistic individualism. The cultural values that support committed human relationships and that support parenting have been eclipsed. Business for profit and working for money have been adulated. It is of interest to note, however, that the dominant emphasis on materialistic individualism in the United States has not been matched by the economic success desired by most individuals and by our nation, and certainly has not fostered safe and fulfilling lives for most of our citizens.

The Interplay of Social and Cultural Values

We currently are in a phase in the United States in which our social values have become detached from our cultural values in critical ways. Yet our society and our culture still are interacting in an evolving pattern so that our social and cultural values continue to influence each other to varying degrees over time.

The most obvious example of the detachment of social and cultural values is in our underclass. The historian Carl Nightingale spent six years with young African American people in a Philadelphia ghetto and described how they were saturated with materialistic social values and were strongly influenced by the advertising and marketing of status symbols.[7] From designer sportswear to gold jewelry, the African American children he knew turned to expensive material goods to find a sense of self-worth and resorted to violent and illegal means of obtaining money to buy them. Many of them aspired to move to better neighborhoods and to improve their lives. To compensate for the humiliation and frustration of poverty and racism, they turned to our society's traditions of consumerism and violence. Nightingale clearly pointed out the detachment of these young people from our cultural values bearing on personal and collective responsibility because of both their lack of experience and their disillusionment with them.

In a broader sense, the contemporary dominance of social over cultural values in the United States has devalued parenting, so that many aspects of our society do not support, and actually undermine, family life. Consequently, commitments to community relationships have diminished as individualistic materialism and competitiveness have been overemphasized. Because the adult capacities for cooperative personal and community living depend upon having formed affectionate attachment bonds with adults early in life, only strengthening parent–child relationships can reverse this trend in the long run.

The objectives of childrearing in the United States could be drawn from the interplay of our social and cultural values. Because of its dependence on the advocacy of competing interests and the lack of advocacy for children, however, our society has never clearly articulated its cultural childrearing objectives, and there has been little public or lobbying pressure to do so. The general assumption is that parents will raise their children as they wish, although there are expectations that children will be educated. The lack of articulated cultural goals for childrearing in the United States does not mean that they do not exist.

As our society has become more involved in childrearing, underlying related cultural values have been codified in legislation and reiterated and refined in court decisions, as noted in chapter 8. The expectation that children will become competent, committed, and compassionate citizens seems clear, in that order of desirability. We expect adults to be competent in their work. We expect adults to be committed to their obligations to others. We expect people to care for each other, especially within families. Each of these expectations may not be met by everyone, but that does not detract from their importance as cultural ideals.

In contrast with other societies that give more weight to one than the other, childrearing in the United States emphasizes the autonomy of both adults and children. In this context, the overall aim of childrearing in the United States is the balanced development of both children's and parents' potentials to function competently within our social and economic system. Both childhood and parenthood are developmental stages in life. Rewarding family relationships are as important for adults as they are for children, and the family still is the only institution that provides unconditional acceptance for both adults and children.

There is a palpable yearning for a sense of family and of community throughout the United States. There is a desire for fulfilling family lives and fulfilling careers. Aligning our social and cultural values that impact on families would relieve the conflicts between these goals.

Supporting Competent Parenting as a National Policy

The impediments to fulfilling family and career goals for parents lie in the long-standing difficulty in formulating a national family policy in the United States. This has left many parents without adequate support at home, in their communities, and in their workplaces.

One of the reasons why we have not developed a coherent family policy is the controversy over what constitutes a family. Because of the many problems involved in defining families, a more accurate and feasible approach would be to focus on the parent–child relationship and design funding, services, and benefits around the goal of promoting competent parenting rather than around the ambiguous and controversial image of a family.

Persons who have not experienced competent parenting tend to have difficulties in childrearing themselves. Such links between childhood experiences and subsequent parental behavior are not inevitable, however. Even in multiproblem families, affectionate bonds between parents and their children may well be the starting point for improving childrearing practices. Parents can be motivated to improve their skills and family relationships by drawing upon their affection for their children. Unfortunately, many social and public policies ostensibly devoted to helping families have foundered because they have focused on either the parent or the child, as if each were freestanding individuals. Those policies actually have undermined the parent–child relationship because they have not focused on parenting.

Welfare requirements are moving toward expecting parents to be employed and placing young children in subsidized day care rather than on helping parents to raise their own children. Such "little picture" policies focus on the employment of parents and force parents to be employed away from home while others care for their children, when they could be helped to more competently rear their own children. The expectation that adults on welfare should be employed when possible is laudable. When that adult is the parent of a young child, however, a separate approach to the parent and to the child incurs greater costs because day care of high quality is expensive and in itself may not be in the interests of children and their parents. Turning the care of their children over to others does not improve the skills of parents or foster parent–child relationships.

A more realistic "big picture" approach for social policies is to recognize that the parent–child unit is irreducible. By definition a child is dependent upon a parent until that child becomes an adult. A focus on the child–parent unit rather than on the ambiguous concept of the family would mean that financial resources, services, and the workplace would be designed to support competent parenting. It would draw attention to remedying the environmental, societal, economic, workplace, and personal impediments to being a competent parent. Then parenthood could be seen as a beneficial growth experience for both children and parents and as an essential social role for society as well.

As it now stands our "little picture" social policy toward child abuse and neglect is to punish or treat parents who are abusive or neglectful. This approach reinforces the tendency to wait until children are damaged before intervention occurs and then overlooks the need to repair the damage done to the children.[8] A more logical and responsible "big picture" policy would be to focus on providing competent parenting for all children through setting expectations for parents and thereby preventing the damage to children by parental abuse and neglect.

James Q. Wilson, the criminologist, is convinced that the key to reducing crime, educational failure, and chronic welfare dependency is the improvement of individual character in the sense of self-discipline and prosocial values. After surveying all of the evidence, Lizbeth and Daniel Schorr also concluded that the federal government must play a role in strengthening the formation of character in young children by supporting programs to better prepare children for school entry and to help parents whose children are at risk.[9] The key lies in helping parents become competent so that they can prepare their children for competent citizenship as adults.

The fundamental questions of social policy, as the educational historian Michael Katz points out, are not about how to spend governmental revenues.[10] They are, rather, about citizenship and the achievement of human dignity. They are about what we want for our people and how willing we are to set priorities for our society in order to attain those goals.

THE SOCIETAL GOAL OF COMPETENT CITIZENSHIP

In the past, technology and the material comforts that evolve from it have stimulated changes in our society. Now that many of us are freed from the "little picture" constraints of our personal wants and are able to engage in "big picture" thinking about the welfare of the society in which we live, the next century could well be devoted to enhancing the emotional and physical security of our lives. We then would be able to focus on self-fulfillment and on the importance of children in our lives. More of us would be able to discover that self-fulfillment lies in being needed by others. Because they naturally need us, children can provide that fulfillment for those of us who are parents and for those of us who are not as well.

In order to live in our free society in which adults do much as they please, children need competent parents to protect them and to help them develop the competencies and the values they need to resist the prevalent forces that would exploit and harm them. At the same time, our democratic society requires competent citizens who can create and maintain committed relationships with other people. As a consequence, both children and our society need competent parents. More fundamentally, our society cannot prosper, or even survive, unless the parenting needs of our children are met. We must recognize that incompetent parenting is at the root of our social problems.

Because of the "little picture," crisis–recoil nature of political responses in the United States to social problems, such as crime and welfare dependency, there is a compelling need for an overall strategy to guide public policies for parenting. That "big picture" strategy could be based on the goal of achieving competent citizenship for all adults by providing competent parenting for all children. Reaching that goal could be furthered by articulating social values that will foster the promise of opportunities for individuals of all ages to become competent citizens, which is implicit in American cultural values. Those values must be more fundamental than, and thereby include, values specifically devoted to reducing the racial discrimination, poverty, and domestic abuse that underlie crime and welfare dependency.

Our societal and cultural expectations that children will become competent, committed, and compassionate citizens seems clear. Accordingly, the goal of competent citizenship for all adults to be achieved by insuring the competent parenting of all children could be the basis for articulating social values that support childrearing families as mediating institutions in our society. The competent parenting of our children would insure the development of affectionate attachment bonds that, in turn, enable the cooperative adult relationships that mitigate against crime and welfare dependency.

Mobilizing the following social values would support competent parenting in our society and thereby further the goal of competent citizenship for all:

1. Children are entitled to competent parenting.
2. Fathers have essential parenting roles.
3. Government policies should strengthen parenting households.
4. The workplace should accommodate parenting responsibilities.

Support for these values cannot be mandated by government alone, but must come from popular sentiment. Yet when majority sentiment and state power converge on a moral issue, such as slavery, racial discrimination, or the inequality of women, the resulting social changes can be dramatic. Like these other pivotal issues there is enough popular concern about the social problems resulting from incompetent parenting to widely publicize that link and to justify interventions to strengthen parenting now. At the very least we must change governmental policies that undermine parenting.

Hopefully, the human need for committed human attachments and the natural affection most adults have for children will ensure that altruistic cultural values supporting parenting will prevail over the individualistic social values that undermine parenting. This will not happen in our democratic republic, that operates through the advocacy of competing interests, unless there is a national parenting policy that builds support for parenting into governmental policies.

Chapter 11

A National Parenting Policy

> . . . *Causing the existence of a human being is one of the most responsible actions in the range of human life. To undertake this responsibility—to bestow a life which may be either a curse or a blessing—unless the being on whom it is to be bestowed will have at least the ordinary chances of a desirable existence, is a crime against that being.*
>
> —JOHN STUART MILL, *On Liberty*, 1859[1]

One day a six-year-old girl told me in all seriousness that she was worried about her mother. Referring to her four-year-old brother and her baby sister, she said that her mother shouldn't have children because she couldn't take care of them. The sad fact was that this six-year-old knew that her mother was incompetent, but her mother did not.

When people talk about the right "to have children," they often do not take into account the fact that children are brought up, as well as brought into, the world. They assume that the right to procreate includes the right to rear a child as one wishes without special obligations to society. They are mistaken. In fact, "having a child" includes obligations that hinge on three separate rights.

First is the right to conceive a child. At one extreme is a desired conception consummated by the mutual assent of a female and a male. At the other extreme is forced conception through rape, which may be regarded as a reason for terminating a pregnancy. In between are accidental and unconsciously motivated conceptions. In each of these instances there are obligations that accompany the biological right to conceive a child, as illustrated by the duty of an unmarried father to financially support a child he conceives.

Second is the right to bear a child, but even this right includes obligations to protect the fetus on the part of the mother. There is a growing tendency to regard the rights of a mother and the rights of a fetus as respectively decreasing and increasing as a pregnancy progresses. In addition a host of questions about who has parental rights and obligations are being raised by the availability of artificial insemination and surrogate childbearing with different ways of uniting eggs and sperm. In each of those instances the obligations to the resulting offspring on the part of various parents have as yet to be completely ascertained.

Third is the right to the custody and rearing of a child. The trend is away from assuming that a parent has a biological right to possess the child as property toward recognizing parenthood as the earned result of affectionate bonding with a child. Although the biological parent has a right to establish a relationship with a child by virtue of genetic and prenatal connections, the psychological, or "real," parent of a child is the person with whom the child actually forms an affectionate attachment bond after birth. Consequently, the parent–child relationship is defined by life experience not by the event of birth. This redefinition of parenthood from simply being a question of biological conception and giving birth to a child to that of a life style of childrearing is an essential way of thinking if our society is to value the competent parenting of children.

The traditional mystique of biological parenthood needs to be placed in perspective, so that parenthood can be seen accurately, not as a state determined by conception and birth but as a relationship based upon a parent–child affectionate bond with reciprocal obligations between parents and children. As adoptive parents well know, parenthood really is a relationship and is not simply a status awarded by conceiving or giving birth to a child.

There are three models for parenthood as a relationship between parents and children. One that has been largely discredited in the

United States is that children are the property of their parents. The second model is that parents are solely responsible for rearing their children, and society intervenes only when children are maltreated. The third model is that parents and society share responsibility for rearing children.

The third model is implicit in the United States because the education of children is generally regarded as a public responsibility. As it now stands, however, our society's interest in childrearing is not explicitly defined. Many adults also are uncertain about their preparation for parenthood, as illustrated by the following excerpt from the novel *Breathing Lessons* by Anne Tyler:[2]

> I remember leaving the hospital with my first child, Jesse, and thinking, "Wait. Are they going to let me walk off with him? I don't know beans about babies! I don't have a license to do this. You're given all these lessons for unimportant things—piano playing, typing, and balancing equations. But how about parenthood? Or marriage, either, come to think of it. Before you can drive a car you need a state-approved course of instruction, but driving a car is nothing, nothing compared to living day in and day out with a husband and raising up a new human being.

The vast majority of adults learn how to be competent parents without society's intervention. A comparatively small, but critical, number of people are unable to competently parent their children, however, because they cannot manage their own lives responsibly, much less the lives of their children. As it now stands, these people must be found to be unfit as parents after their abuse and neglect have damaged their children. Much of this damage to children could be prevented by expecting parents to be competent before damage from abuse and neglect takes place.

The fact that children now must suffer from incompetent parenting until they are damaged instead of expecting parents to be competent is a flagrant expression of juvenile ageism. This is the consequence of the lack of a clear-cut national policy that expects and promotes competent parenting. Society must establish a clear connection between the public interest and competent parenting so that childrearing is regarded as more than simply a life style option.[3] Because children are not the property of their parents but are our future citizens, the parenting they receive has definite implications for society. An explicit legal relationship between parent and child would establish that connection.

THE CONCEPT OF PARENT LICENSURE

Although the desirability of setting expectations for parents has been suggested from time to time in the past, the idea of certifying the childrearing competence of future parents was proposed in 1973 by the psychologist Harriet Rheingold.[4] The legal recognition of parenting through licensing to protect children from abuse and neglect was proposed in 1980 by the philosopher Hugh La Follette.

In 1986, Senator Daniel Patrick Moynihan concluded that a credible family policy should insist that responsibility for a child begins with the individual parent, next the child's family, and then the child's community.[5] He called for public policies and practices that would provide status, encouragement, stability, and time for parenthood.

Since we have child abuse and neglect laws, you might reasonably ask why parent licensing is being raised as an issue now. You can say that we have managed without it. But we have not managed well without it. Children have no protection from damage by their parents before it occurs. As a result large numbers of damaged children have grown up to be unable to live successfully as adults, threatening the very fabric of our society.

Our society simply allows parents to rear their children as a private matter. At the present time any male and any female at any age are free to conceive a child and to assume complete parental rights to the custody and rearing of the child without any expectation that they should be competent to parent the child. They are free to conduct their lives and to do as they wish with the child, with public financial support if needed, until the child shows evidence of sufficient damage to warrant state intervention through child abuse and neglect statutes. Then the state both defends the parents and attempts to prove that they are unfit.

At no time before a child is damaged is it incumbent upon the male or the female to demonstrate that they possess minimal competencies, as they must do in order to obtain a motor vehicle operator's license, to marry, or to join the military forces.

Behind this situation is the general disengagement of our society from cultural values that emphasize the responsibilities of parents and children to each other. This has led to an intolerable level of incompetent parenting. This absence of societal support for competent parenting calls for developing social values that define and expect competent parenting. As is the case with any social value, the articulation of social values that support parenting will require persuasion, education, and legislation.

Although education and persuasion are important, the implementation of any societal value also requires regulation, because not everyone can be depended upon to be sufficiently influenced by knowledge. For those who do not respond to persuasion or education, a clear statement of each child's right to competent parenting with enforcement capacities is necessary in order to convey the value society places on parenting.

The idea of licensing parents may seem to be an outrageous intrusion into individual rights and the privacy of families. Yet in effect social agencies and courts already are licensing parents. Potential adoptive parents are screened intensively by social agencies, and laws mandate the assessment of parenting when children are alleged to have been maltreated by their parents. Furthermore, the family's absolute right to privacy is not guaranteed by the Constitution.

Child abuse and neglect laws are used now to prevent a mother from taking her newborn infant home from the hospital when her condition or home environment would place the child in jeopardy. In these instances the state seeks custody of the child under the applicable law, and a court decides whether or not the child will be endangered if placed in the parent's custody.

The concept of licensing parents applies to the stage of parenthood, not to the conception or birth stages of life. It would designate parenthood as a privilege for which one is qualified rather than as a right that accompanies the event of childbirth. It would define parenthood realistically as a relationship rather than as a biologically determined state. It would provide an opportunity to inform parents of available parenting resources. In addition, becoming and being licensed parents would provide a basis for eligibility for governmental financial aid and supportive services in order to insure that public funding supports competent and not incompetent parenting.

At the societal level licensing would symbolically convey the message that parenting is at least as important as such things as marriage, military service, voting, access to alcohol and cigarettes, driving a motor vehicle, access to pornography, consent to health care, and all other age-graded activities. It also would be a concrete expression of a parenting policy based on a child's right to competent parenting and a parent's right to be competent. It would implement expectations of parents that already exist in child abuse and neglect statutes.

Most importantly, the process of licensing parents would focus attention on the importance of parenting in our society and would be the rallying call for a series of essential multilevel interventions to promote competent parenting.

A MULTISYSTEM APPROACH TO IMPROVING PARENTAL COMPETENCE

A multisystem national parenting policy with the aim of supporting competent parenting for all children at societal, community, and family levels is needed to replace the present fragmented public policies that actually support incompetent parenting and foster the very social problems they are intended to alleviate.

In 1979, on behalf of the Carnegie Council on Children, Richard de Lone pointed out that attempts to alleviate the suffering of children fail because they are not accompanied by rectifying the inequities in our society.[6] He noted that almost every index of physical and developmental harm to children is strongly associated with inequalities of income and race. There is no question that prosperous parents are better able to raise their children than those who are not.

Yet rectifying economic inequities alone will not be sufficient to help all children. Inequities in parental competence are even more important. In fact parental competence exists in most poor families, and parental incompetence exists even in affluent families. The focus must be on strengthening the contexts in which parenting and child development occur. The answers lie in altering the policies of our nation so that they value competent parenting economically and socially by extending civil rights to all children.

More specifically, a multisystem approach is essential to prevent the ill-fated reliance on one system to solve all of our social problems. At the present time, there is great danger that schools will be seen as the answer to the deterioration of families, communities, and religious organizations. Such a direction reinforces the trend to reduce expectations of parents; it encourages parents to further relinquish their responsibilities for childrearing; and it diverts attention from supporting parenting. Instead of expecting schools to take the place of parents, we should see schools as complementing and supplementing parenting.

A multisystem approach also is needed to provide a continuum of coordinated services in communities for all children and for all families who need them.

Societal Level

First of all, our society must recognize that the quality of parenting has social consequences. We must recognize that competent parents strengthen society and that incompetent parents weaken society.

Recognizing parenting as an important responsibility in society is to the advantage of all children, all parents, and society. The problems of our young are not limited to disadvantaged groups. We need to design a comprehensive policy that upgrades the chances of success for all American children.

The lack of expectations of parents in the United States reflects the legal presumption that favors the privacy of families in childrearing.[7] This general policy certainly has merit. Nonetheless, society has a compelling interest in monitoring the rearing of its children. For this reason, public policies are needed that recognize that children are citizens. This recognition means clarifying the rights of children and supporting parents in their homes, communities, and workplaces in their efforts to rear their children.

It is even more important to stimulate public awareness that parental competence is the single most critical variable in promoting adult competence in our society. With some exceptions, competent parenting outweighs biological, social, economic, and ecological variables in the development of the characters and work skills of adults. Incompetent parenting is harmful to children and increases our society's criminal and welfare dependency burdens. Not only does our society need competent, productive citizens, but it also needs to reduce the numbers of dangerous and dependent adults. Most importantly, expecting parental competence is far less costly than public interventions after children have been damaged by incompetent parenting.

All of these considerations point to a need to more clearly define what our society expects of parents, so that children are not prevented from becoming contributing members of our society because of coercion or neglect.

Urie Bronfenbrenner, a leading authority on child development, has pointed out that studies of the socialization of children reveal that they need to have reasonable expectations set for them by their parents.[8] In the same way, many parents need to have reasonable expectations set for them by society. Two of these fundamental expectations that children need can be translated into standards that society could set for parents as well.

The first expectation that parents need to set for their children is that privileges are awarded when the ability to accept responsibility for them is demonstrated rather than prior to that time. The second expectation is to consider the interests of others in the exercise of one's own interests since the pursuit of one person's interests inevitably leads to conflicts with the interests of other persons.

Applied to parents, the first standard is demonstrating the capacity to be responsible for the life of a child. The second standard is the capacity of a parent to take the needs of a child into account while meeting the parent's own needs. The expectations of parents in our society could be based upon these two standards.

Setting standards for parents would not only benefit children. It also would protect people from assuming parenting burdens that restrict their own personal development and that cause stresses and failures in their own lives. This especially is the case with teenage mothers who have not completed their own adolescent development and who have their own emotional, social, and educational needs to meet. For this reason, incentives for delaying childbirth and the responsibilities of parenting can be provided by educational and employment opportunities for both male and female teenagers and young adults and by public service programs, such as the National Youth Service.[9] In addition, a national child protection policy is needed as proposed by th U.S. Advisory Board on Child Abuse and Neglect.

The objective of ensuring competent parenting for all children could be the central theme of a national parenting policy. This objective would elevate the focus from preoccupation with defining families to the unambiguous concept of parenting. Instead of a national family policy the focus could be on a national parenting policy. Society could clearly state its expectations of parents and then support them in meeting those expectations. This would be consistent with the growing consensus that the economic solutions to the poverty of children and adults should not be targeted on the poor but should be addressed through universal programs that benefit all people.[10] The need for this is particularly evident when fully employed parents live at the poverty level but are not eligible for governmental benefits. Governmental programs for families could be organized around the theme of supporting parental competence rather than simply around the existence of a child, as is now the case.

Examples of universal program proposals that would help all children and their parents are child support assurance programs and joint cash allowance programs for a child and adult as a unit. The former would withhold child support from the wages of noncustodial parents who are delinquent in their child support payments.[11] The latter would provide cash payments or tax credits through the Internal Revenue Service to the licensed parent of each child and to each adult as replacements for dependent and personal tax deductions. This would apply to everyone and would provide income for the poor who now receive nothing for dependent children because they are not now eligible for tax deductions. Most Western nations have such arrangements.

Another way to provide public financial recognition of parenting would be through a Child Allowance Trust fund as proposed by Edward Zigler, Director of the Bush Center of Child Development at Yale University.[12] It would draw upon the original mandate of the social security system to relieve families from the economic burdens of supporting family members who are not able to support themselves.

Zigler points out that when the social security system was established, the support of children was not considered to be an extraordinary burden unless a wage earner died or became unable to work. At the present time, the support of children does constitute an extraordinary burden for parents who must compete economically with adults who do not have childrearing responsibilities. A self-sustaining Child Allowance Trust could provide cash payments to all licensed parents to be used at their discretion. Through funding of the Child Allowance Trust by the social security tax, the current workforce would contribute to the welfare of those who will support them in later life.

Another universal support of parenting could be in the workplace. The recognition of parenting as a valuable part of the lives of employees would promote policies that support rather than undermine parenting, such as family leaves, flexible work schedules, and child care accessible to the workplace.

Whenever governmental funds are disbursed or governmental programs are offered at taxpayer expense, accountability is essential. For this reason, the present method of determining eligibility for family entitlements and programs simply because a child exists in a household cannot insure that the support provided will further the competent parenting of that child. Eligibility for a parenting license would provide that essential accountability.

Community Level

Public policies mean little, however, unless they actually affect the communities in which people live.

The community factors that interfere with parenting and with the development of children are dangerous neighborhoods; dilapidated, overcrowded housing; and geographic and social isolation.[13] In addition there are grave environmental hazards, such as lead poisoning which has been identified as the most important ecological threat to American children. Of even greater immediate importance is dealing with the root causes of youth violence, as proposed by the public health physician Deborah Prothrow-Stith.

The most important concept is providing a nurturing environment for children. Before anything substantial and enduring can be done to help families in urban ghettos, social order must be established so that the streets are safe for children. Vibrant, connected neighborhoods with parks and libraries are needed to provide stability for families.

Fortunately, even in crime-infested neighborhoods, there is a fund of human decency and courage that can be used as a force for change.[14] Research carried out by the Center for Urban Affairs and Policy

Research at Northwestern University has demonstrated that organizing and building upon the strengths of people is the key to community development. Urban authorities and community residents can reverse undesirable trends by forming citizen groups to reclaim their embattled neighborhoods through cooperation with adequate numbers of law-enforcement personnel. Beyond that there are a variety of community development programs, such as Habitat for Humanity and the Child Watch Visitation Program that helps community leaders address the problems of families and children.

The collaboration of schools and all community agencies involved in the lives of children and families is essential. A continuum of services that integrates the legal, health, mental health, social service, educational, vocational, recreational, and other support systems can be used to expand prevention efforts to support parenting without straining public coffers through interdisciplinary teamwork. Anything short of comprehensive, interdisciplinary treatment is ineffective and fiscally wasteful. This means applying the principles of individual and class child advocacy in order to ensure the coordination and continuity of services. At the individual case level, this can be done most effectively by child advocacy teams composed of all professionals relevant to a particular family. In child abuse and neglect cases a child advocacy team functions as follows:[15]

> When parental abuse or neglect is suspected, children are referred to the protective services division of a county department of human services. This invokes a fact-finding investigative process that culminates in a judicial finding of abuse or neglect. A child advocacy team composed of the social worker, a mental health professional, and other professionals involved in the case then is organized by the attorney representing the interests of the child, the guardian *ad litem*. The team formulates a life plan for the child which includes the changes that the parents must make in order to have the child removed from protective custody. The team proceeds with treatment of the family and arranges for adjunctive therapeutic and educational programs. The progress of the parents and child is assessed in accordance with applicable state statutes. When the parents have demonstrated their competence, the protective services action is discharged. If parents are unable to become competent, a termination of parental rights action is instituted to

permit the adoption of the child. Throughout this process the child advocacy team bridges the legal, social service, mental health, and educational systems to insure the continuity and coordination of care.

None of this can occur without the availability of well-trained professionals. Consequently, federal, state, and local resources should be devoted to hiring and training caseworkers who are protected from caseloads that make sound judgments difficult because the workers are unable to adequately serve each family.

There are a growing number of interdisciplinary models.[16] For example, the Oregon Children's Service Division operates with a comprehensive family evaluation of parent–child attachments, kinship and community resources, parental self-esteem, parenting skills, and personal addictions. Treatment services include case management, systemic family therapy, group and "in home" parent training, and funding to alleviate severe financial crises.

No amount of professional intervention with multiproblem families is likely to have a lasting effect if informal networks that sustain the families are unavailable.[17] The attitudes of children toward learning and toward society are strongly influenced by the attitudes of all of the peers and adults in their lives. More ways are needed to involve neighborhood and grass-roots groups, particularly church-related, in mentoring and support networks for multiproblem families who need help in childrearing on a day-to-day basis.

One way of supporting parents is through their involvement in the education of their own children, particularly young children.[18] Programs such as Operation Headstart have demonstrated their value in this regard.

Family Level

The first needs of parents include adequate housing, food, and health care for themselves and for their children. When these requirements are met, in addition to parenting support networks of both a professional and volunteer nature, self-help programs are needed.[19] Early-intervention parent-support programs that strengthen parent-infant bonds during the first three years of life are essential for vulnerable parents. This is particularly important for infants and toddlers at risk for developmental and educational problems. The parenting unit should be the focus of direct treatment, support, and supervisory services to improve homemaking and parenting skills.

The home-based prevention program of the Parsons Child and Family Center in Albany, New York, is an example of a successful early intervention program.[20] Making this kind of service available across the country is the mandate of Public Law 99–457 with its commitment to helping young children and their families with special needs. Seven such undertakings in different parts of the country designated as Child Survival/Fair Start programs have been sponsored and evaluated by the Ford Foundation. The common denominator of successful programs is the personal relationship established between program staff and the participants.

Childrearing modeling, along with commonsense techniques and easily acquired skills, could be made more accessible through health care clinics.[21] Much can be done to improve the parenting skills of parents who are motivated and able to do so. Since a significant number of parents are not so motivated, these services should be available on both a voluntary basis and under the aegis of protective services for children. The goal of meeting parent-licensing standards through provisional and probationary licensing would provide a concrete basis for deploying treatment resources and financial aid for incompetent parents and for evaluating their progress.

We should bear in mind that parent support and education programs cannot be expected to significantly alter the social ecology of people's lives. These programs do not change the basic life situations that confront poor families each day, nor can they be expected to alter personalities and parenting styles acquired through a lifetime of experiences and continually reinforced in the present.

Finally, the importance of preparing adults for employment should not be forgotten. Reaching the functionally illiterate through volunteer efforts can bring reading skills to people who need them in order to obtain appropriate employment.[22] Overcoming the reticence of individuals to acknowledge their illiteracy is important in this regard, as is mobilizing volunteers to teach reading skills.

The Precedents for Licensing Parents

The law could be used much more effectively than it is in influencing parenting in the United States.

Laws are more than instruments for punishing behavior. In fact, society expresses its values and influences behavior through the simple existence of its laws more than through actual enforcement of them. Traffic laws determine which side of the road cars drive on and organize traffic flow with little actual need for enforcement. In the same way civil rights laws have created a consciousness of racism and sexism so that few people publicly advocate discrimination against adults today, and attitudes have changed without the actual need for enforcement of these laws. A similar outcome could be anticipated if there were legal expectations of parents.

The precedents for setting expectations for parents through the persuasive, educational, and enforcement aspects of laws are so plentiful that the fact that we do not have expectations of parents in our society is a clear-cut reflection of juvenile ageism. No one can deny that we really do not protect children from incompetent parenting, especially by their biological parents.

There is a long list of precedents for licensing parents that includes adoptive and foster parent licensing, marriage licensing, day care licensing, parental liability laws, child support enforcement laws, laws that mandate compulsory parental cooperation with schools, skill and professional licensing, competency procedures for executing contracts and wills, grandparent liability laws, termination of parental rights statutes, drug and pollutant regulations, and, ironically, pet-owner requirements.

Adoptive and Foster Parent Licensing

Well-established adoption laws do recognize that not everyone is capable of rearing children, so that the investigation of the parenting abilities of adults who want to adopt children usually is required. In fact stringent requirements for adoption are designed to protect children from being adopted by incompetent parents and from being casually transferred by their biological parents to the custody of others. The adoptive process is much more rigorous than any parent licensing procedures envisioned. In fact, it has been carried to unreasonable extremes at times.

Foster parents also are supposed to meet rigorous standards.[23] In most communities in order to obtain a foster parent license one must (1) be 18 years old or over; (2) be in good health; (3) meet the state's home-safety standards; (4) have sufficient income for family needs; (5) be emotionally stable and have character references; (6) have no criminal record; (7) have sufficient bedrooms; (8) be willing to work with social workers; (9) agree to discipline without physical punishment; and (10) agree to attend foster parenting workshops.

There is an obvious double standard for adoptive and foster parents and for biological parents. No one is permitted to raise someone else's child without meeting standards in a screening process. Yet anyone can raise their own child without any questions being raised about their ability to do so.

If we think it is important to protect adopted and foster children, who are less likely to be maltreated than the children of biological parents, is it not reasonable to afford the same protection to children reared by their biological parents?

Marriage Licensing

Historically, marriage licensing has been a means of defining inheritance rights. It also has been a means of ensuring that adults are ready to handle the responsibilities of childrearing.

The legal requirements for obtaining a marriage license and filing certification of the marriage are found in the marriage laws of each state.[24] Premarital physical examinations have been required by law in most states since 1913 and culminated in the Michigan Premarital Physical Examination Law of 1937. Although the actual effect of these laws has been to screen for sexually transmitted diseases, the Michigan statute also was described in legislative proceedings as creating a marriage counseling opportunity. Over the years, however, marriage licensing has become less of a statement of society's expectations of marriage and more of a registration process that establishes a legal contractual relationship between a married couple.

Most states impose conditions for marriage. There usually are waiting periods to reduce impulsive unions. There also are restrictions on kinship, on already being married, on perpetrating fraud in entering the marriage agreement, and on mental competence at the time of marriage. The local licensing authority receives marriage applications and informs the applicants of the waiting period, of the need for parental consent when appropriate, of premarital examinations, and of other legal requirements for obtaining a license. After both parties have completed the required documents, the license is issued. They are informed about the period of time and the geographic area for which the license is valid. The person performing the marriage ceremony receives the license and completes the marriage certificate, which is registered locally, in the state, and with the National Center for Health Statistics.

A reform in welfare eligibility related to marriage licensing is the "bridefare program" in which the disincentive to marriage in the Aid to the Families of Dependent Children regulations is removed by allowing fathers to be included in the AFDC grant if the parents marry.[25] In addition, the usual increases in AFDC grant levels are limited by half when a second baby is born and are frozen for subsequent children.

The progressive shift away from the expectation of commitment in adult relationships in our society has diluted the significance of marriage and its implied commitment to childrearing, so that increasing numbers of children are being born into unmarried situations. This trend increases, rather than decreases, the need for parenting licenses as statements of the commitments of parents to their children.

Day Care Licensing

Although the licensing of day care has concentrated largely on the physical facilities and the ratios of children to adults, there is a growing emphasis on the qualifications of day care workers. In fact, an entire field of child development specialists has emerged with the setting of standards for their education and practice.

As the regulation of the quality of day care has become a public issue, regulating the quality of parent–child relationships logically follows, especially because even without day care worker certification requirements, there are parents who are rejected as supervised day care workers but who still have the unsupervised care and custody of their own children.

Legal Parental Liability

Strangely perhaps, common law has never imposed a duty on parents to provide financial support for their children, but it has penalized parents who neglect children to the point of death or physical injury and suffering.[26] For example, the 3rd District Court of Appeals in Wisconsin ruled that a man whose car accident led to the premature birth of his son and the baby's death two days later could be charged with vehicular homicide by driving while intoxicated.

Negligence occurring in the context of parenting generally has been protected by the principle of parental immunity. Consequently, successful proceedings by children for injuries caused by their parents have been infrequent and have been limited to gross negligence or intentional wrongdoing resulting in physical injury, such as the failure to lead a young child in crossing a street or the damage to a fetus due to an attempted abortion.

At the same time a body of law is developing in which parents can be held accountable more generally for their roles in harming children.[27] In a proceeding initiated by a minor, the Washington Supreme Court upheld a finding that she was incorrigible because of her parents' behavior. The court supported her refusal to return to her parents and affirmed the local court's decision to remove her from her parents' custody.

Traditionally, laws against contributing to the delinquency of minors have been enforced when adults contribute to the delinquency of someone else's child but not to the delinquency of their own child. Holding parents responsible for their behavior toward their own children can be seen as an extension of protecting children from the acts of adults in general.

State laws are beginning to assign specific responsibilities to parents. In California parents can be fined or jailed for allowing their children to participate in antisocial gangs. In Wisconsin and Hawaii they can be required to support the children of their own children. In Arkansas they can be fined when their children skip school. In Florida they can be jailed if their child hurts another person with a gun left accessible by the parent. In Wisconsin parents can lose welfare benefits if their children fail to attend school.

Across the nation parents are increasingly being held liable, sometimes even in a criminal sense, for the misbehavior of their children.[28] This has been the case particularly in tort law in which parents have been successfully sued for injury and damage to others caused by their children. Adults abused as children also have been permitted to sue their parents or relatives for harm inflicted upon them during their formative years.

All of these developments reflect a trend toward holding parents accountable for their behavior with their children. The legal system is defining expectations of parents in a negative sense. Parent licensing would express positive expectations for parents.

Child Support Enforcement

The need for state interventions in some families is dramatically illustrated by the fact that left to their own devices many unmarried and divorced parents would not meet their child support financial obligations through persuasion or education. Law enforcement procedures are necessary in those instances.

Without strict enforcement procedures most fathers have been found to neglect their child support obligations.[29] The threats of jail and the garnishing of wages have been necessary in order to obtain payment. This is a concrete example of how laws are required to effectively enforce society's expectations of parents and to prevent parents from avoiding their responsibilities to their children.

Compulsory Parental Cooperation with Schools

Further evidence of the fact that parenting responsibilities require societal support through legislation is illustrated by a 1989 California law based on the fact that compulsion is necessary to gain the cooperation of some parents with their children's schools and to induce employers to permit parents to do so during working hours.[30] The statute authorizes teachers to compel a parent or guardian to attend one of their child's classes following the child's suspension on the grounds of obscenity, habitual profanity, disruption of school activities, or defiance of school authorities. Employers are prohibited from using such school-required absences from work as reasons to discharge or otherwise to discriminate against affected employees.

In addition in California the Quality Education Project, a federally funded program to gain parental participation in the education of their children, requires parents to pledge to provide the time, space, and materials for their children to do homework.[31]

Public health experts say that state laws that require that children be immunized against infectious diseases prior to school entry have been remarkably successful.[32] They suggest that similar requirements of parents for their preschool children by welfare and Medicaid programs would be effective too.

These statutes and regulations illustrate the degree to which legal expectations beyond persuasion and education must be set to induce some parents to assume responsibilities for their children.

Skill and Professional Licensing

States do not hesitate to license and monitor activities that have far less potential for harm to others and society than does incompetent parenting. In fact licensing or certification is expected for any person's activities that are potentially harmful to other people—except when those persons are parents and when other people are their children.

Any activities that are potentially harmful to others are regulated by requiring the demonstration of minimal levels of competence. We require automobile operators to qualify for licenses. We require professionals, such as real estate agents, physicians, lawyers, and pharmacists, to meet licensing requirements. All of these expectations require the demonstration of competence in activities that affect other people before damage has been caused to them.

Competence to Execute Contracts and Wills

The competence to make decisions is routinely required in the execution of legal contracts, most commonly in the legal status of wills. The decision-making power that parents hold over their children is far more important than any of these contractual matters.

Grandparent Liability Legislation

Legislative action has been taken to hold the parents of minors who conceive and give birth responsible for their grandchildren.

The grandparent liability provisions of Wisconsin's Family Responsibility Act of 1985 hold both sets of grandparents of a baby born to their unmarried minor offspring financially responsible for that baby's support.[33] One of the intents of the Act was to promote communication between parents and teenagers, especially males, about the consequences of sexual behavior and about parental responsibilities.

Holding expectations for the parents of minors who become parents is a step toward setting expectations for all parents.

Termination of Parental Rights Statutes

The courts have held that before it may permanently terminate a parent's rights to a child, a state must show abandonment or harm to a child sufficient to support a compelling interest of the state in doing so.[34] Parents must be afforded procedural protections as well.

In order to establish grounds for the termination of parental rights in most jurisdictions, the following must be demonstrated:[35] (1) a repeated or continuous failure to meet the basic needs of a child; (2) evidence that this pattern has been damaging to the child; and (3) evidence that the parent–child interaction is not amenable to treatment nor likely to change in the natural course of events soon enough to benefit the child. The first of these criteria corresponds to the definition of incompetent parenting used in this book.

When the termination of parental rights is being considered, the gross failure of the parent to meet the basic needs of a child usually is obvious to any fully informed, objective observer. The termination of parental rights is supposed to take into account the fact that the irreplaceable passage of time in children's lives limits the amount of time parents can be given to improve their parenting abilities. An adult may be incompetent for a limited period of time to parent a child, but that time may be critical from the point of view of that child's development. A parent's incompetence during the early years of a child's life precludes that parent from forming affectionate attachment bonds with that particular child and becoming that child's psychological, or real, parent.

The existence of termination of parental rights statutes attests to the fact that there are parents who are unable or unwilling to become competent. As knowledge of the damaging effects of incompetent parenting on society accumulates, the compelling interest of society in identifying incompetent parents through a licensing process and preventing the abuse and neglect of children before they are damaged is evident.

Drug and Pollutant Regulation

Drugs and pollutants that threaten the lives of children, as well as adults, have been regulated through legislation.

In 1938 the U.S. Congress passed the Food, Drug, and Cosmetic Act as a result of the deaths of more then one hundred children from a liquid form of sulfanilamide.[36] The Act requires firms to submit applications to the Food and Drug Administration before introducing pharmaceuticals into interstate commerce. Later in 1962, following fetal deformities in Europe from the administration of thalidomide, the Act was amended to require proof of a new drug's efficacy through regulated clinical testing as well.

In 1990 the federal government began a broad effort to eliminate lead poisoning of children based on the conclusion of the U.S. Centers for Disease Control that lead poisoning is the most important environmental problem facing children.[37] Twenty years before, Congress had declared lead-based paint a health hazard and ordered it stripped from federally subsidized housing. It banned the use of lead-based paint completely ten years ago.

These actions are illustrations of the willingness of the federal government to take regulatory action to protect children when dangers to them from material causes are demonstrated.

Pet Owner Requirements

The fact that the Society for the Prevention of Cruelty to Animals existed before the Society for the Prevention of Cruelty to Children is a revealing aspect of the history of juvenile ageism. Even today more attention is devoted to ascertaining the competence of those who care for pets than of those who rear children.

The San Francisco Society for the Prevention of Cruelty to Animals requires that persons adopting pets be adults and that they agree to: (1) give the animal proper and humane care, food, water, shelter, exercise, and all the other necessities; (2) provide it with veterinary care both on a regular basis and when the animal becomes ill or injured; (3) keep the animal as a pet and companion and never allow it to be used as a guard dog, fighting dog, or for experimentation; and (4) comply with all city, state, and federal laws relating to animals.[38]

Ironically, we continue to see more public outrage over the abuse of animals than the abuse of children, as is evident in antivivisection protests.

CHILDLESS AND CHILDREARING MARRIAGES

Proposals that implicitly license parents have been made in the past. They distinguished between childless and childrearing marriages, both as a means of accommodating the interests of children and as a means of separating sexual behavior from procreation.

The most notable statements of these themes were made by Judge Benjamin Lindsey in the 1920s and by Margaret Mead in the 1970s.

"Companionate" Marriage

Because of his work as a juvenile and family court judge in the 1920s, Judge Benjamin Lindsey presciently saw that the most effective remedy for social problems was for children to spend their early years in homes in which they could thrive. His central objective was to encourage and legalize birth control to ensure that children were wanted. This occurred in the general context of a social movement to reduce venereal diseases through medical examinations prior to marriage.

Judge Lindsey was moved to put an end to the hypocritical pretense of marriage, which in the 1920s was supposed to be permanent and a vehicle for childbearing but in fact was pervaded by divorce and birth control.[39] The widespread use of birth control then made possible a sexual relationship that never before was practical for many people. Lindsey proposed that the de facto "companionate" marriage of educated people who practiced contraception and employed skilled lawyers in obtaining divorces ought to be made legally and openly available to all people—particularly to the poor who needed it the most.

Lindsey's "companionate" marriage was a state of lawful wedlock, entered into for love, companionship, and cooperation by persons who for reasons of health, finances, or temperament did not plan to have children at the time of their marriage. His companionate marriage for childless couples with birth control and the right to divorce by mutual consent, usually without alimony, would have been an alternative to traditional marriage.

Lindsey's hope for traditional, or "family," marriage was that it would weather all storms through adjustments by both parties. He recognized the risk of marital failure, but "stoutly proposed to overcome and nullify that risk." Family marriage was not to include the possibility that divorce would be sought the moment the flame of romantic passion began to cool.

Lindsey's companionate marriage was a compromise between trial marriage and traditional marriage. It would have encouraged women and men to enter marriage under conditions that would afford a line of retreat in case the marriage failed. They would not have children until they had been married long enough to be reasonably sure of their ability to live together and to afford a family. If the couple desired, the marriage could be changed to a family marriage at a later time.

Lindsey's proposal depended upon foolproof contraception and obviously went unheeded. The availability of modern contraceptives and the potential for pharmaceutical abortions has created a different climate today.

"Individual" and "Parental" Marriages

In the 1970s Margaret Mead urged society to put more emphasis on relationships in marriage and less upon sex.[40] She encouraged finding a congenial partner and cultivating a deeply personal relationship. Sex, then, would take its place within an enduring relationship and would not be sought as an end in itself. She also hoped that children would be assured a life-long relationship with both of their parents even if divorce occurred.

Mead suggested two types of marriage. The first she called "individual" marriage—a licensed union in which two individuals would be committed to each other as long as they wished to remain together, but not as future parents. There would be no long-range economic or legal commitments between them.

In contrast, the second type would be "parental" marriage with the explicit intent of founding a family. It could follow an individual marriage and would have its own license, ceremony, and responsibilities. In order to enter a parental marriage, a couple would be expected to demonstrate their ability to support a child. The parental marriage would be a binding contract that was not easily disrupted. The legal aspects of divorce would protect the children for whose sake the marriage was undertaken in the first place.

In a sense, the spirit of Mead's proposal of individual marriage has been informally realized in the contemporary tendency to engage in cohabitation prior to marriage.

Mead's concept of parental marriage did specify parenting as an aspect of the marital contract. It did not, however, establish a contract between parent and child. It could provide a standard for parenting by incorporating the criteria for parent licensing. Still, it would not apply to parents who do not choose to be married.

The most effective way to assure children of competent parenting is to have the obligation of a parent to meet standards begin at the time of a child's birth or adoption, that is, as a contract between the parent and the child rather than between the mother and the father, as it would be with a parental marriage.

PROCEDURES FOR LICENSING PARENTS

Although possibly seeming like an onerous task, procedures for licensing parents actually would entail little more administrative effort than currently is involved in marriage licensing, birth registration, and protective services for children. The idea of licensing is to accord parenting appropriate status in society, not to create a new bureaucracy. With a licensing process the question of parental fitness would be faced before rather than after damage to a child. Licensing would hold a parent responsible for being competent rather than forcing children to endure incompetent parenting until they themselves show publicly recognized signs of damage. The responsibility for demonstrating parental competence before a child is damaged would be with the parent, rather than the responsibility being with the state to demonstrate parental incompetence after a child has been damaged, as now is the case.

The practical aspects of licensing parents would include its timing, eligibility criteria, administration, the consequences of denial of licensure, and the question of testing for parental competence.

The Timing of Licensure Application

There are three circumstances under which the time for parent licensing would arise. The first time is prior to conception either at the time of marriage, on acceptance for adoption, or at the time of an unmarried person's decision to have a child. This could be handled through the existing marriage license procedures.

The second time is during the pregnancy. Unlike the marriage license, there is no existing point for providing a license under this circumstance. One would need to be established so that application for a license could be made, such as during prenatal care as an early extension of birth registration.

The third time is at the birth of a child. The already established procedure for registering births provides a structured point of contact at which the existence of a license could be ascertained; if necessary a license could be obtained then.

Criteria for Licensure

The requirements for obtaining a parenting license would be simple and straightforward so that they could be easily met, as they are now for a marriage license Unlike the marriage license, it would be obtained for each parent and validated for each child.

The first criterion would be the attainment of adulthood. Eighteen would be a reasonable age based on physical, social, and emotional maturity and the likelihood of completion of a high school education. For parents under the age of eighteen, as now with marriage, parental consent and parental assumption of responsibility for the minor and the child would be required so that the minor could obtain a provisional parenting license that would be fully validated when the minor becomes an adult.

The second criterion would be certification by the applicant that he or she agrees to care for and nurture the child and to refrain from abusing and neglecting the child. If this agreement was broken at a later time, the intervention upon a parent's rights then would be based upon the failure of that parent to fulfill a contractual commitment to the child with revocation of the license rather than on an adversarial quasi-criminal action, as is now the case.

The third, possibly optional, criterion would be completion of a parenting course or its equivalent. Family life education already is provided in many communities and public schools.[41] Every middle school and high school in the country could require courses that prepare young people for the responsibilities of parenthood. The laboratories for these courses could be in day care settings. This requirement would not be retroactive and would depend upon the availability of such courses.

In all likelihood, parent licensing would stimulate the development of family life education. Although the actual benefit of education in influencing parenting behavior is uncertain, the mass impact of such a program would be likely to discourage premature marriages and reinforce awareness of the gravity of childrearing responsibilities. From the point of view of the educational curriculum, the importance of the subject matter to society is greater than any other academic subject. Moreover, the need for education in parenting is widely perceived today.

The Administration of Licensing

The administration of parent licenses would be at the level of state and local governments, although enabling federal legislation, such as requiring licensure for the receipt of federal funds, would be helpful in encouraging nationwide consistency. A new bureaucracy would not be needed, since licensing would involve revising the mandate of the existing marriage licensing, birth registration, and child protection systems.

First, the license application process could be handled through the framework of marriage licensing and birth registration, since it essentially would be a question of credentials. Second, questionable situations and the appeals–intervention process could be handled through currently existing protective services for children in county departments of human services guided by state statutes. The shift of protective services for children from an adversarial criminal focus after children have been damaged to a preventive focus would reduce the need for extensive interventions years later. Vulnerable parents and children would be identified at the outset of the children's lives and parent support services could be offered earlier than is now possible.

A general parenting license for each mother and father would be granted on meeting the criteria. It would then be validated for each child, clearly establishing a child–parent contract that includes financial responsibility and expectations of parental competence.

If protective services for a child were invoked by actual child abuse or neglect, the license could be placed on probationary status while treatment was ongoing, or it could be suspended during foster placement of the child and treatment of the parent. When a parent was unable or unwilling to remedy demonstrated incompetence, the license could be judicially revoked for that child through existing termination of parental rights procedures modified to correspond with revocation rather than the present quasi-criminal procedures.

If the parent of a child was ineligible for a parent license because of age or incapacity, that person could be issued a provisional license under the aegis of children's protective services with either concomitant parent training and supervision or foster placement and with a specified time during which that person could qualify for a regular license. If the person proved unable to acquire competency at the end of that time, that person's parental rights would be terminated, and the child would be adopted, as now takes place for parents who voluntarily place their children for adoption.

If a mother could not meet licensing standards, child protection laws would be invoked at the time of the child's birth. The custody of the child would be with an agency, and the child's placement would be determined by the circumstances of the situation, as it is now. Mothers who are minors could obtain provisional licenses underwritten by their own parents who agreed to do so and who met foster parent standards themselves.

The question of whether a child should be removed from an unlicensed mother at birth for adoption or whether the mother should care for the child under a provisional license with support and supervision would hinge on the most likely outcome. If the outlook was favorable and the risk to the child was low, therapeutic support of the mother with a provisional license would be preferable both from the mother's and the child's points of view. On the other hand, if the outlook for the child was poor, the alternatives of maternal or foster care would be less appealing from the child's point of view than adoption. Adoption also would meet the needs of the large pool of qualified adults who wish to adopt infants and young children.

The administration of protective services for children and the enforcement of child abuse and neglect statutes would be facilitated by parent licensing. From the legal point of view, the burden of proof would lie with parents to demonstrate evidence of minimal competence, or of their "parental fitness" in legal terms, rather than on the state, as is now the case, to prove "parental unfitness." If the state required all parents to become licensed before or upon the birth of their children, much later case-by-case adjudication under child protection laws after parents have damaged their children could be avoided, saving enormous amounts of time, financial expense, and other social costs. [42]

Parent licensing would remove protecting the welfare of children from the criminal arena of perpetrator and victim after children have been damaged to the prevention and treatment arena in which expectations are held for parents and in which they can be assisted to be competent parents and helped to avoid damaging their children.

The Denial of Licensure

Parent licensing does not mean attempting to distinguish between "good" and "less good" parents. [43] It would exclude only the obviously incompetent ones. It would not be a birth control measure, although it probably would influence procreation by conveying the message that society values and holds expectations for childrearing. The aim of licensing would be to elevate the status of parenting not to prescribe parenting styles.

Parent licensing also would not be based upon the legal standard of the child's best interests. The practical problem with best interest standards is that they tend to be idealistic and are used to remove children from their homes when less drastic and more effective remedies, such as training, assisting, and supervising foundering parents can be used.

Individuals denied licensure would have opportunities for appeal through the usual legal channels. Those mistakenly denied licenses would be able to demonstrate their competence. Those whose parenting licenses were placed on probationary status or were suspended would be able to obtain treatment in order to qualify for reinstatement.

The denial or revocation of a parenting license would be expected to be a painful experience, particularly for mothers. Still, the fact that disappointment or inconvenience results for people who are denied licenses for other activities does not diminish the conviction that we must regulate activities or occupations that are potentially harmful to others. We also maintain licensing procedures and competency tests even though they sometimes are subject to error. The overall importance of protecting innocent children from incompetent parenting justifies the inconvenience to a few parents and the inevitable imperfections of a licensing system.

Parent-Competence Testing

At this time large-scale testing for signs of parental incompetence is premature. Thus far efforts to predict the parenting potential of pregnant women by testing have yielded inconsistent results.[44] There are apparently satisfactory ways of predicting parental behavior through intensive evaluations, such as the rigorous assessment procedures of those wanting to adopt children; however, those measures are not practical for large-scale use.

At the same time attention should be focused on devising means for the early detection of parental incompetence. This ultimately would enhance the effectiveness of parent licensing and would alert incompetent individuals to their need to examine their motives for rearing children and encourage them to improve their parenting skills.

ALTERNATIVES TO LICENSING PARENTS

The suggestion has been made that rather than licensing parents, children should be monitored to detect deviations in their behavior or development.[45] Services could then be offered when children do not meet certain community standards.

Such family surveillance is part of the existing system in the form of school monitoring of children and provisions for the general reporting of suspected abuse and neglect. It obviously does not protect children from damage and places the responsibility for detecting and proving damage on other people and the state, rather than on parents to refrain from damaging their children in the first place.

Suggestions have been made that less drastic measures than denial of parenting for the unlicensed could be used as incentives. Tax incentives for voluntarily licensed parents and supportive services for unlicensed parents might be seen as adequately protecting children. Compromises of this nature, however, would not affect incompetent parents, who necessitate a licensing process in the first place because they are irresponsible and do not seek supportive services.

Some proposals, such as that both parents' social security numbers be entered on every newborn's birth certificate and that child support be automatically withheld from the wages of all absent parents, would help to bring affected children out of poverty and persuade boys and young men not to father children whom they cannot support.[46] The addition of the social security numbers of both the mother and the father to birth certificates would be a means of establishing paternity and recognizing a child's right to definitive maternity and paternity at the time of birth rather than leaving it to a later initiative, which ordinarily arises now when the state intercedes because of nonpayment of child support.

Measures that try to forestall self-defeating behavior rather than responding to its effects have significant potentials. Rhode Island has devised a plan in which certain children who pass their courses every year, obey the law, avoid pregnancy, and do not use drugs receive special academic help and guidance from a trained mentor throughout their elementary and high school years.[47] Any student who fulfills the contract and is accepted into college or a job-training program receives free education or training. The focus is on parenting the adolescent through a mentor who helps to prevent that teenager from becoming a premature parent.

An intriguing proposal has been made by the political scientist Paul Peterson that minors should be represented in the political process by having their votes cast for them by their parents or by their guardians.[48] This would be an effective means of recognizing that children are indeed citizens of the nation and giving them proportionate political representation.

In the broadest sense, any public efforts to advance the interests of children and to protect the ecological and economic environment of future generations will create a climate in which the needs and rights of children are more likely to be recognized and fulfilled.

THE RATIONALE FOR LICENSING PARENTS

A national parenting policy based on promoting competent parenting is urgently needed. The time has come to seriously consider protecting children from incompetent parenting by licensing parents for four straightforward reasons.

The first reason is the human rights principle that all individuals, including children, should be free from abuse and oppression. As it is now, millions of children are abused and oppressed by incompetent parents. Little is done before children are damaged by abuse.

The second reason is the civil-rights principle that all individuals should have equal access to opportunities to develop their potentials in life, an especially important right for children who are beginning their lives. As it now stands, incompetent parents neglect their children and deprive them of opportunities to learn how to develop their potentials.

The third reason is the common good principle in which society has a right to regulate activities that are potentially harmful to others and to society. As it is now, incompetent parents not only harm their children; they gravely endanger the internal security and productivity of our society by disrupting the safety of our citizens and by creating financial burdens for our nation. The fourth reason is the humanistic principle that the future success of children as citizens and as parents depends upon forming affectionate attachment bonds with their own parents. As it is now, incompetent parents do not form healthy affectionate attachment bonds with their children and thereby deprive their children of forming the capacity to respect others that underlies responsible adult citizenship and competent parenting.

Licensing parents would concretely articulate society's expectations of parents and provide an incentive for parents to be competent. It would accord parenting the status of a privilege rather than a right and would reduce the hazards of incompetent parenting for children. It would establish the existence of children as citizens with certain civil rights. Most importantly, it would demonstrate that society values and supports competent parenting.

Just as a marriage license signifies a contractual relationship between spouses, a parent license would establish a contractual relationship between parent and child. It would elevate childrearing from the realm of caprice, accident, and ulterior motives by according parenting the dignity and legitimacy it deserves. It would require that parents complete their own growth and development before assuming childrearing responsibilities. It would set the standard that parents be able to assume responsibilities for their own lives before assuming responsibility for the life of a child. If parents are unable to meet these criteria, society would help them. If that fails, society would arrange for adoption of the children by competent parents.

Parent licensing would be the symbolic basis for a multilevel approach to families that articulates society's respect for parenting as an important social role and society's expectation that parents will be competent. For those who are not, financial aid, educational programs, social services, and, when necessary, relief from the responsibilities of parenting are required. We know which educational programs and social services effectively help incompetent parents. We know that the success of these programs depends upon building safe, caring communities. What is lacking is an organizing theme to give these programs direction and to provide parenting-based criteria for evaluating their efficacy.

Parent licensing would place the responsibility on adults to be competent parents rather than on the state to financially support incompetent parenting and its consequences. It also would lay the foundation for dramatically reducing the need for costly and ineffective governmental welfare and correctional programs. Rather than only focusing our limited resources on trying to repair children and adults who have been damaged by incompetent parenting, as we do now, we would be able to increase the general level of competent parenting and positively affect generations to come. Tragically, many of our existing interventions perpetuate and aggravate the very social problems they are intended to alleviate.

The priority given to competent parenting now will determine the future of our nation. Because it does not now manifestly place a high priority on childrearing, the United States faces an uncertain future. There now are few limits to what can be done *to* children. Instead the question should be what needs to be done *for* them. Our children depend upon us to ensure that they all will have a chance to become competent adults and to become competent parents themselves.

In order to move toward a national policy for supporting parenting, we need to identify the barriers that stand in the way. The intensity of emotions associated with those barriers immediately becomes evident when the issue of licensing parents is raised and categorically dismissed. For this reason, a careful examination of the arguments against licensing parents is essential.

Chapter 12

Arguments against Licensing Parents

If men were angels, no government would be necessary. If angels were to govern men, neither external nor internal controls on government would be necessary.

—JAMES MADISON, *The Federalist*[1] (1787)

I wrote this book because of the image in my mind of the millions of children who are being neglected today. That image contains faces I know. They will not leave me, and I cannot turn away from them. I know that these children have no political constituency. I know first hand the enormous resistances to helping them, even on the part of well-intentioned people. But I also know that truth and logic are on the side of these children. I know that we live in a nation in which justice for them has a chance to prevail.

No reasonable person would deny that children should not be neglected and should be competently parented. Yet any effort to ensure that children have competent parents meets strident objections. Such an effort encounters the strongly held sentiments that family life is a private matter and that government already interferes in our lives too much. We are loath to point fingers at parents. Underneath these sentiments lies a disguised but deep-seated presumption that children are the possessions of their parents.

Even more fundamentally, we Americans resist constraints on our lives. We do not like to think of ourselves as controlled by forces that limit our choices. We do not like to think of ourselves as dependent on other people. We prefer to think of ourselves as independent actors free of constraints. We do not want anyone looking over our shoulders as we do anything, especially parent our children. Many people also are weary of our society's emphasis on rights and feel that we do not need additional claims for rights for children now.

The very notion of setting expectations for parenting can readily be construed as "blaming" those of us who are parents. We already are stressed by living in a society that does not support us. We feel stretched to our limits as we try to do our best in meeting the demands of childrearing. We may well fear that if there were public expectations for parents, our own lives would be made even more difficult.

Furthermore, most of us who are or have been parents have acted in ways that have fallen short of our images of ideal parenting. We feel guilty and inadequate when we make mistakes or let our children down. For this reason, the mere mention of parental competence in itself might evoke the fear that we would not qualify as competent.

Actually, a statement by society that parenting is important would have the opposite effect. Because only the most obviously abusive and neglectful parents would not meet the simple expectations of minimal competence, the vast majority of parents would be affirmed. Rather than being taken for granted as a secondary or minor role in our society, parenting would be more realistically appreciated and valued as an essential social institution. Because the requirements for licensing would not be met only by parents who clearly are incompetent, the vast majority of parents would be reassured that they are competent. Furthermore, the due process of law and appeal procedures would insure that a competent parent would not be denied a license.

From the political point of view, those of us who are liberals might be concerned that the emphasis on individual responsibility inherent in licensing parents could be used as an excuse to curtail government support programs. Those of us who are conservatives might regard parent licensing as an objectionable intrusion into our private affairs. Most likely, a parent licensing process really would call attention to foundering parents and provide objectives for government programs designed to help them. It would no more invade the privacy of families than do existing child abuse and neglect statutes.

There is an overwhelming list of reasonable arguments against parent licensing. That list includes the following categories: the imposition of majority standards on minorities; the fear of violating the sacred nature of the parent–child relationship; the fear that licensing would foster blaming parents; the fear of restricting the personal freedom of adults, even to behave unwisely; the fear that licensing would accompany financial child support; the fear of according adult rights to children; the fear of enforcing conformity in childrearing; the political rejection of the family; the belief that rearing a child in itself produces maturity; objections to the prior restraint of adult freedom; the fallibility of prediction and education; the unfeasibility of administrating licensure procedures; the fear that licensing would replace aid to parents; the lack of adoption opportunities; the fact that research on social problems is incomplete; the belief that education and training in parenting are sufficient to ensure competent parenting; the belief that children should not be accorded favored legal treatment; society's inherent need for incompetence; and the belief that drastic social changes cannot occur.

Unless each one of these arguments is carefully analyzed, the sheer number of them seems to be enough to summarily dismiss even the mention of licensing parents. That reaction neatly conceals juvenile ageism because each of these arguments is flawed.

THE IMPOSITION OF MAJORITY STANDARDS

Fears that a licensing process could be used to impose the standards of the majority on minority groups are not to be taken lightly. To dispel fears of this form of intentional manipulation, a parenting licensing system would have to be based upon simple standards free from cultural and socioeconomic biases.

The experience of Nazi Germany stands as a warning that the powers of the state can be used against minorities. Eugenics, or "racial hygiene," became popular and academically respectable in Europe in the late nineteenth century.[2] Until the 1920s racial hygiene focused primarily on counteracting the declining birth rate and on reducing mental and physical degeneracy. Thereafter, the presumed Jewish threat to Aryan supremacy preoccupied the racial hygiene movement in Germany and resulted in a distinctively Nazi category—"life unworthy of life."

Germany's ills at that time were attributed by the Nazis to threats to the "folk body" from the growing number of the "unworthy"—the handicapped, criminals, and the inferior yet dangerous races. By medicalizing social problems in the name of improving their race, the Nazis justified the isolation or elimination of those whom they considered to be undesirable. The Nazis encouraged the procreation of people they called Aryans and the rearing of children by the state.

The possibility of such abuse of government powers is remote in the United States because of Constitutional guarantees and the modus operandi of our democratic government. More specifically, licensing parents to raise children would not limit the ability of individuals to conceive or to give birth to children, nor would it necessarily affect the life styles of individuals.

In fact, because their right to competent parenting is not recognized, incompetently parented children in disadvantaged minority groups are the victims of racial, sex, and age discrimination now. Incompetent parenting forecloses the opportunities of these children and perpetuates their disadvantaged minority status. Licensing parents actually would enhance, rather than threaten, the survival and the quality of life of minority groups.

VIOLATING THE SACRED PARENT–CHILD RELATIONSHIP

Some people might protest that licensing parents would be like licensing cars, bicycles, and dogs. It would demean children by treating them like property and demean parents by treating them like animals. Comparing licensing parents with these other forms of licensing certainly does trivialize the sacred bond between parents and children. Parenting is a much greater responsibility and deserves even more attention by society than anything else that we license.

Yet simply mentioning parent licensing can evoke the image of taking a baby away from a weeping mother and completely block rational consideration of the matter. This actually happens when an irresponsible, but tearful mother sways a jury in a termination of parental rights proceeding more than the facts of the case and the pursuit of the child's and the parent's actual interests. It is difficult for many people to accept the fact that mothers can seriously harm their own children. The powerful emotional investment of a mother in the image of having a child, even though she is unable to care for one, is one of the most important barriers to social service and legal efforts to act in the interests of neglected children.

There is no question that the emotional resistance of a mother who has given birth to a child to relinquishing that child can override both her own and her child's interests. That emotional reaction is not sufficient, however, to assure her competence as a parent or that an affectionate attachment bond exists between her and her child. The strength of the emotional feeling of a mother for her child at a particular time cannot be the sole basis for judging her parenting competence or the bonding of her child with her.

A mother who truly loves her child and recognizes her inability to rear her child is more likely to desire placement for the child than an emotionally immature or disturbed mother who is unrealistic about her capabilities and disregards the child's needs. Most adopted children have been placed voluntarily by parents who desire a better life for their children.

Another circumstance that is mistakenly construed to indicate that a child should remain with an abusive or neglectful parent is that many abused and neglected children suggest through their words and their behavior that they want to remain with their incompetent parents. The reasons for this vary, but these children usually are clinging to an idealized image of their parents and are fearful of alternatives that are unknown to them and that mean leaving a familiar situation, however inadequate it may be. Some older children may feel a responsibility to care for their foundering parents. As with the motives and statements of parents, those of children in abusive and neglectful circumstances need to be evaluated clinically, particularly in the light of a strong social policy bias toward family preservation.

The tension between the right to bear children and judgments about the competence required to rear them is illustrated by the case of Debra Ann Foster.[3] In the summer of 1988 in Mesa, Arizona, she was sentenced to use birth control for the rest of her childbearing years because she had repeatedly neglected her sons. The court concluded that she was incapable of rearing children. The American Civil Liberties Union protested that the order violated her reproductive freedom, and the Roman Catholic Church objected because it violated her religious beliefs.

Because people have rights to free speech, free religious expression, and to conceive and bear children, one can argue that people have a right to parent children as well. The right to free speech does not include slander, the right to freedom of religion does not include the mistreatment of human beings or animals, and the right to bear children does not include harming them.

All rights are limited and entail responsibilities in order to protect the innocent. Most importantly, in reality the sacred parent–child relationship is earned through affectionate attachment bonding between parent and child over time. It does not automatically follow the biological conception of, and giving birth to, a child.

LICENSING WOULD FOSTER PARENT BLAMING

There is an understandable reason to fear that licensing might increase parental guilt because parents are susceptible to feeling guilty—and they already consciously or unconsciously feel guilty enough.

Licensing would hold parents responsible for their children. Some parents might fear being wrongly blamed for their children's misbehavior. At the same time those parents may well be the ones who are inclined to blame their children for their own childrearing difficulties. They are likely to believe that the behavior problems of children are caused solely by factors in the children, such as by diseases, brain damage, or chemical imbalances in their brains, not by parental influences.

Underlying these sentiments lies a juvenile ageist rejection of the contribution parents make to the fate of their offspring. This comes in the context of a general abdication of personal responsibility for our own actions in our society. This attitude is reflected when the responsibility for problems in childrearing is placed on institutions other than families or on factors within the children themselves. Because they are helpless and unable to protest, children are ready targets for this form of scapegoating. They, not their parents, are regarded as the causes of their own problems. This attitude is reinforced by the reactions of the children in the form of withdrawing from, or rebelling against, the scapegoating. The children thereby confirm their culpability by further misbehaving. The circle is tightly closed as abused and neglected children are seen as thorns in the sides of their parents and are blamed for their own situations. Historically, the same dynamics of the acquiescence or rebelliousness of victims have justified discriminatory practices of the prejudiced against their victims in general.

Acceding to the fear that licensing would encourage blaming parents and heighten parental guilt might relieve the anxieties of some parents, but it would ignore the interests of children. A more humane and realistic approach to relieving parental anxiety and guilt is through social policies that support rather than undermine parenting and by recognizing parental competence through a licensing process that would affirm the vast majority of parents as competent.

RESTRICTING THE RIGHT OF ADULTS TO FREEDOM OF ACTION

There is a fundamental and necessary resistance in the United States to forcing well-intentioned ideas for personal behavior on other people. The civil right to freedom of action has been construed to include the right of adults to live dangerously, and even foolishly, provided their actions do not injure others. This point has been raised successfully as an argument against laws mandating the use of automobile seat belts and motorcycle helmets.

The purpose of parent licensing is not to restrict the freedom of parents by prescribing parenting behaviors. It is simply to protect children from harm. The principles that parents are not free to harm their children nor to intentionally permit children to harm themselves are well accepted in the United States.

Still there is an understandable reluctance to restrict the actions of a person unless there is a "clear and present" danger that harm to others will result from those actions. Actually the degree of harm required to evoke a sanction depends on public sentiment. The regulation of smoking did not take place until public sentiment rose to a level that justified intervention on the basis of inconvenience without a "clear and present" danger to the health of each nonsmoker. The grave import of incompetent parenting for society justifies interventions before there is clear and present danger of abuse or neglect, and certainly before abuse and neglect actually occur. As it now stands, interventions occur after abuse and neglect have taken place.

Another freedom-based objection to licensing parents is an outgrowth of the argument that our society is moving toward less formal forms of cohabitation and that even marriage constitutes too much restriction of individual freedom. To the extent that this trend continues without the contractual relationship of marriage, the need for protecting the civil and legal rights of children becomes more, not less, important. The interests of children are not inherently recognized nor assured when the liaisons of their parents shift. It is the contemporary lack of commitment to parenting and the irresponsibility of a few parents that has created the current impetus for licensing parents.

An obtuse freedom-based resistance to licensing parents involves fear of the loss of the freedom of adults to use corporal punishment in the parent–child relationship. On the one hand, physical child abuse is deplored, but on the other hand, parents know that some form of physical management of children is necessary. The idea of licensing parents might evoke the fear that there would be an increased risk that someone will allege child abuse whenever a parent lays a hand on a child. This possibility would be no greater with licensing than it is now.

LICENSING WOULD ACCOMPANY FINANCIAL CHILD SUPPORT

The basic thrust of parent licensing is to encourage the formation of child–parent affectionate attachment bonds by drawing upon the natural affinity of parents for their offspring. The tragic fact for children, however, is that avoiding parental responsibilities can be the primary aim of a biological parent. Many fathers, and some mothers, do not wish to parent their children and must be legally forced to financially support them.

In the light of mandatory child support, a parent license might be construed as being automatically given to a biological parent who provides financial support for a child. This would not be the case. Financial responsibility for a child's support and the privilege of parenting the child are separate issues which do not necessarily overlap. Financial responsibility for a child does not make one competent to parent nor does it necessarily mean that the interests of a child are served by a relationship with that parent. Equating financial support with custody or visitation treats the child as chattel for which financial responsibility implies the rental or possession of the child as property.

The separation of financial responsibility and a child's relationship with a parent rests on a fundamental distinction between a monetary relationship with a child and an affectionate attachment bond relationship. The purpose of licensing a parent is to foster the affectionate attachment bonding aspect of the parent–child relationship that may or may not accompany financial responsibility. Eligibility for licensing would not be based solely on financial responsibility for a child. It would be based upon the simple licensing criteria: majority age, commitment to parent and to not abuse or neglect the child, and possibly completion of parenting education.

The licensing of parents is a separate issue from mandated financial support of a child. The appropriate procedure, from a child's point of view, when a parent wants to avoid financial responsibility for a child, is to terminate that parent's parental rights and release the child for adoption, thus relieving the biological parent of unwanted financial responsibility for the child.

FEAR OF ACCORDING ADULT RIGHTS TO CHILDREN

Some people fear that according civil rights to children would mean giving them all of the rights of adults. This attitude reflects a misunderstanding of child advocacy based on the literal transfer of the legal concept of advocacy for adults to children. It construes child advocacy as following the wishes of children. This fear is a reaction against those who mistakenly believe that children should be treated as adults. Actually equating adults' and children's rights represents a subtle juvenile ageist position that ignores the differences between childhood and adulthood and that ignores the need of children for nurturance, protection, and guidance.

The civil rights of children include both freedom from oppression and access to the adult guidance and limit setting inherent in competent parenting. Appropriate and informed child advocacy involves advocating the developmental needs of children not their immediate wishes; it is not a question of according them all of the rights of adults. A child's civil right to competent parenting reified by a licensing process would not inappropriately accord children adult rights.

Still there is the argument that the children's rights approach is not the most appropriate way to recognize the needs of children in our society. That argument holds that resources should be redistributed so as to equitably support all children and parents as contributing members of society. It envisions a society in which resources are allocated according to humane priorities rather than by the advocacy of competing rights. It reflects ideals that favor the common good side of the individual versus collective rights equation.

Reallocating resources according to society's priorities can be achieved through entitlement programs and through tax relief and credits. In the United States, as a capitalistic democracy, those priorities are determined by the vigorous representation of the interests and rights of affected groups. But the allocation of financial resources is less important than society's values in determining how children are parented.

Because financial entitlements for children and parents can be abused, as illustrated by some of the effects of the Aid to the Families of Dependent Children program, standards are needed for the quality of parenting that society is willing to support financially. The reallocation of financial resources more equitably for parents and children in itself would not insure that children would be competently parented.

ENFORCING CONFORMITY IN CHILDREARING

For some people the idea of licensing parents conjures up images of a totalitarian state in which parents are forced to raise their children in a uniform way with the prospect of producing conforming masses of adults who lack originality and creativity. That scenario would have no room for the mavericks and creative geniuses who are so essential to the evolution of a democratic society. That feared outcome of conformity is particularly envisioned whenever prosocial values are mentioned as a desirable ingredient of competent parenting.

The criteria for licensing parents would only restrain those who abuse or neglect their children. Licensing would not prescribe childrearing practices. It would not affect those who seek to change society or who are unhappy with the status quo. It probably would facilitate social change by fostering the development of adults with the characters and coping skills needed to effect change.

THE POLITICAL REJECTION OF THE FAMILY

In recent years the family has been portrayed as a repressive institution that fosters the dependency of women. It also has been recognized accurately as the main site of violence against women and children. Domestic relationships have been unpleasant, painful, and even damaging for many people.

For critics of the family, the abuse and neglect of children by their parents is seen as signaling the need to shift the responsibility for the care of children from parents to society in a collective sense.[4] More fundamentally, through the years there have been persistent tensions between political ideals of equality and the elitism of families. This tension is based on the fact that the opportunities of children raised by their families can never be equal when they become adults, because families vary so much in their access to resources. Even when the access to resources is equal, the motivations of parents to further the interests of their children vary widely.

Equal treatment in a society, in a strict sense, probably is incompatible with family ties. Family loyalty treats people on the basis of kinship and affection. Family members usually make no pretense of treating people outside of the family the same as themselves for better or for worse. For these reasons, some people hold that families are incompatible with modern life and represent archaic holdovers from the past that need not be taken seriously. For them licensing parents would prolong the natural death of the family. They would favor an emphasis on the societal rearing of children in standardized ways rather than supporting parents in different styles of childrearing.

The realities of family life cannot be dismissed so simply. Some degree of family feelings are essential, biologically based parts of the lives of all but a few human beings. The ethics that govern relationships between people who love or care for each other inevitably intrude into public life, coloring peoples' perceptions of what they and others ought to do. It is appropriate to expect public officials to avoid favoritism, but it is a completely different matter to expect all human beings to relate to each other with emotional detachment, whether or not they are related by family ties. To imagine stripping human relationships of their emotional and familial components is to imagine a world of robots rather than human beings. Family relationships really do not assure success in life nor does the lack of family ties assure failure.

When oppressive discrimination is minimized, our ability to deal with the differences in opportunities and in the treatment we receive in life makes it possible to progress in a competitive world that depends on each one of us to shape our own destinies. Among those differences in opportunities in life are those determined by personal relationships. Each one of the many political efforts to abolish the family as a social institution from the time of ancient Greece to the present has failed because it did not face this reality. The family as a cultural institution probably will survive with or without the licensing of parents.

The Maturing Influence of Childrearing

Another objection to parent licensing is that it is not needed because the presence of a child in itself will cause a mother or father to become a competent parent.

Not all jurisdictions have been willing to prohibit parents from taking custody of their infants when circumstances indicate that the infants' safety or health would be jeopardized if placed in the parents' custody, as illustrated by the opinion of a Washington Appellate Court:[5]

> A parent's right to custody and control of his or her child should not be abridged except for the most powerful reasons . . . It may well be, as the social workers and psychiatrists opined below, that the odds do not favor that a petitioner because of youth and a history of avoiding responsibility will become a good parent. Fortunately for the preservation of the human species, however, a lot of people who would rate poorly on any scale of parental

prospects have done rather well at it when confronted by the reality
of a baby, in a crib, in the home . . .

There is no question that the presence of a baby can stimulate
personal growth in a parent. There also is evidence that significant
changes in some women and men do occur following childbirth, such as
the discontinuation of substance abuse.[6]

Our culture encourages an optimistic belief in the future for all
Americans. This is the land in which anyone can succeed if given the
opportunities to do so. If anyone can become President, certainly
anyone can become a competent parent. This optimism fosters hope for
improvement in the lives of incompetent parents, but it also blocks
awareness that there are some people who are incapable of changing
their lives in time to benefit their children.

The courts are beginning to recognize the need to intervene in the
lives of children when the likelihood of abuse or neglect exists. In the
case of *In re East* the Court of Common Pleas of Ohio held that a child
should not have to endure harm in order to give a mother an opportunity to prove her ability to parent the child.[7] The Court held that the
law did not require courts to experiment with a child's welfare to see if
the child will suffer "great detriment or harm."

The idea that the welfare of a child should be risked solely because
of the possibility that the presence of that child might cause an incompetent parent to become competent in the face of evidence to the contrary
is a clear-cut expression of juvenile ageism.

OBJECTIONABLE PRIOR RESTRAINT

Because of its preventive purpose, a parent licensing program
would deny licenses to people judged to be incompetent even though
they had never maltreated children and, therefore, such licensing could
constitute objectionable prior restraint of the freedom of adults. Prior
restraint is used commonly, however, when the restricted activity is one
which could lead easily to serious harm.

We hospitalize people judged as potentially harmful to themselves
or others, and we withhold professional licenses prior to an individual
making errors as a practitioner. The potential of harm to a child and

society by an incompetent parent is a much more serious matter than either of these examples.

THE FALLIBILITY OF PREDICTION AND EDUCATION

A major objection to licensing is the presumed difficulty in identifying incompetent parenting. Other than age, demographic factors in themselves are not sufficiently reliable to identify potentially incompetent parents.

When demographic data are supplemented by the use of individualized screening methods, such as the Child Abuse Potential Inventory, the combination seems to have predictive power.[8] Testing instruments, however, assess knowledge rather than skills. They also are subject to all of the issues of fairness and distortion inherent in testing procedures. Basing licensing parents on knowledge testing alone would introduce an unacceptable degree of unreliability. Even a license to drive a motor vehicle does not depend solely on knowledge testing; a demonstration of actual driving skill is necessary.

There is no assurance that making education in parenting a requirement for licensing would reduce the risk to children. Parenting involves more than knowledge; it requires intuition and mature judgment.

Still, by developing a body of family life knowledge, by training teachers of parenting skills, by promulgating parenting curricula, and by certifying mastery of this knowledge, we might hope for a change in prospective parents' appreciation of the importance of competent parenting. Some might learn enough about children's needs to decide to defer childrearing until they were ready to meet its demands. Many might profit from an introduction to parenting skills prior to having to use them.

For all of these reasons, parent licensing criteria should be simple and straightforward as proposed in chapter 11, rather than based on knowledge testing procedures. The analog is a marriage license rather than a license to practice a profession. The objection of fallibility can be raised for all licensing procedures, which essentially are audits of present knowledge and performance to decrease potential harm and thereby are predictive. The fact that they are not infallible does not detract from their usefulness. No licensing program is completely successful. Licensing motor vehicle operators has not eliminated hazards on the roads or insured the competence of drivers. Without such regulation, however, motor vehicle hazards would be much greater.

The Unfeasibility of Administration

Another objection to licensing parents is the unfeasibility of its implementation. The specter of an enormous and inflexible bureaucracy needed to deal with the myriad of issues surrounding licensing is frightening enough in itself. But the prospect of dealing with millions of existing incompetent parents all at once is absolutely overwhelming.

Any kind of parent licensing program would encounter many problems and exceptions. What about a situation in which one parent qualifies for licensing, but the other does not? What if a mother is licensable, but she lives with a man who abuses her and her child? Should licensing be repeated at intervals, or does a single licensing permanently qualify one as a parent?

Not all children are alike in temperament; in the simplest terms some are "easy," and some are "difficult" to parent. It is plausible that some parents could rear an "easy" child but would be likely to neglect and abuse a "difficult" child. Would we license a parent only to bring up an "easy" child? Another consideration is the situation of handicapped children who have special needs and pose challenging parenting issues.

These practical questions highlight the importance of basing licensing on simple criteria, as we do marriage licenses, rather than upon detailed definitions of competence or incompetence and upon specific testing procedures. Using the simple criteria of age, parenting pledge, and possibly educational certification accomplishes this.

Most of the complications that would arise from licensing parents would be the result of the inconvenience of introducing the rights and needs of children into situations and activities now dominated by juvenile ageism that leads society to behave as if children do not have these rights. The whole idea of licensing is based upon the interests of children. Our society would profit from addressing, rather than avoiding, questions raised by the issue of licensing parents.

A new bureaucracy would not be needed for licensing parents because specific situations that require individual judgments would be handled by child protective service systems that already are available and most likely are involved already with questionable parents. The credentialing process itself could be handled by the existing birth and marriage registration and licensing processes.

The fear that licensing parents would make it easier for bureaucratic social workers to remove children from their families is not justified because legal safeguards and appeal procedures would remain in place as they are now. The same safeguards apply to fears that social workers would be given inordinate powers to dictate childrearing practices.

As it commonly is for other credentialing procedures, a parent licensing system would need to be prospective rather than retroactive. It could be applied first to parents who receive governmental financial support for rearing children to ensure that incompetent parenting is not encouraged and actually supported by public funds.

If parent licensing were to be seriously undertaken, it would take years to develop the system. Decisions also would have to be made about ways of handling the transition from the present situation in which there are no parental expectations to one in which expectations for parents would be implemented. The fact that reducing the federal debt takes years of planned adjustments should not preclude the mission of protecting the national economy. The prospect of a lengthy process in developing a parent licensing system should not preclude protecting our economy and the quality of our lives in a much more fundamental and enduring way.

Licensing Would Replace Helping Parents

An important concern about licensing is that in itself it could be regarded as the solution to the personal and social problems associated with incompetent parenting and thereby permit bypassing the obvious needs for the support and treatment of foundering parents and for the improvement of their socioeconomic conditions.

An example of a superficial legislative approach to human behavior problems is the West Virginia school attendance law that suspends the driver's licenses of students who drop out.[9] This law has been criticized because it does not address and deflects attention from the school-based reasons for dropping out, even though it does provide an incentive to remain in school for students and actually has reduced school dropout rates. In contrast, with this kind of legislative sanctioning licensing parents would address fundamental family problems.

Because of the possibility that it could be regarded as the only necessary governmental response to incompetent parenting, it is essential that licensing be seen as a standard-setting vehicle for deploying resources to help parents to become and remain competent. It would be the symbolic element of the multilevel national parenting policy described in chapter 11.

INSUFFICIENT ADOPTION OPPORTUNITIES

Another important concern about licensing parents is that there would be no adoptive parents for the children who would be made available for adoption when parents were found to be intractably incompetent. There even are those who question the validity of adoption itself as an institution.[10]

A definitive answer to the adoption question is not possible now. The contemporary pool of potential adoptive parents is large, and there is considerable interest in transracial adoptions.[11] On the positive side, there are about 200,000 women who begin actively seeking to adopt children each year. On the negative side, in 1986 the nation's foster-care system harbored at least 36,000 adoptable "special needs" children, but only 13,500 found families.

Yet, according to the National Council for Adoption, there are 1 million infertile couples and 1 million parents who seek an additional child. The Council estimates adoption possibilities for 2 million children, particularly if adoption occurs shortly after birth rather than after children have been damaged and are designated as having "special needs." As it is now, homes must be found for seriously impaired babies because of brain damage, physical handicaps, and AIDS.

At the present time there are only about 60,000 legal adoptions annually in the United States; 50,000 of the children are from the United States and 10,000 from foreign countries. About one quarter of all of these adoptions are transracial. These data suggest that the adoption pool seeking one million children is large enough to absorb the number of neglected children and that the races of the children would not pose insurmountable barriers if a shift in attitudes toward adoption took place.[12] To illustrate this point, in the most unlikely event that all babies born to mothers between the ages of fifteen and nineteen were placed for adoption, the total number according to 1990 statistics would be about 227,000 Caucasian, 96,000 African American, and 43,000 Hispanic children.

Serious questions have been raised about the advisability of transracial adoptions. There is anecdotal evidence that some transracially adopted children have experienced adjustment problems. There is a strong belief within some minority groups that in order to preserve their cultural heritage their children should not be raised by parents from other racial backgrounds. This viewpoint was codified in the 1978 Indian Child Welfare Act that generally gives tribal courts exclusive power to make custody and foster care decisions for children considered to be legal residents of a reservation, regardless of where they live. The argument also has been made that only an African American family can equip an African American child with the psychological armor needed to fight racial prejudice.[13] This may be feasible because of the finding that, when properly recruited, there are substantial numbers of African American adults who seek to adopt African American children.

On the other hand, longitudinal studies of transracial adoptions reveal that they generally have been successful and that transracial adoption, although posing problems in our society, is a viable means of providing stable homes for children.[14] The adoption of high-risk children also has been more successful than anticipated during its early trials; their adoption disruption rate has been reported to be between 8 and 13 percent in long-term follow-up studies. Adoption also has been found to be superior to long-term foster care and residential placement. Waiting for a same-race adoption can be an injustice to the affected children.

In the light of all of this evidence and the contemporary political climate, the Child Welfare League of America has taken the following position on transracial adoptions: "Children in need of adoption have a right to be placed into a family that reflects their ethnicity or race. Children should not have their adoption denied or significantly delayed, however, when adoptive parents of other ethnic or racial groups are available."

The point also can be made that maintaining racial and cultural purity is contrary to the pluralistic values of the American culture and is negated ultimately by the inevitability of interracial marriages in the United States. Furthermore, the birth mother has emerged in many instances as a significant participant in selecting the adoptive parents of her child.

The evidence suggests that ample opportunities for the adoption of children from all backgrounds exist in the United States, particularly by identifying incompetent parents before children are damaged and thereby become "high-risk" candidates for adoption.

Licensing parents would raise the question of parental competence before or at birth and result in larger numbers of babies available for adoption. It would serve the needs of both the babies and the competent parents who seek to adopt children.

RESEARCH IS INCONCLUSIVE

You have two choices. You can accept the conclusion of some researchers, such as the authors of *Pathways to Criminal Violence*,[15] that we do not know enough about why people become criminals or welfare dependent and wait for the results of further research. You also can rely upon your own judgment about the effects of parental incompetence.

Although some hardy individuals do not seem to be adversely affected by abuse or neglect, the mistreatment of children is neither to their advantage nor to society's advantage. Further research will help us to understand the details, but it certainly is not needed to prove that incompetent parenting is harmful to both children and adults. It is a reflection of juvenile ageism that research questions are framed in terms of whether or not there is evidence that abuse and neglect harm children rather that in terms of whether or not it is in the interests of children to be abused and neglected.

Another viewpoint of some researchers is that values should not interfere with empirical research in child development. This is reflected in the following statement by the child psychologist Jerome Kagan:[16]

> The findings of future empirical inquiry may affirm the popular belief that surrogate care of infants has psychological dangers [but] even the most traditional student of child development would

admit that these beliefs remain largely unproven . . . A combination of emotional conviction and frail evidence often betrays the
fact that a deep value is being threatened . . . I believe that the
possibility that the biological mother might be partially replaced
bothers a great many citizens.

This statement reveals the underlying belief that cultural values
should not play a governing role in establishing childrearing objectives,
in influencing childrearing methods, or in evaluating parental competence. This viewpoint has been interpreted by those who disparage
parenting to imply that childrearing should be guided by "scientific"
rather than "sentimental" factors. They hold that establishing sentimental affectionate attachment bonds between parents and children is
not a valid objective in childrearing.

The ethical question for social scientists is the same as for environmental scientists. Do we have to wait for future research to show that
the environment or society have been damaged before concluding that
environmental pollution or incompetent parenting are harmful? The
answer to this question must consider the readiness of many people
to use the need for more research as an excuse for inaction or as a
justification for funding the research enterprise.

EDUCATION, TRAINING, AND CLINICAL SERVICES ARE SUFFICIENT

Most thinking about improving parental competence focuses on
education, training, and clinical services. The reasoning is that the
positive reinforcement of voluntary behavior is more effective than
coercive regulation. There is a reluctance to legislate expectations of
parents because the educational and clinical approaches are seen as more
humane and as potentially more effective.

Yet the fact that educational and clinical services are necessary but
are not enough to prevent damaging others because of addiction to
alcohol, drugs, and smoking is well known, so that public regulation of
those activities is accepted. School-based educational programs can be
useful in reducing undesirable behavior, such as smoking, alcohol
consumption, and substance abuse, for many children and adolescents.[17] However, there is a core group for whom adhering to antisocial

peer pressures has overriding importance in spite of the persuasive and educational efforts of adults. Those youngsters, who are more susceptible to peer pressure than to the influence of parents and schools, are either unaffected by educational efforts or are more strongly motivated to pursue self-defeating behavior by them. They are the youngsters who are prone to become incompetent parents. The most effective approach to them is to ensure that they receive competent parenting themselves. When that is not available, law enforcement is necessary.

Persuasion and education also are recognized as insufficient to protect the public from incompetent motor vehicle operators, so laws that license them are necessary. No one questions that the licensing of professional activities is required beyond the education of the professionals.

The damage to other persons by incompetent parenting far exceeds in scope and severity the damage caused to others by alcohol, drug, and smoking addictions; by incompetent motor vehicle operation; and by incompetent professionals. Yet the call for remedies to incompetent parenting usually is limited to education and professional services with the glaring omission of placing expectations on parents through regulation. This is particularly ill-informed in the case of teenage parents, because it overlooks the inherent sense of invulnerability in adolescents that impairs their judgment and that in itself in other aspects of their lives requires parental and societal regulation.

Any activity that can adversely affect other people is subject to some form of regulation beyond persuasion and education—except parenting. Our society financially and educationally supports parents who are not permitted to operate motor vehicles or care for the children of other parents. This is an obvious expression of juvenile ageism when the devastating and widespread consequences of incompetent parenting for children and for the incompetent parents themselves are recognized.

FAVORED LEGAL TREATMENT IS UNDESIRABLE

The political and legal systems of the United States are strongly biased against providing favored treatment for any particular individual or group and toward favoring equal treatment of everyone.

The exception to the equal treatment principle is that all individuals are presumed to be equal unless they have "disabilities." This legal doctrine has been applied to the obvious inequality of children, who are regarded as growing progressively out of the "disabled" state of legal "infancy" and gradually acquiring the rights of adults by being "emancipated" from the "disabilities" of childhood.

The doctrine of disability has justified the protection of children from responsibilities and from dangers. It has given rise to child labor and child abuse and neglect laws, but it also has been used inappropriately. For example, the mistreatment of children can be concealed because they are regarded as "disabled" dependents on their parents. In those instances the child's dependence on the parent conceals the parent's oppression and abuse of the child.

From the theoretical point of view, confusion arises when the legal and political rights of children are equated with their human and civil rights. The legal principle of equal treatment does require the limitation of children's legal and political rights because of the inherent "disability" of their immaturity. It does not require limitation of their human and civil rights, which should apply to anyone regardless of age.

The principle of equal treatment can be used spuriously to avoid the restriction by society of adult behavior in order to accommodate children because such restriction would "favor" children. Restricting adult behavior that is harmful to children actually would give children equal treatment in accordance with the same human and civil rights that now apply only to adults. It would not accord children favored treatment in legal and political matters.

The doctrine of avoiding favored treatment underlies the segregation of children from undesirable adult influences. Rather than providing favored treatment for children by restricting adult behavior, children are segregated from adult influences that are harmful to them. The result is that adults are accorded favored treatment over children. If, as with antismoking laws that protect nonsmokers, public sentiment favored regulation of adult behavior that was inimical to children, the society of the United States could accommodate the presence of children, as do the majority of other societies, without giving them favored treatment in the legal sense. Both adults and children could be accorded equal treatment by restricting the behavior of each class that is offensive or harmful to the others.

From another perspective, licensing parents might be construed as according parents favored status over adults who are not parents. If that did occur, it would be an appropriate outcome, because the contribution that competent parents make to the greater good of society would be more formally recognized.

SOCIETY'S NEED FOR INCOMPETENCE

The communications expert Lee Thayer pointed out that if thousands, if not millions, of people are not to be thrown out of work, future parents must be at least as incompetent as present parents.[18] The deficiencies of their offspring provide employment for legions of social service, mental health, educational, law enforcement, legal, and correctional personnel and for related businesses. Incompetent adults further reduce competition in the work force.

All prevention efforts meet covert but formidable resistance from professions and industries. In this instance, professionals need not fear the loss of employment, as health care workers have found in the effective prevention of physical illnesses. A societal emphasis on competent parenting would not reduce the need for human services because of the continued need for services to help parents be competent. Competition in the work force also is not an issue because projections are for future labor shortages rather than surpluses.

There is another factor that favors employing professionals to repair damage rather than placing expectations on people to prevent problems. It is the thinking of the Industrial Age that has led us to believe that scientific methods and technological devices and services are the solutions to human problems. We rely excessively on experts to provide services and to answer questions that really can only be answered by ourselves. Prime examples are what kind of a life we want to lead, what kind of society we want to live in, what kind of environment we want to surround us, what kind of citizens we want in our society, and how we should raise our children. These are value-based rather than science-based questions.

If our society wants to improve the quality of its citizens and the competence of its parents, the answers lie in the realm of social values and public policies not just in professions that repair damage and in the methods of experimental science. On the contrary, science and technology need ethical guidance. In addition the industries and professions that service incompetent parents and their products need to consider their ethical responsibility to include prevention in their aims and practices.

Professional interventions are inadequate when whole populations do not follow, or even want to follow, competent childrearing practices.[19] The answers for them lie in changing their values and living conditions. The rapid assent up the economic ladder of Asian Americans without public or professional assistance in the face of racist resentment against them is an affirmation of cultural values that serve that group well: respect for the family, valuing education, and bootstrap entrepreneurship.

The responsibility lies with our society, not with scientists or professionals, to develop and implement proparenting policies to reduce incompetent parenting. If that happens, the service professions and industries certainly still will have enough to do. Contractors can shift from building prisons to family homes.

DRASTIC CHANGES IN PUBLIC POLICY DO NOT OCCUR

The argument is advanced that a change in public policy, such as licensing parents, is too drastic, and therefore, cannot occur. Contradicting this belief are a number of examples of major shifts in public policies occasioned by changes in social attitudes.

The most comprehensive examples of changes in public policy have been stimulated by women's movements from the turn of the century to the present time.[20] Earlier in this century women's movements were responsible for the passage of legislation that benefited women and children. In recent years they have pressed for affirmative action and equal rights legislation that has dramatically changed the role of women in our society. Similar innovations have improved the status of children.

The most recent example of drastic change in public policy is the regulation of smoking, so that an activity that once was regarded as socially desirable has become socially undesirable. Significantly, that change involves persuasion and education but ultimately requires local and national regulation for its implementation.

A similar shift has occurred in the public attitude toward the degradation of the environment. One indication of the intensity of this sentiment is the success of The Nature Conservancy, which has become a powerful private resource for acquiring land in conjunction with local, state, and federal agencies.[21] Even with many voluntary efforts such as this, however, legislative regulation of environmental pollutants has been required with substantial enforcement provisions.

ARE THESE ARGUMENTS OBSTACLES OR HURDLES?

The most important obstacle to recognizing the civil rights of children by licensing parents is the implication that doing so entails additional responsibilities and burdens for adults. The expectation of competency in parenting runs counter to our yearning to lessen our personal responsibilities and to our distaste for external regulation.

Our society, devoted as it is to the free pursuit of adult interests, already has enough difficulty expecting us to be responsible for our actions. The dominant sentiment is one of feeling overburdened and stressed, particularly for those of us who are parents. Many of us have had painful experiences in our own families and do not want to even think about the interests of other parents and children. Yet our society's support of the competent parenting of children would relieve much of that stress, which is caused by the social and economic problems of our nation that result from incompetent parenting.

All of the objections to licensing parents can be regarded as insurmountable obstacles, or they can be seen as hurdles to be taken into account in designing and implementing licensing procedures. If undertaken, a process for licensing parents should carefully consider all of the potential problems. It should not be ruled out simply because it has not been done before or because it would be too much trouble. The excuse that according parenting the same status as marriage or the same status as operating a motor vehicle would be too difficult or is unnecessary is a clear expression of juvenile ageism.

Even if the ideas that children have a right to competent parenting and that licensing parents would be useful are accepted, both can be dismissed as idealistic and impractical. That attitude betrays a lack of vision for the future which depends upon the competent parenting of children at the present time. This finally leads us to the question: Will the United States value parenting?

Conclusion

Will the United States Value Parenting?

. . . the future of a society may be forecast by how it cares for its young.
—DANIEL PATRICK MOYNIHAN, 1986

This book ends with a question: Will our nation value parenting? That question cannot be answered with words, only by actions. I know that we can answer by actions because I have seen dramatic changes take place in the lives of particular children. Those changes have resulted when courts have intervened early in their lives and placed expectations on their parents who then received effective help. It would be much better for all of our children and for our society if we held expectations for their parenting before they require court intervention because they are damaged.

In spite of the frequently heard phrase "children are our most precious national resource," our actions and inactions speak otherwise. At the root of this misfortune are the lack of recognition of the civil right of children to competent parenting and the lack of enforcement of the legal right of children to be protected from incompetent parenting.

Anyone who conceives and gives birth to a child is entitled to raise that child and may be entitled to receive governmental financial and possibly educational support. No one asks if that person is capable of parenting that child.

This situation results from popular views of parenthood that emphasize the freedom of adults to do as they wish and that emphasize the privacy of family life. Those views really regard children as the property of their parents. The principle of a child's interests and the principle of the common good of society are seldom applied to family life.

The United States is the only Western nation that does not significantly accommodate the workplace or governmental finance to the responsibilities of parenting. There is no credible statement of our society's interest in rearing children to become competent citizens. More significantly, there is little recognition of the connection between our social problems and incompetent parenting.

The Social Costs of Incompetent Parenting

The enormous financial and human costs of incompetent parenting, especially for high-risk, disadvantaged children are beginning to come to light at two levels.

The first level is the professional recognition that adult criminal recidivism and intergenerational welfare dependency are products of incompetent parenting, and that competent parenting protects even the biologically vulnerable and socioeconomically disadvantaged from those adult outcomes.

The second level is the growing public awareness of the obvious damage to children from the abuse, neglect, and sexually transmitted diseases of incompetent parents. This was signaled in 1991 by the National Commission on Children, appointed by Congress and by the President.[1] The Commission called attention to the growing number of mothers and fathers who lack both the commitment and the ability to be competent parents.

There is a dawning awareness that juvenile ageism is as virulent a prejudice as racism and as pervasive a prejudice as sexism. Not only are children unrepresented in political processes, but many are neglected, damaged, and killed with little political response. As those who survive disadvantaged childhoods enter adulthood without coping and vocational skills, they are denied opportunities to succeed in our competitive society.

Underlying the mounting and costly social problems in the United States is a lack in many people of the elements of character so essential to a democratic way of life—honesty, self-control, and fidelity. At the same time the scientific evidence confirms the age-old observation that the foundations of character and of later productive citizenship are laid in the formation of affectionate attachment bonds between parents and young children.

Most children who live in poverty, most children who come from "broken" homes, most children who receive welfare, most children who have been abused, and most children who have criminal relatives do not become habitual criminals or chronic welfare cases. When any of these factors converge with parental neglect, however, a significant number of children are destined for criminality or welfare dependency. This happens because these children do not learn how to relate to other people and to become responsible citizens.

We now can add incompetent parenting to the list of factors that adversely affect the development of children. The past exclusive focus on socioeconomic, racial, educational, marital, gender, biological, and ecological factors has obscured the most important and obvious element in child development—parenting. The time to help children is before and as their problems appear by redressing incompetent parenting, not after damage has been done. We cannot be reassured by the fact that some adults succeed in life in spite or because of childhood adversity; the vast majority do not. Incompetent parenting is a damaging reality that society can no longer afford to ignore, much less support.

The effects of incompetent parenting are devastating for millions of children who do not have the opportunity to learn from their parents the values and skills necessary for survival in modern society. Instead, many of these children are handicapped by brain damage caused by such factors as maternal drug abuse and alcoholism and inadequate prenatal care. Later they are further damaged by neglect and physical and sexual abuse. Then they are influenced by antisocial peers rather than by competent parents. They do not acquire social and work skills, and they lack access to effective education or to later employment opportunities.

Their incompetent parents are permitted to fail without opportunities to improve their own lives.

Those who question the social and economic costs of incompetent parenting need not be deterred by the lack of complete answers. If we take only the most clear-cut evidence from the lives of incompetently parented habitual criminals, the financial cost to society of almost $2 million for each one contrasts dramatically with the contribution to society of over $1 million by competent parents for each child they raise.

OUR SOCIETY MUST VALUE PARENTING

Because we already have statutes that mandate intervention in families in which child abuse and neglect take place, you might ask why we need to do more.

The answer is that our present approach is dominated by juvenile ageism and does not recognize the basic human and civil rights of children. Our society sets no positive standards for parenting and requires damage to children before it intervenes. Because there are no articulated expectations of parents before they damage their children, we place the responsibility on our government to protect children after abuse and neglect have occurred rather than on parents to refrain from damaging their children in the first place.

In 1989 the Committee for Economic Development, a national organization of leaders in education and business, noted that children are a shrinking proportion of our population and that by the year 2020 40 percent of the population will be composed of what are now called minorities.[2] The Committee warned that unless preventive investment in early childhood is made a national policy, our future labor force will be disproportionately poor, unhealthy, untrained, and uneducated. We will not be competitive in the global arena. We cannot continue to be economically productive when a fifth of our children live in poverty and a third of them grow up without learning the skills necessary to function in modern society.

Against this grim forecast, one might ask how the evident deterioration in public health, public education, and public safety can be occurring along with the greater emphasis on hard work and the apparent affluence of most people in the United States.

One fundamental answer is that only financially remunerated work is valued. Parenting is not appreciated as an essential societal function. This is reflected in the general lack of recognition in the workplace of the responsibilities of parents and in the specific lack of articulated expectations of parents. The prevailing attitude appears to be that the way in which children are reared has no consequences for society.

The facts are otherwise. In 1987 the National Council of Juvenile and Family Court Judges reported the following conclusions about the status of parenting in our society:[3]

> Society must engender within its citizens the awareness of what it is to be a good parent. No public or private agency, child caregiver, social worker, teacher, or friend can replace the parent in the child's mind. To the extent that family life is damaged or failing, our children, their children, and the nation will suffer. The high calling of "parenthood" must be more adequately recognized, respected and honored by our society. Therein lies the future of our nation.

Our society must clearly state that competent parenting is essential to our democratic way of life and ultimately to the preservation of our species. When the sole emphasis of solutions to social problems is technological in the form of increasing professional services, education, and financial aid, the call for society's valuation of parenting is obscured. Because there has been no national recognition that competent parenting is vital to the integrity of our society, social services for families and education for children actually have deteriorated. The effectiveness of services for children and families depends upon a supportive social context that values parenting. Because persuasion and education in themselves are insufficient measures to ensure general compliance with a social value, parenting needs to be accorded a legal status that recognizes the reciprocal obligations of parents and children to each other.

If public policies shift toward valuing parenting as an essential social role and toward remedying incompetent parenting, the need for preventive, educational, and treatment services and for financial aid for parents would become more evident. Those interventions then could be based on the rationale of supporting competent parenting rather than on simply financing the existence of a child, as our present welfare system does.

Social Welfare Is Not Enough

Although social welfare policies in the United States have been successful in many respects, few question the need for reform in our welfare system and in our approach to poverty.[4] The programs implemented and expanded during the War on Poverty era reshaped our social safety net. As bad as the child poverty situation is now, it would be more severe if there were no programs such as Head Start, food stamps, basic educational opportunity grants, Medicare, Medicaid, and low income energy assistance.

Still, a new concept of public welfare is sorely needed. The polarized images of the poor as being either lazy and exploitative or downtrodden and exploited tend to block constructive changes. This polarization is expressed in the views that either the poor themselves or "the system" are the problems. Missing are means of ensuring that opportunities for self-improvement are available to all citizens, including the socioeconomically disadvantaged.

Private funds and voluntarism alone cannot solve all of our social problems. Public funds always have been essential for the support of certain segments of the population. Despite its flaws government has been, and can be again, the moving force in social progress in the United States, if its programs and policies rest on solid foundations. That they do not at the present time is becoming increasingly evident.

The Midwest American Assembly in 1990, sponsored by the University of Wisconsin Institute for Research on Poverty, concluded in its report, *The Future of Social Welfare in America*, that the current welfare system fosters dependency.[5] It recommended that the principles of individual responsibility and accountability for one's own well-being should guide changes to improve the system. This position reflects the consensus of current welfare reform proposals.

The main issue is no longer how much to do for the poor but whether and how much to require them to do in return for support. The federal government is moving in the direction of linking accountability to the receipt of financial support. This has taken the form of expecting welfare recipients to obtain training and to be employed to the extent of their abilities. Recipients are expected to contribute to their own support and to manage public assistance responsibly. Consistent with this trend, eligibility for aid to the parents of dependent children could be based upon ensuring the recipients' minimal competence as parents through a licensing process.

The answers to our society's problems do not lie at either end of a continuum of either giving money to poor people or punishing crime. There is a critical middle ground that would focus on building the characters of our children. The means of doing this lie in encouraging and expecting the competent parenting of our children. Anthony Bouza, former head of the Bronx and Minneapolis Police Departments, put it this way:[6] "A nation full of zest and vigor, growing under values that emphasize 'us' rather than 'me,' altruism over hedonism, sacrifice over pleasure, and service over self, will provide for a much safer society than the one we have today, which is fast sinking into dissolution in the pursuit of happiness."

The readiness of our society for change in its attitude toward parenting children is reflected by the emergence of outcries against unethical behavior and against widespread violence. This concern reveals a yearning for an ethical and safe society, which depends upon an ethical and responsible citizenry.

When the links between incompetent parenting and these social problems are fully appreciated, the focus can be placed on insuring competent parenting for all children. In the process the fact that parenting is a fulfilling career will become evident.

PARENTING CAN BE SELF-FULFILLING

Modern technology has enabled a degree of affluence that now permits many people to look beyond the satisfaction of their immediate material needs to the meaning and purpose of their lives. Public attention is being drawn ineluctably toward self-fulfillment through the rewards of personal relationships.

The most meaningful rewards for adults derive from being significant to other persons, as they are in parenting children. Because significance to others derives from meeting the needs of others, parenting abundantly affords this opportunity.

Parenthood is the most fulfilling when embarked on by those who are prepared to handle its challenges and responsibilities. Caring for children implies that parents also must care for themselves. Adolescents need to know that premature parenthood is unwise for both themselves and their babies. They need encouragement to delay parenting until they have attained adulthood themselves and are ready to become competent parents. Once a child enters a parent's life, the next ten to twenty years will be the most responsible and rewarding of that parent's life. It is important to be prepared for the challenges of parenting and also to recognize that parenting is a temporary stage of life. Even those who wish to devote themselves completely to parenting during their children's early years need to anticipate the future when their children are independent adults.

If parents cannot lead their lives without unmanageable strain on themselves and on their children, parenting can be frustrating and unfulfilling. Child abuse and neglect are common consequences. Society in turn loses in productivity and the quality of life of future generations.

The United States Needs a National Parenting Policy

The United States has been devoting its attention to its external strength and to its security in the world while its internal strength and the personal security of its people have suffered.

The current plight of our children could be a stimulus for our society to heal itself by dealing with the institutional defects of our society—inadequate schools, housing, public welfare, control of violence and disorder, and ethics in government. That healing could take place if we devote our attention to articulating our societal and cultural objectives for our citizens by expecting and supporting competence in the parenting of our children. The ability to cooperate with others resulting from competent parenting is essential to the survival of individuals in a modern, democratic society—indeed, to the survival of individual freedom itself.

The societal objectives of childrearing in the United States are to produce competent, productive consumers, who also are educated citizens. The American cultural childrearing objectives are to produce autonomous, responsible persons capable of self-fulfillment and of contributing to the common good.

The United States has not clearly recognized that competent parenting is an essential foundation for competent citizenship. This is a reflection of juvenile ageism—the subtle, but profound, prejudice and discrimination against children, particularly for the disadvantaged where it is compounded by racism and sexism. Because of juvenile ageism our society operates as though children do not have human and civil rights.

When the repercussions of juvenile ageism are faced, we can begin to find ways to accord children the same civil right expected by adults: the opportunity to be free of insurmountable barriers to the pursuit of developing one's talents in life. This can be done by asking if public and private programs for children strengthen or weaken the child-parent affectionate attachment bond and if they strengthen or undermine parenting. This can be done by according legal status to parenting as a simple, but clear, expression by society that parenting is to be taken seriously as a privilege rather than as a biological right.

A national policy for supporting parenting could target our resources on promoting, supporting, and expecting competent parenting and the converse of identifying, remediating, and, when necessary, replacing incompetent parenting. Its repercussions would extend throughout society by recognizing that parenting is as important to society as is remunerated employment.

Because it would mean preparing young people for parenthood, the national objective of competent parenting for all children would focus attention on the importance of providing an adequate education for everyone. Because poverty is harmful to children, it would focus attention on the socioeconomically disadvantaged segments of the population. Because the demands of childrearing and employment away from home often conflict, it also would focus attention on the importance of accommodating the workplace to parenting.

At the level of the states, a national parenting policy could be implemented by licensing parents. By doing so the United States would lead other nations in according civil rights to children and, because few will admit to being against the interests of children, would further enhance respect for human rights in general.

A licensing process for parents would recognize parenting as a relationship sanctioned by society in the same sense that licensing marriage does. It would encourage people to become more responsible in their sexual behavior and in their rearing of children. It would focus public policies on supporting competent parenting and on remedying or replacing incompetent parenting.

Important in all of these considerations are value judgments based upon the civil rights inherent in American culture: that every individual, regardless of sex, race, or age, should have the opportunity to pursue life, liberty, and happiness. In order to realize these ideals, there are times when the interests of society must take precedence over a particular individual's wishes or emotional state. One of those times is when an incompetent parent interferes with a child's opportunity to develop in life so as to become a competent adult.

Any effort to help children and foundering parents must have clear and measurable objectives. It is not enough to draw upon charitable impulses or appeals for social justice. Furthermore, simply increasing income or the employment of parents are not sufficient objectives, because they do not necessarily directly benefit the target of the aid—the children. Objectives based on the principles that each child has a right to competent parenting and a right to be protected from incompetent parenting would insure that children are helped.

Even if the licensing of parents were never implemented, debates about it would focus public attention on the importance of parenting and would bring expressions of concern about children down from abstract rhetoric to reality. It would expose juvenile ageism. It would call attention to the political disenfranchisement of children and the possibility of supporting parenting through such means as parents casting votes for their children.

GLOBAL LEADERSHIP IN HUMAN RIGHTS FOR CHILDREN

Of all nations, the United States has come the closest to articulating the ideals of human fulfillment. Its leadership in advocating international human rights and national civil rights has resulted in progress toward the goals of freedom, justice, and equal opportunity for adults both here and abroad. We risk losing these gains and our standard of living if we do not secure these same human and civil rights for all of our own children.

The United States needs a vision for the future. Our flawed society fosters an underclass by holding no standards for the parenting of its children. The future holds the demise of public education in a two-class society, the further deterioration of public safety, and the loss of economic productivity. We do not need to continue to be "number one" in the world, but we should not lose control of our future by ignoring our next generation. The economist Paul Krugman reminds us that maintaining the constructive growth of our economy is important for our own sake not just to keep up with international competition.[7]

There is hope. The dire outlook could be reversed if we honored each child's right to competent parenting and each child's right to be protected from incompetent parenting. The United States is the most economically dynamic and technologically innovative nation on Earth. It is an evolving experiment in human relations watched intently by the rest of the world. Because the United States is ethnically diverse, everyone on the face of the Earth can identify with being American. We have the opportunity to expand our global influence by emphasizing both the human rights of adults and the human rights of children.

Although competitive individualism seems to characterize short-term success in the United States, there is ample evidence that self-fulfilling teamwork actually lies behind the long-term success of our free enterprise system. In contrast with societies that depend upon duty to others as the basis for cooperation, America could set forth self-fulfillment as the motive for the global cooperation required for the survival of humankind. The United States could do this by visibly pursuing its own social and cultural objectives through supporting the development of the affectionate attachment bonds between parents and children that undergird our capacities as adults to engage in self-fulfilling teamwork.

In the 1890s, children captured the energy and attention of social reformers in the United States with an unprecedented intensity. The historian Michael Katz wrote about that period:[8] "Almost overnight it seemed, children became the symbol of a resurgent, reformed spirit, the magnet that pulled together a diverse collection of causes and their champions into a new, loose, informal but effective coalition." This could happen again in the 1990s.

Although inevitable conflicts exist between the interests of older and younger generations, it seems that America's latent will is to promote the healthy development of all of our children. The problem lies in finding feasible ways to do so. If we do nothing to protect our children from abuse and neglect, future generations will wonder how we permitted anyone to rear children without considering their competence to do so. They will know the consequences of ignoring incompetent parents until they irretrievably damage our children and our society.

Appendix

Calculating the Costs of Incompetent Parenting (Wisconsin—1994 Estimates)

1. AFDC Payments
   Single parent with two children: $419/ Month or $5023/year

2. Foster Home Care
   Regular foster care
     0–4 years old: $230/month
     5–11 years old: $277/month
     12–14 years old: $339/month
     15–17 years old: $350/month
   Treatment foster care: $1007/month
   Group home: $2545/month

3. State Mental Hospital (Mendota Mental Health Institute)
   $11,880/month ($396/day)

4. Juvenile Correctional Institutions
   Ethan Allen/Lincoln Hills: $3524/month
   Child caring institution: $4040/month

5. Adult Correctional Institutions
   Average cost: $1838/month

6. Jail Detention
   $108/day

7. Juvenile Shelter Home
   $108/day

8. Home Detention
   $22/day

9. Juvenile Court Intake (arrested by police for offense) $216/
   incident

10. Dane County Juvenile Court
    Social services: $1536/juvenile
    Juvenile division of the public defender's office: $448,000/year
    Juvenile division of the district attorney's office: $448,000/year
    Juvenile court salaries, equipment, & supplies: $576,000/year
    Of 3142 juvenile petitions filed, 1900 went to court.
    Individual juvenile court system cost = total court cost ÷ number of juveniles + social service cost:

$$\frac{\$448,000 + \$448,000 + \$576,000}{1900} + \$1536 = \$2,311$$

11. Dane County Department of Social Services
    Budget of Service Division
      Administration: $ 1,413,760
      Facilities: $ 285,440
      Salaries: $ 3,325,524
      Travel reimbursement: $ 108,800
    Total: $ 5,133,524
    $2633/juvenile

12. Federal Income Tax
    Mean annual income: $ 21,936
      Federal tax: $ 2381

Notes

Please note that in order to reduce distractions in reading, the superscripts in the text direct you to all of the references cited in a particular paragraph.

1. The Eroding Quality of Life in the United States

1. Lisbeth B. Schorr & Daniel Schorr (1988). *Within our reach: Breaking the cycle of disadvantage*. New York: Anchor Press, Doubleday, pp. xix–xx.
2. National Commission on Children (1991). *Opening doors for America's children*. Washington, DC: National Commission on Children.
3. William Kenkel (1966). *The family in perspective*. New York: Appleton-Century-Crofts, pp. 77, 87.
4. Carnegie Corporation of New York (1994). *Starting points: Meeting the needs of our youngest children*. Waldorf, MD: Carnegie Corporation of New York. David A. Hamburg (1992). *Today's children: Creating a future for a generation in crisis*. New York: Times Books/Random House.
5. Fred G. Gosman (1992). *Spoiled rotten: Today's children and how to change them*. New York: Villard Books. James A. Michener (1993). After the war: Victories at home. *Newsweek*, January 11, pp. 26–27. Kenneth L. Woodward (1990). Young beyond their years. *Newsweek: The Family in the 21st Century*, Winter/Spring, pp. 56–68.
6. Kris Rudolph (1990). Bad homes sabotage education. *Wisconsin State Journal*, February 25, p. A7.

7. Peter Sipchen (1988). Fear and loathing in the suburbs. *U.S. News and World Report*, July 11, p. 6.
8. Jack C. Westman (1979). *Child advocacy*. New York: Free Press, pp. 3–29. Thomas M. Achenbach, & Catherine T. Howell, (1993). Are American children's problems getting worse?: A 13-year comparison. *Journal of the Academy of Child and Adolescent Psychiatry, 32*, 1145–1154.
9. National Center for Education Statistics (1993). *Youth Indicators–1993*. Washington, DC: U.S. Department of Education, pp. 4–5. Victor R. Fuchs & Diane M. Reklis (1992). America's children: Economic perspectives and policy options. *Science, 255*, 41–46.
10. Urie Bronfenbrenner (1986). Testimony before U.S. Senate Committee on Rules and Administration, "A Generation in Jeopardy: America's Hidden Family Policy," Washington, DC, July 23.
11. Business-Higher Education Forum (1990). *Three realities*. Washington, DC: Business-Higher Education Forum.
12. Council on Competitiveness (1991). *Competitiveness index–1991*. Washington, DC: Council on Competitiveness. MetLife (1991). Historical perspective. *Statistical Bulletin, 72*, 38.
13. Southport Institute for Policy Analysis (1992). *Missing link*. Washington, DC: Southport Institute for Policy Analysis. U.S. Department of Labor (1992). *Report of commission on achieving necessary skills*. Washington, DC: U.S. Department of Labor.
14. U.S. Census Bureau (1992). *School enrollment—Social and economic characteristics of students*. Washington, DC: U.S. Government Printing Office. For mathematics proficiency levels see: *1992 National assessment of educational progress*. Washington, DC: National Assessment Governing Board. National Assessment of Educational Progress (1985). *The reading report card: Progress toward excellence in our schools, trends in reading over four national assessments, 1971–1984*. Princeton, NJ: Educational Testing Service. For reading performance of eighth and twelfth graders see: National Center of Education Statistics (1993). *Reading report card for the nation and the states*. Washington, DC: U.S. Department of Education. Richard L. Venesky, Carl F. Kaestle, & Andrew H. Sum (1987). *The subtle danger: Reflections on the literacy abilities of America's young adults*. Princeton, NJ: Educational Testing Service.
15. A.E. Lapointe, N.A. Mead, & G.W. Phillips (1989). *A world of differences: An international assessment of mathematics and science*. Princeton, NJ: Educational Testing Service. Harold W. Stevenson, Chuansheng Chen, & Shin-Ying Lee (1993). Mathematics achievement of Chinese, Japanese, and American children: Ten years later. *Science, 259*, 53–58.
16. Ina V.S. Mullis, Eugene H. Owen, & Gary W. Phillips (1990). *Accelerating academic achievement: A summary of findings from 20 years of NAEP*. Princeton,

NJ: Educational Testing Service. For SAT scores see: Department of Education (1988). *Youth indicators–1988.* Washington, DC: Office of Educational Research and Improvement, pp. 67–69. Mike Rose (1988). *Lives on the boundaries: The struggles and the achievements of America's underprepared.* New York: Free Press. Mike Dorsher (1992). UW report cites remedial needs. *Wisconsin State Journal,* December 4, p. 3D.

17. Carnegie Council on Adolescent Development (1989). *Turning points: Preparing American youth for the 21st century.* Washington, DC: Carnegie Corporation of New York. Irwin S. Kirsch & Ann Jungeblut (1986). *Literacy: Profiles of America's young adults.* Princeton, NJ: Educational Testing Service.

18. Janet E. Gans (1990). *AMA profiles of adolescent health, Volume 1. America's adolescents: How healthy are they?* Chicago, IL: American Medical Association. Office of Technology Assessment (1991). *Adolescent health, Volume 1, Summary and policy options.* Washington, DC: U.S. Government Printing Office. Janet M. Simons, Belva Finlay, & Alice Yang (1991). *The adolescent & young adult fact book.* Washington, DC: Children's Defense Fund. Fred M. Hechinger (1992). *Fateful choices: Healthy youth for the 21st century, executive summary.* New York: Carnegie Council on Adolescent Development. National Center for Educational Statistics (1988). *Youth indicators–1988.* Washington, DC: Department of Education, p. 98. For recommendations see: Carnegie Council of Adolescent Development (1992). *A matter of time: risk and opportunity in the nonschool hours.* New York: Carnegie Corporation of New York. National Research Council (1993). *Losing generations: Adolescents in high-risk settings.* Washington, DC: National Academy Press.

19. J. Larry Brown (1992). *Report to Honorable Tony Hall, Chair of the House Select Committee on Hunger.* Boston, MA: Tufts University Center on Hunger, Poverty, and Social Policy, September 8.

20. National Center for Health Statistics (1993). *Health, United States, 1992.* Hyattsville, MD: U.S. Department of Health and Human Services, Public Health Service, CDC, Publ. No. (PHS) 93–1232

21. Nicholas Eberstadt (1991). America's infant-mortality puzzle. *The Public Interest,* Fall, pp. 52–64.

22. J.G. Dryfoos (1990). *Adolescents at risk.* New York: Oxford University Press. For adolescent contraceptive usage see: Freya L. Sonenstein, Joseph H. Pleck, & C. Ku Leighton (1989). Sexual activity, condom use and AIDS awareness among adolescent young males. *Family Planning Perspectives, 21,* 152–158. For the incidence of sexually transmitted diseases in adolescents see: M.A. Shafer & A.B. Moscicki (1990). Sexually transmitted diseases in adolescents, in W.R. Hendee (Ed.), *The health of adolescents.* San Francisco: Jossey-Bass. For AIDS and adolescents see: Select Commitee on Children, Youth, and Families (1992). *A Decade of denial: Teens and AIDS in America.* Washington, DC: U.S. Government Printing Office, p. 20. David Michaels

& Carol Levine (1992). Estimates of the number of motherless youth orphaned by AIDS in the United States. *Journal of the American Medical Association, 268*, 3456–3461. Richard M. Chu, Susan Y. Selik, & James W. Buehler (1993). HIV infection as leading cause of death among young adults in U.S. cities and states. *Journal of the American Medical Association, 269*, 2991–2994. Fred J. Hellinger (1993). The lifetime cost of treating a person with HIV. *Journal of the American Medical Association, 270*, 474–478.

23. For adolescent sexual behavior see: Janet E. Gans, Blyth, Dale A., Elster, Arthur, & Gaveras, Lena Lundgren (1990). *America's Adolescents: How Healthy are They?* Chicago, IL: American Medical Association. HHS News, RP 0810 (1993). *National high school senior survey on drug abuse.* Washington, DC: U.S. Public Health Service .

24. Committee on Trauma Research of the National Research Council and Institute of Medicine (1985). *Injury in America: A continuing public health problem* Washington, DC: National Academy Press. National Highway Traffic Safety Administration (1987). *Fatal accident reporting system, 1985* Washington, DC: U.S. Department of Transportation. For the behavior problems of adolescent alcoholics see: L. Buydens-Branchey, M.H. Branchey, & D. Noumair (1989). Age of alcoholism onset. *Archives of General Psychiatry, 46*, 225–230.

25. National Advisory Mental Health Council (1990). *National plan for research on child and adolescent mental disorders.* Washington, DC: U.S. Department of Health and Human Services, Publication No. (ADM) 90–1683. Centers for Disease Control (1991). Attempted suicide among high school students in the United States–1990, *Centers for Disease Control Surveillance Summaries MMWR, 90*(37), Atlanta, GA.

26. Children's Defense Fund (1989). *A vision for America's future.* Washington, DC: Author, pp. 5, 7. Centers for Disease Control (1992). Summary of notifiable diseases common in the United States–1991, *Centers for Disease Control Surveillance Summaries MMWR, 40*(53), Atlanta, GA. Centers for Disease Control (1994). Reported vaccine-preventable diseases—United States, 1993, and the Childhood Immunization Initiative. *Journal of the American Medical Association, 271*, 651–652.

27. Anna E. Waller, Susan P. Baker, & Andrew Szocka (1989). Childhood injury deaths: National analysis and geographic variations. *American Journal of Public Health, 79*, 310–315. P.W. O'Carroll (1988). Homicides among black males 15–24 years of age, 1970–1984. *Centers for Disease Control Surveillance Summaries MMWR, 37*(5), 53–60, Atlanta, GA.

28. Leonard A. Sagan (1987). *The health of nations: True causes of sickness and well-being.* New York: Basic Books, pp. 4–5. National Center for Health Statistics (1993). *Advance report of final mortality statistics for 1991, Monthly vital*

statistics report, Volume 42, No. 2 suppl. Washington, DC: U.S. Government Printing Office. National Center for Health Statistics (1993). *National health interview survey–1991, Series 10, No. 184* Washington, DC: U.S. Government Printing Office. The life expectancy is 79.1 years in Japan, 76.5 years in Canada, and 75.0 years in the United States: Centers for Disease Control (1990). *Comparative life expectancies.* Atlanta, GA: Author, April 6.

29. Metrolife (1990). Major improvements in life expectancy: 1989. *Statistical Bulletin,* July-September, p. 13. See also: E. Fuller Torrey (1988). *Nowhere to go: The tragic odyssey of the homeless mentally ill.* New York: Harper & Row.

30. J.H. Knowles (1977). The responsibility of the individual. *Daedalus, 106,* 57–80. R. Karasek, & T. Tores (1990). *Healthy work: Stress, productivity and the reconstruction of working life.* New York: Basic Books. J. Michael McGinnis & William H. Foege (1993). Actual causes of death in the United States. *Journal of the American Medical Association, 270,* 2207–2212.

31. D.H. Schetky (1985). Children and handguns. *American Journal of Diseases of Children, 139,* 229–231. U.S. Office of Budget and Management (1993). *Annual Hospital Costs of Gun Injuries.* Washington, DC: U.S. Government Printing Office.

32. Tim Weiner (1991). Report: U.S. leads all in crime. *Wisconsin State Journal,* March 13, p. A1.

33. Arlene Levinson (1992). Murder leveling off; other crimes rise. *Wisconsin State Journal,* December 11, p. 8A.

34. Crime Statistics (1987). Crime in the United States–1986. *FBI Law Enforcement Bulletin,* September, pp. 5–12.

35. Federal Bureau of Investigation (1986). *Age-specific arrest rates and race-specific arrest rates for selected offenses 1965–1985.* Washington, DC: U.S. Department of Justice. Bureau of Justice Statistics (1992). *Criminal victimization in the United States–1991.* Washington, DC: U.S. Department of Justice, p. 55.

36. The figure of 2 percent includes juveniles taken into custody (1,185,770). and juveniles in institutions (49,322); adults on parole (391,840); adults on probation (2,638,720); and adults in jails (223,551) and in prisons (481,616). Together these total 4,970,819, or 2 percent of the population of the United States: Bureau of Justice Statistics (1989). *National crime survey.* Washington, DC: U.S. Government Printing Office.

37. Beverly Sweatman (1994). Personal communication, Interpol, Washington, DC. Lois A. Fingerhut & Joel C. Kleinmen (1990). International and interstate comparisons of homicide among young males. *Journal of the American Medical Association, 263,* 3292–3295.

38. G.J. Wintemute, S.P. Teret, J.F. Kraus, M.A. Wright, & G. Bradfield (1987). When children shoot children. *Journal of the American Medical Association, 257,* 3107–3109. Center for Disease Control (1992). Unintentional firearm-

related fatalities among children, teenagers; United States, 1982–1988. *Journal of the American Medical Association, 268,* 451–452. David A. Brent, Joshua A. Perper, Christopher J. Allman, Grace M. Moritz, Mary E. Wartella, & Janice P. Zelenak (1991). The presence and accessibility of firearms in the homes of adolescent suicides: A case-control study. *Journal of the American Medical Association, 266,* 2989–2995.

39. Eloise Salholz (1992). Deadly lessons. *Newsweek,* March 9, pp. 22–30. For Seattle survey see: Charles M. Callahan & Frederick P. Rivara (1992). Urban high school youth and handguns: A school-based survey. *Journal of the American Medical Association, 267,* 3038–3042. Robert Byrd (1991). Centers for Disease Control study: Many teens carry guns, knives. *Wisconsin State Journal,* October 11, p. 1A.

40. S.P. Baker (1985). Without guns, do people kill people? *American Journal of Public Health, 75,* 587–588.

41. Shari Hamilton (1992). Domestic violence: An overview. *Wisconsin Medical Journal,* June, 279–280. M.P. Koss (1990). Hidden rape: Sexual aggression and victimization in a national sample of students of higher education, in A.W. Burgess (Ed.) *Rape and sexual assault.* New York: Garland, 2, 3–25. National Center on Child Abuse Prevention Research (1992). *Current trends in child abuse reporting and fatalities: The results of a fifty-state survey.* Chicago, IL: The National Committee for Prevention of Child Abuse. U.S. Advisory Board on Child Abuse and Neglect (1990). *Child abuse and neglect: Critical first steps in response to a national emergency.* Washington, DC: U.S. Government Printing Office, No: 017-092-00104-5.

42. Select Committee on Children, Youth, and Families (1989). *U.S. children and their families: Current condition and recent trends.* Washington, DC: U.S. Government Printing Office. Sheryl Stolberg (1990). Report on child abuse finds agencies deluged. *Los Angeles Times,* November 14, p. A12.

43. Associated Press (1992). Japan top competitor as U.S. falls. *Wisconsin State Journal,* June 22, p. 1A.

44. Clifford M. Johnson, Andrew M. Sum, & James D. Weill (1988). *Vanishing dreams: The growing economic plight of America's young families.* Washington, DC: Children's Defense Fund. Frank Levy (1988). *Dollars and dreams: The changing American income distribution.* New York: Norton. Katherine S. Newman (1993). *Declining fortunes: The withering of the American dream.* New York: Basic Books.

45. U.S. Census Bureau (1992). The shriveling middle class. *U.S. News & World Report,* March 2, p. 12. Kevin Phillips (1992). *Boiling point: Republicans, Democrats, and the declining middle-class propsperity.* New York: Random House. For poverty statistics see: Committee on Ways and Means (1989). *Background material and data on programs within the jurisdiction of the Committee*

on Ways and Means WMCP: 101-4 Washington, DC: U.S. Government Printing Office, p. 943. Jonathan Kozol (1988). *Rachel and her children: Homeless families in America.* New York: Crown.

46. Bryce Christensen, Allan Carlson, Maris Vinovskis, Richard Vedder, & Jean Bethke Elshtain (1988). *The family wage: Work, gender, and children in the modern economy.* Rockford, IL: The Rockford Institute. For Bureau of Labor Statistics see: Steven Greenhouse (1992). Income data show years of erosion for U.S. workers. *New York Times,* September 7, p. 1.

47. Juliet B. Schor (1991). *The overworked American: The unexpected decline of leisure.* New York: Basic Books. Jo Ann Tooley (1989). Roper survey: Grumbling in the office. *U.S. News and World Report,* September 18, p. 77.

48. Dave Skidmore (1991). Census Bureau: Most of us can't afford to buy a house. *Wisconsin State Journal,* June 14, p. 3A.

49. Kenneth L. Woodward (1989). Young beyond their years. *Newsweek: The Family in the 21st Century,* Winter/Spring, pp.54–68.

50. Scott Lautenschlager (1990). More kids at work is a worry. *Wisconsin State Journal,* May 15.

51. William J. Baumol, Sue Anne Batey Blackman, & Edward N. Wolff (1989). *Productivity and American leadership.* Cambridge, MA: MIT Press, p. 209. The Secretary's Commission on Achieving Necessary Skills (1992). *Learning a living: A blueprint for high performance.* Washington, DC: U.S. Department of Labor. For intergenerational equity see: Constance Holden (1990). Multidisciplinary look at a finite world. *Science, 249,* 18–19.

52. Vance Packard (1983). *Our endangered children.* Boston, MA: Little, Brown. Examples of earlier books on the plight of children in the United States are: (1) David McKay & Joint Commission on the Mental Health of Children (1969). *Crisis in child mental health.* New York: Harper; (2) Howard James (1970). *Children in trouble: A national scandal.* New York: David McKay Company; and (3) Paul L. Adams, Lisa Berg, Nan Berger, Michael Duane, A.S. Neill, & Robert Ollendorff (1971). *Children's rights: Toward the liberation of the child.* New York: Praeger. U.S. Bureau of the Census (1992). *Household and family characteristics: March 1991–Series P, No. 458* Washington, DC: U.S. Government Printing Office.

2. The Proximate Cause: Incompetent Parenting

1. Carnegie Foundation for the Advancement for Teaching (1988). *An imperiled generation: Saving urban schools.* Princeton, NJ: Carnegie Foundation for the Advancement of Teaching.

2. Jack C. Westman (1979). *Child advocacy*. New York: Free Press, pp. 132–133. Sula Wolf (1989). *Childhood and human nature: The development of personality*. London: Routledge. George W. Albee (1980). A competency model must replace the defect model, in Lynne A. Bond & James C. Kosen (Eds.), *Competence and coping during adulthood*. Hanover, NH: University Press of New England, p. 96.
3. Sander J. Breiner (1990). *Slaughter of the innocents: Child abuse through the ages and today*. New York: Plenum. Brigitte Berger (1988). Multiproblem families and the community, in James Q. Wilson & Glenn C. Loury (Eds.), *From children to citizens, Volume 3, Families, schools, and delinquency prevention*. New York: Springer-Verlag, p. 277. Jack C. Westman & David Kaye (1990). The termination of parental rights as a therapeutic option, in Jack C. Westman (Ed.), *Who speaks for the children?* Sarasota, FL: Professional Resources Exchange, Inc., pp. 257–259. Bette Keltner (1990). Family characteristics of preschool social competence among black children in a Head Start program. *Child Psychiatry and Human Development, 21*, 95–108.
4. Kim Oates (1986). *Child abuse and neglect: What happens eventually?* New York: Brunner/Mazel. David A. Wolfe (1992). *Preventing physical and emotional abuse of children*. New York: Guilford, pp. 19–43.
5. Abe Fosson & John Wilson (1987). Family interactions surrounding feedings of infants with nonorganic failure to thrive. *Clinical Pediatrics, 26*, 518–523.
6. Children's Division (1993). *America's children: How are they doing? Fact sheet #8*. Englewood, CO: American Humane Association.
7. In 1990 there were 63,604,432 children under the age of eighteen in the United States.[a] In 1991 there were 2,694,000 reported cases of child abuse and neglect; 39%, or 1,050,660, were substantiated. Of those 53%, or 556,849, were cases of neglect.[b] In estimating the prevalence of child neglect, the redundant reporting of the same cases, the repeated reporting of the same cases, the responsiveness of families to treatment, the severity of the neglect, the preponderance of reporting between birth and 10 years of age, unsubstantiated cases that are later substantiated, and statistical errors should be taken into account. In order to conservatively estimate the number of substantiated neglect cases, I accommodated the foregoing mitigating factors by taking the substantiated neglect figure for an eight-year period from 1983 to 1991.[b] Rather than including all seventeen of the dependent years of childhood, I took only eight in order allow for a wide margin of error. That calculation yielded 17,440,000 reported cases of child abuse and neglect of which 6,801,600 (39%) were substantiated and of which 3,604,848 (53%) were cases of substantiated neglect. According to this estimate about 3.6 million children in the United States have been

neglected, or approximately 5.6% of all children. Of the neglected children 51%, or 1.84 million, are from single-parent, and 49%, or 1.76 million, are from two-parent households. [c] Assuming two children in each household, a total of 1.8 million households are involved, of which .92 million would be single-parent and .88 million would be two-parent. By adding the single-parent and two-parent households the total number of neglectful (incompetent) parents then would be 2.68 million, or 4% of all parents. [d] This would involve 8% of single-parent and 3% of two-parent households. [d]

References: (a) U.S. Bureau of the Census (1991). *Census Bureau complete distribution of 1990.* Washington, DC: U.S. Bureau of the Census, Table 1-A; (b) The National Center on Child Abuse Prevention Research (1992). *Current trends in child abuse and fatalities: The results of the 1991 Annual Fifty-State Survey.* Chicago, IL: The National Committee on the Prevention of Child Abuse; (c) American Humane Association (1989). *National analysis of official child neglect and abuse reporting.* Denver, CO: American Humane Association; and (d) U.S. Bureau of the Census (1992). *Household and family Characteristics: March 1991, Series P-20, No. 458.* Washington, DC: U.S. Government Printing Office, p. 7.

The above estimates are conservative. An analysis by a private firm WESTAT of 1986 survey data from children's-protective-service and other professional agencies on the national incidence of child abuse and neglect estimated that only 40 percent of known child abuse and neglect cases are reported each year. Significantly only 32 percent of physical and emotional neglect cases are reported compared to 52 percent of physical abuse cases. This means that there are two additional neglected children known to professionals for each one reported each year. In other words, it is suspected that some 3.3 million children are neglected each year. In addition there are neglected children who are neither known to professionals nor reported to child-protection agencies. Moreover, the number of neglected children appears to be increasing: Andrea J. Sedlak (1989). *Supplementary Analysis of Data on the National Incidence of Child Abuse and Neglect.* Rockville, MD: WESTAT, Inc.

8. David Quinton & Michael Rutter (1988). *Parenting breakdown: The making and breaking of intergenerational links.* Aldershot, UK: Avebury, p. 200. National Research Council (1993). *Understanding child abuse and neglect.* Washington, DC: National Academy Press.

9. Henry P. David, Z. Dytrych, Z. Matejcek, & V. Schuller (1988). *Born unwanted: The developmental effects of denied abortion.* New York: Springer.

10. Judith Areen (1978). *Cases and materials on family law.* Mineola, NY: The Foundation Press, pp. 906–962.

11. Mary Jo Bane & David T. Ellwood (1989). One fifth of the nation's

children: Why are they poor? *Science, 245,* 1047–1053. Leroy H. Pelton (1991). Poverty and child protection. *Protecting Children,* 7, 3–5.

12. U.S. Bureau of the Census (1991). Poverty in the United States. *Current Population Reports, Consumer Income, Series P-60, No. 175.* Washington, DC: U.S. Department of Commerce, p. 98.

13. Ibid., p. 7.

14. Lisbeth B. Schorr & Daniel Schorr (1988). *Within our reach: Breaking the cycle of disadvantage.* New York: Anchor Press, Doubleday, p. 18. National Center for Children in Poverty (1990). *Five million children: A statistical profile of our poorest young citizens.* New York: School of Public Health, Columbia University, p. 41.

15. U.S. Bureau of the Census (1993). Poverty in the United States. *Current Population Reports, Consumer Income, Series P-60, No. 175.* Washington, DC: U.S. Department of Commerce, pp. 4, 8.

16. Ibid., pp. 7, 116. National Center for Children in Poverty (1993). *Five million children: A statistical profile of our poorest young citizens.* New York: School of Public Health, Columbia University.

17. U.S. Bureau of the Census (1993). Poverty in the United States. *Current Population Reports, Consumer Income, Series P-60, No. 175.* Washington, DC: U.S. Department of Commerce, p. 127.

18. Ibid., pp. 1–2. Sandra K. Danziger & Sheldon Danziger (1993). Child poverty and public policy. *Daedalus, 122,* 57–84.

19. U.S. Bureau of the Census (1993). Poverty in the United States. *Current Population Reports, Consumer Income, Series P-60, No. 175.* Washington, DC: U.S. Department of Commerce, p. 4.

20. Urban Institute (1989). Urban Institute research on the underclass: A summary and selected readings. *Urban Institute Policy and Research Report, 19,* 11–12.

21. Sandra K. Danziger & Sheldon Danziger (1993). Child poverty and public policy. *Daedalus, 122,* 57–84, 71.

22. U.S. House of Representatives Committee on Ways and Means (1989). *Background material and data on programs within the jurisdiction of the Committee on Ways and Means WMCP: 101-4.* Washington, DC: U.S. Government Printing Office, p. 974.

23. Ken Auletta (1982). *The underclass.* New York: Random House, pp. 25–26. Elijah Anderson (1990). *Streetwise: Race, class, and change in an urban community,* Chicago, IL: University of Chicago Press. Christopher Jencks & Paul E. Peterson (Eds.) (1991). *The urban underclass.* Washington, DC: The Brookings Institution.

24. Erol R. Ricketts & Isabel V. Sawhill (1988). Defining and measuring the underclass. *Journal of Policy Analysis and Management,* 7(2). Ronald B. Mincy,

Isabel V. Sawhill, & Douglas A. Wolf (1990). The underclass: Definition and measurement. *Science, 248,* 450–453. William R. Prosser (1991). The underclass: Assessing what we have learned. *Focus, 13,* 1–18 (University of Wisconsin-Madison Institute for Research on Poverty).

25. William P. O'Hare & Brenda Curry-White (1992). *The rural underclass: Examination of the multiple-problem populations in urban and rural settings.* Washington, DC: Population Reference Bureau.

26. Michael B. Katz (1989). *The undeserving poor: From the war on poverty to the war on welfare.* New York: Basic Books, pp. 195–235. James Garbarino, Kathleen Kostelny, & Nancy Dubrow (1991). *No place to be a child.* Lexington, MA: Lexington Books. Christopher Jenks & Paul E. Peterson (Eds.) (1991). *The urban underclass.* Washington, DC: Brookings Institution. Alex Kotlowitz (1991). *There are no children here: The story of two boys growing up in the other America.* New York: Doubleday. Massey, Douglas S. & Denton, Nancy A. (1989). Hypersegregation in U.S. Metropolitan Areas: Black & Hispanic Segregation Along Five Dimensions, *Demography 26,* 373–391. Jennings, James (Ed.) (1992). *Race, Politics, and Economic Development.* New York: Verso.

27. National Advisory Commission on Civil Disorders (Kerner Commission) (1968). *Report of the National Advisory Commission on Civil Disorders.* New York: Bantam Books. William P. O'Hare & Brenda Curry-White (1992). *The rural underclass: Examination of the multiple-problem populations in urban and rural settings.* Washington, DC: Population Reference Bureau. Ronald B. Mincy (1991). *Underclass variations by race and place: Have large cities darkened our picture of the underclass?* Washington, DC: The Urban Institute. National Rural Development Institute (1990). *National study regarding at-risk students.* Bellingham, WA: Western Washington University.

28. Nicholas Lemann (1991). *The promised land: The great black migration and how it changed America.* New York: Alfred A. Knopf. Jacqueline Jones (1992). *The dispossessed: America's underclasses from the Civil War to the present.* New York: Basic Books.

3. The Benefits to Society of Competent Parenting

1. James P. Comer (1972). *Beyond black and white.* New York: Quadrangle Books.

2. J. L. Reiss (1976). *Family systems in America, 2nd Edition.* Hinsdale, IL: Dryden, pp. 11–44.

3. Harry F. Harlow (1974). *Learning to love.* New York: Jason Aronson. T. Alloway, P. Pliner, & L. Krames, (1977). *Attachment behavior.* New York:

Plenum. Harry F. Harlow & Clara Mears (1979). *The human model: Primate perspectives.* Washington, DC: V. H. Winston & Sons. L. Brothers (1989). A biological perspective on empathy. *American Journal of Psychiatry, 146,* 10–19.

4. John Bowlby (1969, 1973, & 1980). *Attachment and loss; Volumes 1, 2, and 3.* New York: Basic Books.

5. J. Langmeir & Z. Matejecek (1975). *Psychological deprivation in childhood.* New York: Wiley.

6. James Elicker, Michelle Englund, & L. Alan Sroufe (1989). *Predicting peer competence and peer relationships in childhood from early parent-child relationships.* Sula Wolf (1989). *Childhood and human nature: The development of personality.* London: Routledge. Jay Belsky (1990). Parental and nonparental child care and children's socioemotional development. *Journal of Marriage and the Family, 52,* 885–903. Penelope Leach (1994). *Children first: What our society must do—and is not doing—for our children today.* New York: Alfred A. Knopf.

7. Jack C. Westman (1979). *Child advocacy.* New York: Free Press, pp. 3–29. Arnold J. Sameroff & Robert N. Emde (Eds.) (1989). *Relationship disturbances in early childhood: A developmental approach.* New York: Basic Books. American Academy of Child and Adolescent Psychiatry (1990). *Prevention in child and adolescent psychiatry: The reduction of risk for mental disorders.* Washington, DC: American Academy of Child and Adolescent Psychiatry. Cathryn L. Booth, Susan J. Spieker, Kathryn E. Barnard, & Colleen E. Morisset (1992). Infants at risk: The role of preventive intervention in deflecting a maladaptive developmental trajectory, in Joan McCord & Richard E. Tremblay (Eds.) *Preventing antisocial behavior: Interventions from birth through adolescence.* New York: Guilford. Michael Rutter (1989). Psychiatric disorder in parents as a risk factor in children, in David Shaffer, Irving Phillips, & Norbert B. Enzer (Eds.), *Prevention of mental disorders, alcohol and other drug use in children and adolescents.* Rockville, MD: U.S. Department of Health and Human Services. Peter S. Jensen, Linda Bloedau, James DeGroot, Todd Ussery, & Harry David (1990). Children at risk: I. Risk factors and child symptomatology. *Journal of the Academy of Child and Adolescent Psychiatry, 29,* 51–59.

8. Alice S. Rossi & Peter H. Rossi (1990). *Of human bonding: Parent-child relations across the life course.* New York: Aldine de Gruyter, p. 492.

9. M.G. Goertzel, V. Goeertzel, & T.G. Goertzel (1978). *Three hundred eminent personalities.* San Francisco, CA: Jossey-Bass.

10. Marc Pilisuk & Susan Hiller Parks (1987). *The healing web: Social betworks and human survival.* Hanover, NH: University Press of New England, p. 15.

11. Leonard A. Sagan (1987). *The health of nations: True causes of sickness and well-being.* New York: Basic Books.

12. John Boswell (1988). *The kindness of strangers: The abandonment of children in Western Europe from late antiquity to the Renaissance.* New York: Pantheon.
13. Leonard A. Sagan (1987). *The health of nations: True causes of sickness and well-being.* New York: Basic Books, pp. 28–29.
14. Ibid., p. 127. For a discussion of psychoimmunology see: S. Locke & D. Colligan (1986). *The healer within.* New York: Dutton. Norman Cousins (1989). *Head first: The biology of hope.* New York: Dutton.
15. Leonard A. Sagan (1987). *The health of nations: True causes of sickness and well-being.* New York: Basic Books, pp. 110.
16. Marc Pilisuk & Susan Hillier Parks (1987). *The healing web: Social networks and human survival.* Hanover, NH: University Press of New England, pp. 29–61. Christopher Peterson & Lisa M. Bossio (1991). *Health and optimism.* New York: Free Press.
17. Emmy E. Werner & Ruth S. Smith (1992). *Overcoming the odds: High risk children from birth to adulthood.* Ithaca, NY: Cornell University Press.
18. David Quinton & Michael Rutter (1988). *Parenting breakdown: The making and breaking of intergenerational links.* Aldershot, UK: Avebury, p. 199. Michael Rutter (1985). Resilience in the face of adversity: Protective factors and resistance to psychiatric disorder. *British Journal of Psychiatry, 147,* 598–611.
19. Janis V.F. Long & George E. Vaillant (1989). Escape from the underclass, in Timothy F. Dugan & Robert Coles (Eds.), *The children in our times: Studies in the development of resilience.* New York: Brunner/Mazel.
20. Sibylle Escalona (1982). Babies at double hazard: Early development of infants at biologic and social risk. *Pediatrics, 70,* 670–676. Melvin D. Levine, Walt M. Karniski, Judith S. Palfrey, Lynn J. Meltzer, & Terence Fenton (1985). A study of risk factor complexes in early adolescent delinquency. *American Journal of the Diseases of Children, 139,* 50–56. The Infant Health and Development Program (1990). Enhancing the outcome of low-birth-weight, premature infants: A multisite randomized trial. *Journal of the American Medical Association, 263,* 3055–3042. J.D. Lloyd-Still (1976). *Malnutrition and intellectual development.* Littleton, MA: Publishing Sciences Group. Leon Eisenberg (1982). Conceptual issues on biobehavioral interactions, in Delores L. Parron & Leon Eisenberg (Eds.), *Infants at risk for developmental dysfunction.* Washington, DC: National Academy Press.
21. Stephen J. Suomi (1983). Short-and long-term effects repetitive mother-infant separations on social development in rhesus monkeys. *Developmental Psychology, 19,* 770–786.
22. Consortium for Longitudinal Studies (1983). *As the twig is bent: The lasting effects of preschool programs.* Hillsdale, NJ: Lawrence Erlbaum. Jack C. Westman (Ed.) (1991). *Who speaks for the children?* Sarasota, FL: Professional Resource Exchange.

4. The Effects of Incompetent Parenting

1. Sybil B.G. Eysenck (1989). Foreword, in Hans J. Eysenck & Gisli H. Gudjonsson, *The causes and cures of criminality*. New York: Plenum.
2. F.G. Bolton, Jr. (1983). *When bonding fails: Clinical assessment of high-risk families*. Beverly Hills, CA: Sage, pp. 26–27. Kenneth Wooden (1980). Case history of Charles Manson, in William Aiken & Hugh LaFollette (Eds.) *Whose child?* Totowa, NJ: Littlefield Adams, pp. 44–54.
3. M.G. Goertzel, V. Goertzel, & T.G. Goertzel (1978). *Three hundred eminent personalities*. San Francisco, CA: Jossey-Bass. For empirical research on childhood resiliency see: (1) Emmy E. Werner & R.S. Smith (1982). *Vulnerable but invincible: A study of resilient children*. New York: McGraw-Hill, p. 163; (2) Ronald Seifer, Arnold J. Sameroff, Clara P. Baldwin, & Alfred Baldwin (1992). Child and family factors that ameliorate risk between 4 and 13 years of age. *Journal of the American Academy of Child and Adolescent Psychiatry, 31,* 893–903; and (3) Peter A. Wyman, Emory L. Cowen, William C. Work, Anisa Raoof, Patricia A. Gribble, Gayle P. Parker, & Michael Wannon (1992). Interviews with children who experienced major life stress: Family and child attributes that predict resilient outcomes. *Journal of the American Academy of Child and Adolescent Psychiatry, 31,* 904–910.
4. Dane Archer & Rosemary Gartner (1984). *Violence and Crime in Cross-National Perspective*. New Haven: Yale University Press. James Q. Wilson & Richard J. Herrnstein (1986). *Criminals born and bred: Crime and human nature*. New York: Simon & Schuster, pp. 526–527.
5. U.S. Department of Justice (1992). *Crime in the United States–1991*. Washington, DC: U.S. Government Printing Office. Bureau of Justice Statistics (1992). *Criminal Victimization in the United States, 1991*. Washington, DC: U.S. Department of Justice.
6. U.S. Department of Justice (1992). *Federal and state prisons inmates in 1991*. Washington, DC: U.S. Department of Justice.
7. Nigel Walker (1987). *Crime and criminology: A critical introduction*. Oxford, U.K.: Oxford University Press, p. 30. Bill Buford (1992). *Among the thugs*. New York: Norton.
8. Alfred, Blumstein, Jacqueline Cohen, Jeffrey A. Roth, & Christy A. Visher (Eds.) (1980). *Criminal careers and "career criminals," Volume 1*. Washington, DC: National Academy Press, p. 94.
9. Tracy L. Snell & Danielle C. Morton (1992). Prisoners in 1991. *Bureau of Justice Statistics Bulletin*, May.
10. L.W. Shannon (1982). *Assessing the relationship of adult criminal careers to juvenile careers: A summary*. Washington, DC: U.S. Department of Justice,

June (505128). For studies that trace habitual criminality to the early years of life see: (1) Brent B. Benda (1979). *Criminal recidivism: From adolescence to adulthood.* Ph.D. dissertation, University of Wisconsin (450373); (2) J. Petersilia, P.W. Greenwood, & M. Lavin (1978). *Criminal careers of habitual felons.* Washington, D.C.: National Institute of Law Enforcement and Criminal Justice; (3) D.G. Rojeck & M.L. Erickson (1982). Delinquent careers: A test of the career escalation mode. *Criminology, 20,* 5–82; (4) J.R. Scanlon & L. Webb (1981). Juvenile offenders who become adult criminals. *Criminal Justice Review, 6,* 1–5; and (5) L.W. Shannon (1982). *Assessing the relationships of adult criminal careers to juvenile careers: A summary.* Washington, DC: U.S. Department of Justice, June (505128). For juvenile arrests see: Office of Juvenile Justice and Delinquency Prevention (1991). *Juveniles taken into custody: Fiscal year 1990 report.* Washington, DC: Author. For the outcomes of incarcerated juvenile delinquents see: Barry Krisberg (1992). *Juvenile justice: Improving the quality of care.* San Francisco, CA: National Council on Crime and Delinquency. For rising violence in juvenile crime see: U.S. Department of Justice (1992). *Crime in the United States–1991.* Washington, DC: U.S. Government Printing Office.

11. For profiles of juvenile delinquents destined to become adult habitual criminals see: (1) D.G. Rojeck & M.L. Erickson (1982). Delinquent careers: A test of the career escalation model. *Criminology, 20,* 5–82; (2) J.R. Scanlon & L. Webb (1981). Juvenile offenders who become adult criminals. *Criminal Justice Review, 6,* 1–5; and (3) L.W. Shannon (1982). *Assessing the relationship of adult criminal careers: A summary.* Washington, DC: U.S. Department of Justice, June (505128). Robert M. Regoli & John D. Hewitt (1994). *Delinquency in society: A child-centered approach, Second Edition.* New York: McGraw-Hill.

12. Cathy Spatz Widom & Ashley Ames (1988). Biology and female crime, in T.E. Moffitt & S.A. Mednick (Eds.), *Biological contributions to crime causation.* Dordrecht, Netherlands: Martinus Nijhoff.

13. Thomas O. Marsh (1981). *Roots of crime: A bio-physical approach to crime prevention and rehabilitation.* Newton, NJ: Nellen, p. xii. Dorothy Otnow Lewis & David A. Balla (1976). *Delinquency and psychopathology.* New York: Grune & Stratton, p. 79.

14. Sheilagh Hodgins & Michael Von Grunau (1988). Biology, mental disorder, aggression and violence: What do we know?, in T.E. Moffitt & S.A. Mednick (Eds.), *Biological contributions to crime causation.* Dordrecht, Netherlands: Martinus Nijhoff. Richard Barnum (1988). Biomedical problems in juvenile delinquency, in James Q. Wilson & Glenn C. Loury (Eds.), *From children to citizens, Volume 3, Families, schools and delinquency prevention.* New York: Springer-Verlag, p. 75. Adrian Raine, Peter H. Venables, & Mark

Williams (1990). Autonomic orienting responses in 15-year-old male subjects and criminal behavior at age 24. *American Journal of Psychiatry*, *147*, 933–937. According to Stephen Soumi, antisocial monkeys have low levels of serotonin; poor nurturing lowers the serotonin level, while good nuturing raises it: William F. Allman (1992). The evolution of aggression. *U.S. News & World Report*, May 11, pp 58–60.

15. Susan E. Folstein, Mary Louise Franz, Barbara Jensen, Gary A. Chase, & Marshal F. Folstein (1985). Conduct disorder and affective disorder among the offspring of patients with Huntington's disease, in S.B. Guze, F.J. Earls, & J.E. Banett, (Eds.), *Childhood psychopathology and development*. New York: Raven.

16. Robert Plomin (1986). *Development, genetics, and psychology*. Hillsdale, NJ: Erlbaum, pp. 291–293. James J. Gallagher & Craig Ramey (1987). *The malleability of children*. Baltimore, MD: Paul H. Brookes.

17. Hans J. Eysenck & Gisli H. Gudjonsson (1989). *The causes and cures of criminality*. New York: Plenum, p. 247. James Q. Wilson & Richard J. Herrnstein (1986). *Criminals born and bred: Crime and human nature*. New York: Simon & Schuster, p. 103.

18. Richard M. Restak (1992). See no evil: The neurological defense would blame violence on the damaged brain. *The Sciences*, July/August, 16–21.

19. Wesley G. Skogan (1990). *Disorder and decline: Crime and the spiral of decay in American neighborhoods*. New York: Free Press.

20. James Q. Wilson & Richard J. Herrnstein (1986). *Criminals born and bred: Crime and human nature*. New York: Simon & Schuster, p. 294. Marvin E. Wolfgang & Franco Ferracuti (1982). *The subculture of violence: Towards an integrated theory of criminology*. Beverly Hills, CA: Sage.

21. James Q. Wilson & Richard J. Herrnstein (1986). *Criminals born and bred: Crime and human nature*. New York: Simon & Schuster, p. 209. Glenn C. Loury (1988). The family as context for delinquency prevention, in James Q. Wilson & Glenn C. Loury (Eds.), *From children to citizens, Volume 3, Families, schools, and delinquency prevention*. New York: Springer-Verlag, pp. 21–22.

22. Travis Hirschi (1969). *Causes of delinquency*. Berkeley, CA: University of California Press. Alfred Blumstein, Jacqueline Cohen, Jeffery A. Roth, & Christy A. Visher (Eds.) (1980). *Criminal careers and "career criminals": Volume 1*. Washington, DC: National Academy Press.

23. James Q. Wilson & Richard J. Herrnstein (1986). *Criminals born and bred: Crime and human nature*. New York: Simon & Schuster, pp. 242, 283, 311. Terrie E. Moffitt (1990). Juvenile delinquency and attention deficit disorder: Boys' developmental trajectories from age 3 to age 15. *Child Development*, *61*, 893–910.

24. Bureau of Justice Statistics (1988). *Survey of youth in custody, 1987*. Washington, DC: U.S. Department of Justice. Summaries of the evidence linking incompetent parenting and criminality can be found in: (1) Lisbeth B. Schorr & Daniel Schorr (1988). *Within our reach: Breaking the cycle of disadvantage*. New York: Anchor Press, Doubleday; (2) James Q. Wilson & Richard J. Herrnstein (1986). *Criminals born and bred: Crime and human nature*. New York: Simon & Schuster, p. 20; (3) Sheppard G. Kellam & Werthamer-Larsson (1986). Developmental epidemiology: A basis for intervention, in Marc Kessler & Stephen E. Goldston (Eds.), *A decade of progress in primary prevention*. Hanover, NH: University Press of New England; (4) L. Rowell Huesmann & Leonard D. Eron (1992). Childhood aggression and adult criminality, in Joan McCord (Ed.), *Facts, frameworks, and forecasts: Advances in criminological theory, Volume 3*. New Brunswick, NJ: Transaction Publishers, pp. 151–152; and (5) Samuel B. Guze (1976). *Criminality and psychiatric disorders*. New York: Oxford University Press.

25. William McCord & Joan McCord with Irving K. Zola (1959). *Origins of crime: A new evaluation of the Cambridge—Somerville Youth Study*. New York: Columbia University Press. D.J. West & D.P. Farrington (1977). *The delinquent way of life: Third report of the Cambridge Study in Delinquent Development*. New York: Crane Russak. Joan McCord (1992). The Cambridge-Somerville Study: A pioneering longitudinal experimental study of delinquency prevention, in Joan McCord & Richard E. Tremblay (Eds.), *Preventing antisocial behavior: Interventions from birth through adolescence*. New York: Guilford.

26. Jose Alfaro (1989). One additional view, in David N. Sandberg (Ed.) *The child-abuse–delinquency connection*. Lexington, MA: Lexington Books, p. 109–121. Schweinhart, Lawrence J. & Weikart, David P. (1983). The Effect of the Perry Preschool Program on Youths through Age 15—A Summary, in Consortium for Longitudinal Studies *As the twig is bent: The lasting effects of preschool programs*. Hillsdale, NJ: Erlbaum.

27. Joan McCord (1983). A forty year perspective on child abuse and neglect. *Child Abuse and Neglect, 7*, 265–270. J. Kaufman & E. Zigler (1987). Do abused children become abusive parents? *American Journal of Orthopsychiatry, 57*, 186–192. David Gelman, Karen Springer, Regina Elam, Nadine Joseph, Kate Robins, & Mary Hagen (1990). The mind of the rapist. *Newsweek*, July 23, pp. 48–52. Barbara K. Luntz & Cathy Spatz Widom (1994). Antisocial personality disorder in abused and neglected children grown up. *American Journal of Psychiatry, 151*, 670–674.

28. J.E. Oliver (1993). Intergenerational transmission of child abuse: Rates, research, and clinical implications. *American Journal of Psychiatry, 150*, 1315–1324. Cathy Spatz Widom (1989). The cycle of violence. *Science, 244*, 160–166. Betsy McAlister Groves, Barry Zuckerman, Steven Marans, & Don-

ald J. Cohen (1993). Silent victims: Children who witness violence. *Journal of the American Medical Association, 269,* 262–264. Lise M. Youngblade & Jay Belsky (1990). Social and emotional consequences of child maltreatment, in Robert T. Ammerman & Michel Hersen (Eds.), *Children at risk: An evaluation of factors contributing to child abuse and neglect.* New York: Plenum.

29. Larry J. Siegel (1983). *Criminology.* St. Paul, MN: West, pp. 211–213. Remi J. Cadoret (1986). Epidemiology of the antisocial personality, in William H. Reid, Darwin Dorr, John I. Walker, & Jack W. Bonner, (Eds.), *Unmasking the psychopath: Antisocial personality and related syndromes.* New York: Norton.

30. Jack Henry Abbott (1981). *In the belly of the beast.* New York: Random House.

31. Alice Miller (1990). *The untouched key: Tracing childhood trauma in creativity and destructiveness.* New York: Doubleday, p. 168.

32. Robert N. Emde (1989). The infant's relationship experience: Developmental and affective aspects, in Arnold J. Sameroff & Robert N. Emde (Eds.), *Relationship disturbances in early childhood.* New York: Basic Books, p. 51.

33. Alan Sroufe (1989). Relationships, self, and individual adaptation, in Arnold J. Sameroff & Robert N. Emde (Eds.), *Relationship disturbances in early childhood.* New York: Basic Books, pp. 92–94.

34. Ernest Hirschbach (1982). Children beyond reach, in Ranae Hanson (Ed.), *Institutional abuse of children and youth.* New York: Haworth. Lea Pulkkinen (1988). Delinquent development: Theoretical empirical considerations, in Michael Rutter (Ed.), *Studies of psychosocial risk: The power of longitudinal data.* Cambridge, U.K.: Cambridge University Press. Manfred S. Guttmacher (1960). *The mind of the murderer.* New York: Farrar, Straus & Cudahy. Stanton E. Samenow (1984). *Inside the criminal mind.* New York: Times Books. Jack Katz (1988). *Seductions of crime: Moral and sensual attractions of doing evil.* New York: Basic Books.

35. Leonard Shengold (1989). *Soul murder and the effects of childhood abuse and deprivation.* New Haven, CT: Yale University Press.

36. Elissa Benedek & Dewey G. Cornell (Eds.) (1989). *Juvenile homicide.* Washington, DC: American Psychiatric Association. Muriel Gardiner (1985). *The deadly innocents.* New Haven, CT: Yale University Press.

37. Karl Zinsmeister (1990). Growing up scared. *Atlantic Monthly,* June, 49–66. Michael T. Kaufman (1993). 21 unfortunate reasons to simply ask "why?" *New York Times,* January 9 OP-ED. The Orlando, Florida case is from: Ken Magid & Carole A. McKelvey (1987). *High risk: Children without a conscience.* New York: Bantam, p. 1.

38. Kip Schlegel & David Weisburd (1992). *White-collar crime reconsidered.* Boston, MA: Northeastern University Press. Stephen Hoar (1991). ATM theft suspects nabbed in Colorado. *Raleigh State Journal,* March 23, North Carolina, p. 89.

39. Jose Sanchez (1986). Social crisis and psychopathy: Toward a sociology of

the psychopath, in W. H. Reid, D. Dorr, J.I. Walker, & J. W. Bonner III (Eds.), *Unmasking the psychopath: Antisocial personality and related syndromes.* New York: Norton, p. 93. Georgette Bennett (1987). *Crimewarps: The future of crime in America.* New York: Doubleday, p. 104. Jack Levin & James Alan Fox (1985). *Mass murder: America's growing menace.* New York: Plenum.

40. *Wisconsin State Journal* (1991). 30 watched soldier's fatal beating. September 25. Bob Lewis (1992). Torture-slaying stuns small town. *Wisconsin State Journal*, June 16, p. 3A. Jerry Thomas & David Ibata (1991). Unreported body lay in woods for months while teens viewed it. *Wisconsin State Journal*, April 18, p. 4A. Linda Deutsch (1993). Rich kids call friends killers. *Wisconsin State Journal*, August 1. Melinda Henneberger (1993). Now sex and violence link at an earlier age. *New York Times*, July 5, p. B1.

41. Jay G. Lindgren (1987). Social policy and the prevention of delinquency, in John D. Burchard & Sara N. Burchard (Eds.), *Prevention of Delinquent Behavior.* Newbury Park, CA: Sage, p. 335.

42. James Q. Wilson (1988). Strategic opportunities for delinquency prevention, in James Q. Wilson & Glenn C. Loury (Eds.), *From children to citizens, Volume 3; Families, schools and delinquency prevention.* New York: Springer-Verlag, p. 294.

43. James Q. Wilson & Richard J. Herrnstein (1986). *Criminals born and bred: Crime and human nature.* New York: Simon & Schuster, pp. 213–263.

44. J.D. Hawkins & J.G. Weiss (1985). The social development model: An integrated approach to delinquency prevention. *Journal of Primary Prevention, 6,* 73–97.

45. Greg J. Duncan, Martha S. Hill, & Saul D. Hoffman (1988). Welfare dependence across generations. *Science, 239,* 467–471. American Association for Protecting Children (1988). *Highlights of official child neglect and abuse reporting–1986.* Denver, CO: American Humane Association.

46. Patricia Ruggles (1988). *Welfare dependency and its causes: Determinants of the duration of welfare spells.* Washington, DC: Urban Institute. Greg J. Duncan & Saul D. Hoffman (1990). Teenage welfare receipt and subsequent dependence among black adolescent mothers. *Family Planning Perspectives, 22,* 16–20.

47. Irwin Garfinkel & Sara S. McLanahan (1986). *Single mothers and their children: A new American dilemma.* Washington, DC: Urban Institute Press, p. 167. Gary Sandefur & Sara S. McLanahan (1993). *Uncertain childhood, uncertain future.* Princeton, NJ: Princeton University Press. Sara S. McLanahan & Gary Sandefur (1994). *Growing up with a single parent: What hurts and what helps?* Cambridge, MA: Harvard University Press. Annie E. Casey Foundation (1994). *Kids count.* Greenwich, CT: Author. American Association for Protecting Children (1988). *Highlights of official child neglect and abuse reporting–1986.* Denver, CO: American Humane Association, p. 21.

48. For relating teenage pregnancy and welfare dependency see: Rebecca M. Blank (1986). *How important is welfare dependence?* Cambridge, MA: National Bureau of Economic Research. Sarah H. Broman (1981). Longterm development of children born to teenagers, in Keith G. Scott, Tiffany Field, & Evan G. Robertson (Eds.). *Teenage parents and their offspring.* New York: Grune & Stratton, p. 222. J. Leventhal (1989). Are children of teenage mothers at increased risk of child maltreatment? *Research grant status report (NCCAN Grant No. 90-CA-1374).* New Haven, CT: Yale University School of Medicine, Department of Pediatrics. For relating unmarried teenage mothers and child abuse see: Judith S. Musick (1990). Adolescents as mothers: The being and the doing. *Zero to Three, 11*(2), 21–28. Cynthia C. Garcia Coll, Joel Hoffman, & William Oh (1987). The social ecology and early parenting of caucasian adolescent mothers. *Child Development, 58,* 955–963.

49. American Association for Protecting Children (1988). *Highlights of official child neglect and abuse reporting–1986.* Denver, CO: American Humane Association.

50. William Julius Wilson (1987). *The truly disadvantaged: The inner city, the underclass, and public policy.* Chicago, IL: University of Chicago Press. William R. Prosser (1992). The underclass: Assessing what we have learned. *Focus, 13,* 16.

51. Mary Jo Bane & David T. Ellwood (1989). One fifth of the nation's children: Why are they poor? *Science, 245,* 1047–1053. Sara McLanahan & Larry Bumpass (1988). Intergenerational consequences of family disruption. *American Journal of Sociology, 94,* 130–152. David T. Ellwood & Mary Jo Bane (1985). The impact of AFDC on family structure and living arrangements, in Ronald G. Ehrenberg (Ed.), *Research in labor economics, Volume 7.* Greenwich, CT: JAI Press.

52. Greg J. Duncan, Martha S. Hill, & Saul D. Hoffman (1988). Welfare dependence across generations. *Science, 239,* 467–471.

53. Carol L. M. Caton (1990). *Homeless in America.* New York: Oxford University Press. National Coalition for the Homeless (1989). *Homelessness in America: A summary.* Washington, DC: Author. Jonathan Kozol (1988). *Rachel and her children: Homeless families in America.* New York: Crown. Urban Institute (1988). *State activities and programs for the homeless: A review of six states (2381).* Washington, DC: Author. Alice S. Baum & Donald W. Burnes (1993). *A nation in denial: The truth about homelessness.* Boulder, CO: Westview Press. Christopher Jencks (1994). *The homeless.* Cambridge MA: Harvard University Press.

54. Carl I. Cohen & Kenneth S. Thompson (1992). Homeless mentally ill or mentally ill homeless? *American Journal of Psychiatry, 149,* 816–823. Margery Austin Turner, Michael Fix, & Raymond J. Struyk (1991). *Opportunities*

denied, opportunities diminished: Racial discrimination in hiring. Washington, DC: Urban Institute, Report 91-9. Ellen L. Bassuk (Ed.) (1986). *The mental health needs of homeless persons.* San Francisco, CA: Jossey-Bass, p. 48. Ellen L. Bassuk (1991). Homeless families. *Scientific American,* December, 66–74. George Thorman (1988). *Homeless families.* Springfield, IL: Charles C. Thomas. Institute of Medicine (1988). *Homelessness, health, and human needs.* Washington, DC: National Academy Press. Bonnie Hausman & Constance Hammen (1993). Parenting in homeless families: The double crisis. *American Journal of Orthopsychiatry, 63,* 358–369.

55. The Stanford Center for the Study of Families, Children and Youth (1991). *The Stanford study of homeless familes, children and youth.* Stanford, CA: Stanford University, p. 11.

56. David Finkel, Gerald Hotaling, & Andrea Sedlak (1990). *Missing, abducted, runaway, and thrownaway children in America.* Washington, DC: U.S. Department of Justice, Office of Juvenile Justice and Delinquency Prevention. Lisa Averson Richette (1969). *The throwaway children.* New York: Dell Publishing.

57. Nikolaos Stefanidis, Julia Pennbridge, Richard G. MacKenzie, & Karl Pottharst (1991). Runaway and homeless youth: The effects of attachment history on stabilization. *American Journal of Orthopsychiatry, 62,* 442–446. The New York study of runaway youths was reported in: Carol L. M. Caton (1986). The homeless experience in adolescent years, in Ellen L. Bassuk (Ed.), *The mental health needs of homeless persons.* San Francisco, CA: Jossey-Bass, pp. 65–66.

58. J.W. Huffman, Sir John Dewhurst, & V.J. Capraro (1981). *The gynecology of childhood and adolescence, 2nd Edition.* Philadelphia, PA: Saunders. Arline T. Geronimus (1987). On teenage childbearing and neonatal mortality in the United States. *Population and Development Review, 13,* 245–279. Arline T. Geronimus & Sanders Korenman (1990). The socioeconomic consequences of teen childbearing reconsidered. *Research Reports No. 90–190.* Ann Arbor, MI: Population Studies Center. Arline T. Geronimus & John Bound (1990). Black/white differences in women's reproductive-related health status: Evidence from vital statistics. *Demography, 27,* 457–466.

59. Claire Brindis & Rita Jeremy (1988). *Adolescent pregnancy and parenting in California: A strategic plan for action.* San Francisco, CA: University of California. Maris A. Vinovskis (1988). *An "epidemic" of adolescent pregnancy: Some historical and policy considerations.* New York: Oxford University Press, p. 216. Ibelice Ripoli-Cespedes (1981). Early motherhood: Some psychosocial and sociological aspects. *Temas de Trabajo Social, 3,* 131-139.

60. E.L. Abel (1984). *Fetal alcohol syndrome and fetal alcohol effects.* New York: Plenum. Heather Carmichael Olson, Donna M. Burgess, & Ann P.

Streissguth (1992). Fetal alcohol syndrome (FAS) and fetal alcohol effects (FAE): A lifespan view, with implications for early intervention *Zero to Three*, *13*(1), 24–29.

61. United States General Accounting Office (1990). *Drug-exposed infants: A generation at risk*. Washington, DC: Author, GAO/HRD-90-138. Ira J. Chasnoff, (1988). *Drugs, alcohol, pregnancy and parenting*. Hingham, MA: Kluwer Academic Publishers.

62. F. Elinore (1991). The consequences of maternal substance abuse for the child exposed in utero. *Psychosomatics*, *32*, 268–271. Claire D. Coles, Kathleen A. Platzman, Iris Smith, Mark E. James, & Arthur Falek (1992). Effects of cocaine and alcohol use in pregnancy on neonatal growth and neurobehavioral status. *Neurotoxicology and Teratology*, *14*, 23–33. Gale A. Richardson & Nancy L. Day (1991). Maternal and neonatal effects of moderate cocaine use during pregnancy. *Neurotoxicology and Teratology*, *13*, 455–460. Fredrik F. Broekhuizen, J. Utrie, & C. Van Mullen (1992). Drug use or inadequate prenatal care? Adverse pregnancy outcome in an urban setting. *American Journal of Obstetrics and Gynecology*, *166*, 1747–1754. Nilda M. Gonzalez & Magda Campbell (1993). Cocaine babies: Does prenatal cocaine exposure to cocaine affect development? *Journal of the American Academy of Child and Adolescent Psychiatry* 33, 16–19. Ciaran S. Phibbs, David A. Bateman, & Rachel M. Schwartz (1991).The neonatal costs of maternal cocaine use. *Journal of the American Medical Association*, *266*, 1521–1526.

63. Centers for Disease Control (1990). HIV prevalance, projected case estimates. *Journal of the American Medical Association*, *263*, 1477–1480. Meade Morgan, James W. Curran, & Ruth L. Berkelman (1990). The future course of AIDS in the United States. *Journal of the American Medical Association*, *263*, 1539–1540. Erik Eckholm (1992). AIDS, fatally steady in the U.S., accelerates worldwide. *New York Times*, June 28, p. 5.

64. Children's Defense Fund (1992). *Children's Defense Fund report*. Washington, DC: Author. Elizabeth R. Zell, Vance Dietz, John Stevenson, Stephen Cochi, & Richard H. Bruce (1994). Low vaccination levels of U.S. preschool and school-age children. *Journal of the American Medical Association*, *271*, 833–839.

65. J.H. Knowles (1977). The responsibility of the individual. *Daedalus*, *106*, 57–80.

66. Commission on Workforce Quality and Labor Market Efficiency (1989). *Investing in people: A strategy to address America's workforce crisis*. Washington, DC: U.S. Department of Labor.

67. U.S. Bureau of the Census (1989). *Current Population Reports, Series P-25, No. 1018 (Middle Series): Projections of the population of the United States by age,*

sex, and race: 1988–2080. Washington, DC: U.S. Government Printing Office.

68. Carnegie Council on Adolescent Development (1989). *Turning points: Preparing American youth for the 21st century* Washington, DC: Carnegie Corporation of America.

69. William B. Johnston & Arnold E. Parker E. (1987). *Workforce 2000: Work and workers for the twenty-first century.* Indianapolis, IN: Hudson Institute, pp. 114, 116.

5. The Costs of Incompetent Parenting

1. Children's Defense Fund (1991). *A vision for America's future.* Washington, DC: Author, p. xii.

2. Vivian A. Zelizer (1985). *Pricing the priceless child.* New York: Basic Books. The conservative figure of $112,000 cost of raising an urban child was estimated for June, 1989, by *Family Economics Review* Volume 2, No. 4, p. 30. Adjusting this figure for inflation to 1994 (26.5%), the amount would be $144,417.

3. Dorothy P. Rice, Thomas A. Hodgson, & Andre N. Kopstein (1985). The economic costs of illness: A replication and update. *Health Care Financing Review*, 7, 61–80. J. Petersilia, P.W. Greenwood, & M. Lavin (1978). *Criminal careers of habitual felons.* Washington, DC: National Institute of Law Enforcement and Criminal Justice. Brent B. Benda (1979). Criminal recidivism: From adolescence to adulthood. Ph.D. Dissertation, University of Wisconsin (450373).

4. Stewart Gabel (1992). Children of incarcerated and criminal parents: Adjustment, behavior, and prognosis. *The Bulletin of the American Academy of Psychiatry and the Law*, 20, 33–45.

5. Office of Family Assistance (1992). *Characteristics and financial circumstances of AFDC recipients–FY 1990.* Washington, DC: U.S. Department of Health and Human Services, p. 30, p. 1. The female adult recipients of AFDC were represented by age as follows: 11–18 (4.2%), 19–21 (13%), 22–24 (14.5%), 25–29 (24.6%), 30–39 (32%), and 40 and over (11.7%). There were 10,832 mothers who were 11 through 14 years of age. The ages of recipient children were as follows: under 2 (16.2%), 2–4 years (22.8%), 5–7 years (18.8%), 8–10 years (16.1%), 11–13 years (12.8%), 14–17 years (12.7%), and 18 years (.5%). The races of recipient children were as follows: Asian (3.9%), African American (41.4%), Hispanic (17.7%), Native American (1.3%), white (33.1%), and unknown (2.7%). U.S. Census Bureau (1988). *Receipt of*

selected noncash benefits: 1987. Washington, DC: U.S. Department of Commerce.

6. Irwin Garfinkel & Sara S. McLanahan (1986). *Single mothers and their children: A new American dilemmma.* Washington, DC: Urban Institute Press, pp. 169–170.

7. U.S. General Accounting Office. (1994). *Costs of welfare programs for families started by teenagers.* Washington, DC: U.S. Government Printing Office; Office of Family Assistance, Administration for Children and Families (1991). *Quarterly public assistance statistics–FY 1990.* Washington, DC: U.S. Government Printing Office.

8. Maureen Hack & Avroy A. Fanaroff (1989). Outcomes of extremely-low-birth-weight infants between 1982 and 1988. *New England Journal of Medicine, 321,* 1642–1647. John C. Sinclair (1987). High technology, high costs and the very low birth weight newborn, in R.C. McMillan, H.T. Englehardt, Jr., & S.F. Spicker (Eds.), *Euthanasia and the newborn.* Dordrecht, Netherlands: Reidel.

9. T. Tatara (1991). Child substitute care flow data for FY 1990 and child substitute care population trend since FY 1986. *UCIS Research Notes,* May 3.

10. Deborah Daro (1988). *Confronting child abuse: Research for effective program design.* New York: Free Press, p 156–157. In 1992, 2.9 million reports of child abuse or neglect were made, according to the National Committee for Prevention of Child Abuse. Of those reports, 39 percent were substantiated, and, of the substantiated cases, 65 percent actually received services. This suggests that some 740,000 children received services. Social service case management costs were taken from an annual estimate of $2,500 for each case from the Dane County Department of Social Services. The court expense of $800 per case was based on data from the Dane County Juvenile and Family Court.

11. D. Jones (1987). The untreatable family. *Child Abuse and Neglect, 11,* 409–420. Peter Reder, Sylvia Duncan, & Moira Gray (1993). *Beyond blame: Child abuse tragedies revisited.* London: Routledge. Deborah Daro (1988). *Confronting child abuse: Research for effective program design.* New York: Free Press, pp. 197–198.

12. U.S. Department of Defense (1982). *Profile of American youth.* Washington, DC: U.S. Government Printing Office.

13. Committee for Economic Development (1987).*Children in need: Investment strategies for the educationally disadvantaged.* New York: Author.

14. U.S. Bureau of the Census (1989). *Current Population Reports, Series P-25, No. 1018 (Middle Series): Projections of the population of the United States by age, sex, race: 1988–2080.* Washington, DC: U.S. Government Printing Office. A. Pine (1989). Quality of the work force: Challenge of the 90's. *Financier,* June: 13–16.

15. Harold L. Hodgkinson (1985). *All one system.* Washington, DC: The Institute for Educational Leadership, pp. 5–9. E.R. Ricketts & I.V. Sawhill (1986). Defining and measuring the underclass. *Journal of Public Policy Analysis and Management,* 7, 316–325.
16. Georgette Bennett (1987). *Crimewarps: The future of crime in America.* New York: Doubleday, p. 104.
17. U.S. News and World Report (1994). Cost of crime: $674 Billion, January 17, pp. 40–41. Edwin Zedlewski estimated that the average cost of a crime is $2300 to each victim; the typical felon committing 187 crimes was estimated to be responsible for $430,000 in victims' costs each year: Edwin W. Zedlewski, (1987). Making confinement decisions. *Research in Brief,* July, Washington, DC: National Institute of Justice (Publication No. 105834).
18. For the thesis that the crime control industry is locked into a capitalistic dynamic and must expand to survive see: Nils Christie (1993). *Crime control as industry.* London: Routledge.
19. Richard J. Zeckhauser & W. Kip Viscusi (1990). Risk within reason. *Science,* 248, 559–564. Allan M. Brandt (1990). The cigarette, risk, and American culture. *Daedalus,* 119, 155–176, p. 161. Kyle Steenland (1992). Passive smoking and the risk of heart disease. *Journal of the American Medical Association,* 267, 94–99.

6. *The Tolerance of Incompetent Parenting*

1. Alexis de Tocqueville (1969). J.P. Mayer (Ed.), *Democracy in America.* New York: Doubleday, p. 106.
2. For a broad view of the impact of individualism on societies see: R. Lesthaeghe (1983). A century of demographic and cultural change in Western Europe: An exploration of underlying dimensions. *Population and Development Review,* September, 411–435. Hanz Peter Dreitzel (1984). Generational conflict from the point of view of civilization theory, in V. Garms-Homolova, E.M. Hoerning, & D. Schaeffer (Eds.), *Intergenerational relationships.* Lewiston, NY: Hogrefe, pp. 17–26.
3. Benjamin Friedman (1988). *Day of reckoning: The consequences of American economic policy under Reagan and after.* New York: Random House.
4. Michael Crozier (1984). *The trouble with America: Why the system is breaking down.* Berkeley, CA: University of California Press.
5. Howard M. Leichter (1991). *Free to be foolish: Politics and health promotion in the United States and Great Britain.* Princeton, NJ: Princeton University Press.
6. David Popenoe (1988). *Disturbing the nest: Family change and the decline in modern societies.* New York: De Gruyer, pp. 307–341. Kari Schleimer & Valle

Rune (1994). Personal communication, University of Lund, Malmö, Sweden.

7. William Petersen (1990). Malthus: The reactionary reformer. *The American Scholar*, Spring, 275–282.

8. Marc Pilisuk & Susan Parks (1987). *The healing web: Social networks and human survival.* Hanover, NH: University Press of New England.

9. Gunnar Heckscher (1984). *The welfare state and beyond: Success and problems in Scandinavia.* Minneapolis, MN: University of Minnesota Press, p. 160. Gopsta Rehn & Helveg K. Peterson (1980). *Education and youth employment in Sweden and Denmark.* New York: The Carnegie Foundation. David Popenoe (1988). *Disturbing the nest: Family change and the decline in modern societies.* New York: De Gruyer. Henry Milner (1989). *Sweden: Social democracy in practice.* New York: Oxford University Press.

10. Daniel P. Moynihan (1986). *Family and nation.* San Diego, CA: Harcourt, Brace, Jovanovich.

11. Arland Thornton (1989). Changing attitudes toward family issues in the United States. *Journal of Marriage and the Family, 51,* 873–893. David Blankenhorn, Steven Bayme, & Jean Bethke Elshtain (1990). *Rebuilding the nest: A new commitment to the American family.* Milwaukee, WI: Family Service of America, p. 252. Sylvia Ann Hewlett (1991). *When the bough breaks: The cost of neglecting our children.* New York: Basic Books, p. 257.

12. Andrew Hacker (1992). *Two nations: Black & white, separate, hostile, unequal.* New York: Scribner's, p. ix. Thomas E. McCollough (1991). *The moral imagination and public life: Raising the ethical question.* Chatham, NJ: Chatham House.

13. Andrew Hacker (1992). *Two nations: Black & white, separate, hostile, unequal.* New York: Scribner's, p. ix–x.

14. Ibid., p. 218. Glenn C. Loury (1993). *One by one from the inside out: Race and responsibility in America.* New York: Free Press.

15. Karl Zinsmeister (1990). Growing up scared. *Atlantic Monthly*, June: 49–66.

16. Jack C. Westman (1989). The risks of day care for children, parents, and society, in Bryce J. Christiansen (Ed.), *Day Care: Child Psychology and Adult Economics.* Rockford,IL: The Rockford Institute, pp. 18–20.

17. Barbara Magrisso (1988). Children, community and the future. *Seeds of Unfolding, 5*(3).

18. U.S. Bureau of the Census (1992). *Current Population Reports, Series P-20, No. 458, Household and family characteristics: 1991.* Washington, DC: U.S. Government Printing Office.

19. Ranae Hanson (Ed.) (1982). *Institutional abuse of children and youth.* New York: Haworth, p. 3.

20. Bruce R. Thomas (1982). Protecting abused children: Helping until it

hurts, in Ranae Hanson (Ed.), *Institutional abuse of children and youth*. New York: Haworth.

21. Justine Wise Polier (1989). *Juvenile justice in double jeopardy*. Hillsdale, NJ: Erlbaum, p. 159. Lois G. Forer (1991). *Unequal protection: Women, children, and the elderly in court*. New York: Norton. Mark D. Jacobs (1990). *Screwing the system and making it work: Juvenile justice in the no-fault society*. Chicago, IL: University of Chicago Press. Jonathan Groner (1991). *Hilary's trial: The Elizabeth Morgan case. A child's ordeal*. New York: Simon & Schuster.

22. *In re Application of Gault*, 387 U. S. 1, 87s. Ct. 1428, 1967.

23. W.C. Rhodes (1972). *Behavior threat and community response*. New York: Behavioral Publications.

24. Elizur, Joel & Minuchin, Salvador (1989). *Institutionalizing madness: Families, therapy and society* New York: Basic Books.

25. Gordon, Diana R. (1990). *The Justice Juggernaut*. New Brunswick, NJ: Rutgers University Press.

26. Arthur Caplan L. (1987). Imperiled newborns, Conclusion. *Hastings Center Report* 17, 30–31.

27. Daniel P. Moynihan (1993). Defining deviancy down. *The American Scholar*, Winter, 17–30.

28. Evoleen N. Rexford (1969). Children, child psychiatry and our brave new world. *Archives of General Psychiatry, 20*, 25–37.

7. Juvenile Ageism

1. Jean-François Revel (1991). *The flight from truth: The reign of deceit in the age of information*. New York: Random House, pp. xi–xiii.

2. Erdman B. Palmore & Kenneth Manton (1973). Ageism compared to racism and sexism. *Journal of Gerontology, 28*, 363–369. Gordon W. Allport (1979). *The nature of prejudice, unabridged*. Reading, MA: Addison-Wesley. Bruno Bettelheim & Morris Janowitz (1964). *Social change and prejudice including dynamics of prejudice*. New York: Free Press. Jack Levin (1975). *The functions of prejudice*. New York: Harper & Row. William Ryan (1971). *Blaming the victim*. New York: Pantheon.

3. For parental ambivalence toward children see: Evoleen N. Rexford (1969). Children, child psychiatry and our brave new world. *Archives of General Psychiatry, 30*, 25–37. For unresolved childhood conflicts of adults see: Michael B. Rothenberg (1980). Is there an unconscious national conspiracy against children in the United States? *Clinical Pediatrics, 19*, 15–24.

4. Robert N. Butler (1969). Age-ism: Another form of bigotry. *The Gerontologist, 9*, 243–246.

5. Group for the Advancement of Psychiatry (1971). *The age and community mental health: A guide to program development, Volume 8.* New York: Author.
6. Select Committee on Aging, House of Representatives (1990). *Elder abuse: A decade of shame and inaction.* Washington, DC: U.S. Government Printing Office, Comm. Pub. No. 101–752.
7. Sander J. Breiner (1990). *Slaughter of the innocents: Child abuse through the ages and today.* New York: Plenum. Linda A. Pollock (1983). *Forgotten children: Parent-child relations from 1500 to 1900.* Cambridge, U.K.: Cambridge Press.
8. Maria Montessori (1974). *Childhood education.* Chicago, IL: Regnery.
9. C.M. Pierce & G.B. Allen (1975). Childism. *Psychiatric Annals, 5,* 266–270. Jack C. Westman (1979). *Child advocacy.* New York: Free Press, p. 39, p. 49. Michael B. Rothenberg (1980). Is there an unconscious national conspiracy against children in the United States? *Clinical Pediatrics, 19,* 15–24.
10. R.J. Kastenbaum (1973). Editorial; Reverse ageism: A temptation. *International Journal of Aging and Human Development, 4,* 283–284. Douglas C. Kimmel (1988). Ageism, psychology, and public policy. *American Psychologist, 43,* 175–178.
11. U.S. House of Representatives Select Committee on Children, Youth, and Families (1989). *U.S. children and their families: Current conditions and recent trends.* Washington, DC: U.S. Government Printing Office. National Commission on Children (1990). *Opening doors for America's children.* Washington, DC: National Commission on Children.
12. Samuel H. Preston (1984). Children and the elderly in the U.S. *Scientific American, 251,* 44–49. For a comparison of federal spending on children and the military see: Children's Defense Fund (1989). *A Vision for America's Future.* Washington, DC: Author.
13. Daniel P. Hanley, Jr. (1990). 4¢ for protecting children. *The Milwaukee Journal,* January 28, p. 23A.
14. Lenore J. Weitzman (1985). *The Divorce Revolution.* New York: Free Press, p. 321.
15. Christopher Lasch (1992). Communitarianism or populism? *New Oxford Review, 59,* 5–12.
16. Jane Jacobs (1961). *The death and life of great American cities.* New York: Vintage Books.
17. L. Genevie & E. Margolies (1987). *The motherhood report: How women feel about being mothers.* New York: Macmillan.
18. Margaret Mead (1976). Society's problem with children, in Jack C. Westman (Ed.). *Proceedings of the University of Wisconsin Conference on Child Advocacy.* Madison, WI: University of Wisconsin-Extension. For the crisis-recoil response see: W.C. Rhodes (1972). *Behavior threat and community response.* New York: Behavioral Publications.

19. Justine Wise Polier (1989). *Juvenile justice in double jeopardy*. Hillsdale, NJ: Erlbaum, p. 159. Peter S. Prescott (1981). *The child savers: Juvenile justice observed*. New York: Simon & Schuster.
20. Lis Wiehls (1990). When a child takes the witness stand: Bill proposes federal guidelines to govern testimony of children. *St. Petersburg Times*, January 12, p. A12.
21. Ranae Hanson (Ed) (1982). *Institutional abuse of children and youth*. New York: Haworth, p. 3. Howard James (1975). *The little victims: How America treats its children*. New York: David McKay, pp. 307–312.
22. Abigail Norman (1985). *Keeping families together: The case for family preservation*. New York: Edna McConnell Clark Foundation. For the pitfalls in family preservation see: Michael Wald (1988). Family preservation: Are we moving too fast? *Public Welfare*, Summer, 33–38. For "witch hunts" occasioned by allegations of sexual abuse see: Paul Eberle & Shirley Eberle (1986). *The politics of child abuse*. Secaucus, NJ: Lyle Stuart Inc. For how the war against child abuse has become a war against children see: Richard Wexler (1990). *Wounded innocents: The real victims of the war against child abuse*. Buffalo, NY: Prometheus Books.
23. Elly Singer (1992). *Child-care and the psychology of development*. London: Routledge, pp. 9–11.
24. Barbara Katz Rothman (1989). *Recreating motherhood: Ideology and technology*. New York: Norton. Bob Lee & Derek Morgan (1989). *Birthrights: Law and ethics at the beginnings of life* London, U.K.: Routledge. For the impact of involuntary childlessness see: Ann Oakley (1984). *Captured womb*. London, U.K.: Blackwell, and James H. Monach (1993). *Childless: No choice, the experience of involuntary childlessness*. London: Routledge.
25. For the psychological issues in reproductive technology see: Lantos, J.D. (1990). Second-generation Ethical Issues in the New Reproductive Technologies: Divided Loyalties, Indications, and Research Agenda, in Stotland, N.L. (Ed.) *Psychiatric Aspects of Reproductive Technology* Washington, DC: American Psychiatric Association Press. *Report of the Committee of Inquiry into Human Fertilisation and Embryology—Warnock Report* (1984). Cmnd 9314, London, U.K.: HMSO. New York Times (1991). France Outlaws Surrogate Moms. *Wisconsin State Journal*, June 2, p. 1B.
26. Arthur Caplan (1987). Imperiled newborns: Conclusion. *Hastings Center Report*, 17, 30–31.
27. National Center for Prosecution of Child Abuse (1992). *Update*, 5(3): 2, and by the Child Abuse Prevention Center in Baltimore, MD. Ann E. Waller, Susan P. Baker, & Andrew Szocka (1989). Childhood injury deaths: National analysis and geographic variations. *American Journal of Public Health*, 79, 310–315.

28. Tamar Jacoby (1988). Is sterilization the answer? *Newsweek*, August 8, p. 59. Anita Clark (1982). Prostitute gets seven years in death of 20-month-old son. *Wisconsin State Journal*, November 4.
29. Child Fatality Review Panel (1992). *New York City Child Fatality Review Panel annual report for 1991*. New York: The City of New York Human Resources Administration, p. 12, Table 6.
30. Ernle W.D. Young (1988). *Alpha and omega*. Stanford, CA: Stanford University Alumni Association.
31. *Webster v. Reproductive Health Services* (1989). 109 S. Ct. 3040. John A. Robertson (1989). Reconciling offspring and maternal interests during pregnancy, in Sherrill Cohen & Nadine Taub (Eds.) *Reproductive laws for the 1990s*. Clifton, NJ: Humana. Susan S. Mattingly (1992). The Maternal–fetal dyad: Exploring the two-patient obstetrical model. *Hastings Center Report*, *22*, 13–18.
32. Barbara Kantrowitz (1991). Pregnant addict. *Newsweek*, April 29, p. 53.
33. Ted Gest (1989). The pregnancy police on patrol. *U.S. News & World Report*, February 6, p. 50.
34. Tamar Lewin (1989). Mother vs. fetus. *New York Times*, January 9.
35. Suzanne D. Dixon (1989). Effects of transplacental exposure to cocaine and methamphetamine on the neonate. *Western Journal of Medicine*, *150*, 436–442.
36. *In the Interest of J. L. W.* (1981). 102 Wis 2d 118.
37. Denise Lavole (1992). Former Chinese prisoner at heart of custody case. *Wisconsin State Journal*, July 8, p. 2A. Laurie Asseo (1993). Court refuses to delay return of child, 2, to her biological parents. *Wisconsin State Journal*, July 31, p. 3A.
38. *Lehr v. Robertson*, 463 U.S. 248 (1983).
39. Associated Press (1989). Baby-swap dad: Ordeal hurt his girl. *Wisconsin State Journal*, November 23, pp. 4–5A.
40. Geoffrey L. Grief & Rebecca L. Hegar (1993). *When parents kidnap: The families behind the headlines, their problems and possible solutions*. New York: Free Press.
41. Philip Greven (1990). *Spare the child: The religious roots of punishment and the psychological impact of physical abuse*. New York: Knopf.
42. Robert H. Bremner (1971). *Children and youth in America: A documentary history, Volume 2, 1866–1932*. Cambridge, MA: Harvard University Press, pp. 666–725.
43. U.S. Department of Labor (1990). *Department of Labor Operation Childwatch uncovers child-labor violations*. Press release, March 15. Richard Eggleston (1991). Law cuts minor's work week. *Wisconsin State Journal*, December 29, p. 1C.

44. Robert H. Bremner (1971). *Children and youth in America: A documentary history, Volume 2, 1866–1932.* Cambridge, MA: Harvard University Press, pp. 1420–1429.
45. Ibid., p. 189, pp. 216–219.
46. Patricia A. Schene (1991). Interventions in child abuse and neglect, in Jack C. Westman (Ed.), *Who speaks for the children?* Sarasota, FL: Professional Resource Exchange. For the ineffectiveness of legislation designed to prevent crime and child abuse see: Ronald Barri Flowers (1986). *Children and criminality: The child as victim and perpetrator.* New York: Greenwood Press.
47. *Prince v. Commonwealth of Massachusetts* (1944). 321 U.S. 158 (170). *Walker v Superior Court* (1988). 253 CA Reporter 1 (19).
48. Elizabeth R. Zell, Vance Dietz, John Stevenson, Stephen Cochi, & Richard H. Bruce (1994). Low vaccination levels of U.S. preschool and school-age children. *Journal of the American Medical Association, 271,* 833–839. Willard, Jr. Cates & Kathleen E. Toomey (1990). Sexually transmitted disease. *Primary Care,* 17, 1–27.
49. Jenny Teichman (1982). *Illegitimacy: An examination of bastardy.* Ithaca, NY: Cornell University Press.
50. *Osborne v. Ohio,* (1990). U.S. Supreme Court, No.88–5986, April 18.
51. Gordon Hawkins & Franklin E. Zimring (1988). *Pornography in a free society.* New York: Cambridge University Press.
52. M. Horn (1991). Salvaging Saturday morning prime time. *U.S. News & World Report,* March 4, p. 54.
53. James R. Kincaid (1992). *Child-loving: The erotic child and the Victorian culture.* New York: Routledge.
54. *United Auto Workers v. Johnson Controls* (1989). U.S. Court of Appeals, 7th Circuit, 886 F. 2d 871. Stephen Wermiel (1991). Justices bar "fetal protection" policies, *Wall Street Journal,* March 21, p. B1.
55. Jack C. Westman (1991). Individual child advocacy, in Jack C. Westman (Ed.), *Who speaks for the children?* Sarasota, FL: Professional Resource Exchange.
56. Generations United, Child Welfare League of America, 440 First Street, N.W., Suite 310, Washington, DC 20001-2085.

8. A Child's Right to Competent Parenting

1. Albert B. Paine (1912). *Mark Twain: A Biography,* Volume 3. New York: Harper and Brothers, p. 1299.

2. M.D.A. Freeman (1983). *The rights and wrongs of children*. London: Frances Printer, p. 150. David Archard (1993). *Children: Rights and childhood*. London: Routledge.

3. D.D. Raphael (1967). *Political theory and the rights of man*. London: Macmillan, p. 54. Laurence D. Houlgate (1980). *The child and the state: A normative view of juvenile rights*. Baltimore, MD: Johns Hopkins Press, pp. 99–100.

4. A.H. Robertson & J.G. Merrills (1989). *Human rights in the world: An introduction to the study of the international protection of human rights*. Manchester, U.K.: Manchester University Press. Louis Henkin (1990). *The age of rights*. New York: Columbia University Press.

5. Leah Levin (1988). The rights of the child, in Peter Davies (Ed.), *Human rights*. London: Routledge, p. 40.

6. For the White House Conferences on children see: Jack C. Westman (1979). *Child advocacy*. New York: Free Press, pp. 257–262. United Nations General Assembly Resolution 1386 (XIV), November 20, 1959, New York, *Official records of the General Assembly, Fourteenth Session, Supplement No. 16. 1960*, p.19.

7. United Nations (1991). *Convention on the rights of the child*. New York: United Nations, No. DPI/1101–December–10M.

8. Charles D. Gill (1991). Essay on the status of the American child, 2000 A.D.: Chattel or constitutionally protected child-citizen? *Ohio Northern University Law Review*, 17, 543–579. David N. Sandberg (Ed.) (1989). *The child abuse-delinquency connection*. Lexington, MA: Lexington Books, p. 15.

9. Franklin E. Zimring (1982). *The changing world of adolescence*. New York: Free Press, pp. 31–32.

10. *Ginsberg v. New York* (1969). 390 U.S. 629, 88 S. Ct. 1274, 20 L. Ed. 2d 195. *Prince v. Massachusetts* (1944). 321 U.S. 158, 170.

11. Samuel M. Davis & Mortimer D. Schwartz (1987). *Children's rights and the law*. Lexington, MA: Lexington Books, pp. 207–208.

12. *Zepeda v. Zepeda* (1963). 41 Ill App 2d 240, 190 NE 2d 849, 379 U.S. 945.

13. *Illinois National Bank & Trust v. Turner* (1981). 38 Ill. Dec. 653, 403 N.E. 2d 1256, 83 Ill. App. 3d 234.

14. Parental immunity was upheld for negligence within the scope of the parental relationship in: *Wilson by Wilson v. Wilson* (1984). C. A. Tenn. 742 F.2d 1004. Robert Horowitz (1992). Families, infants and the justice system. *Zero to Three*, 13, 1–7. George H. Russ (1993). Through the eyes of a child, "Gregory K.": A child's right to be heard. *Family Law Quarterly*, 27, 365–394.

15. *DeShaney v. Winnebago County Department of Social Services*, U.S. Supreme Court No. 87–154. Decided February 22, 1989.

16. *Smith v. Alameda County Social Services Agency* (1979). 90 Cal. App. 3d 929; 153 Cal. Rptr. 712; March.
17. Peter Gorner (1981). How Illinois turned its back on Billy—A case of assault through neglect. *Chicago Tribune*, December 14, p. A2.
18. William Grimm (1992). Recent federal lawsuits prompt child welfare reform. *Protecting Children, 8*, 3–5.
19. Jack C. Westman (1979). *Child advocacy*. New York: Free Press, pp. 107–108.

9. A Parent's Right to Be Competent

1. James P. Comer (1972). *Beyond black and white*. New York: Quadrangle Books, p. xv.
2. U.S. Bureau of the Census (1993). *Current Population Reports P-20, No. 468: Marital status and living arrangements, March 1992*. Washington, DC: U.S. Department of Commerce.
3. Eulah Croson Laucks (1981). *The meaning of children: Attitudes and opinions of a selected group of U.S. university graduates*. Boulder, CO: Westview.
4. Therese Benedek (1959). Parenthood as a developmental phase. *Journal of the American Psychoanalytic Association, 7*, 389–417. E. James Anthony & Therese Benedek (Eds.) (1970). *Parenthood: Its psychology and psychopathology*. Boston, MA: Little, Brown. William Ruddick (1979). Parents and life prospects, in Onora O'Neill & William Ruddick (Eds.), *Having children: Philosophical and legal reflections on parenthood*. New York: Oxford University Press, pp. 124–137.
5. John Dewhurst (1984). *Female puberty and its abnormalities*. Edinburgh: Churchill Livingstone, p. 27.
6. Child Trends (1993). *Facts at a glance*. Washington, DC: Author. Stuart N. Seidman & Ronald O. Rieder (1994). A review of sexual behavior in the United States. *American Journal of Psychiatry, 151*, 330–341.
7. W.A. Schonfeld (1971). Adolescent development: Biological, psychological and sociological determinants, in S. Feinstein, P. Giovacchini, & A. Miller (Eds.), *Adolescent psychiatry, Volume 1*. New York: Basic Books. Frank Falkner & J.M. Tanner (1986). *Human growth, 2nd edition, Volume 2*. New York: Plenum, pp. 389–390. N.J. Anastasiow (Ed.) (1982). *The adolescent parent*. Baltimore, MD: Paul H. Brookes, pp. 2–31.
8. Jay Belsky, Laurence Steinberg, & Patricia Draper (1991). Childhood experience, interpersonal development and reproductive strategy: An evolutionary theory of socialization. *Child Development, 62*, 647–670.
9. Laurence Steinberg (1991). Developmental considerations in youth advo-

cacy, in Jack C. Westman. *Who speaks for the children?* Sarasota, FL: Professional Resource Exchange, pp. 26–27.

10. David Bakan (1971). Adolescence in America: From idea to social fact. *Daedalus, 100,* 979–995. For a detailed account of adolescent development see: Jane Kroger (1990). *Identity in adolescence: The balance between self and other.* London: Routledge. For a concise summary see: Mihaly Csikzentmihalyi (1993). Contexts of optimal growth in childhood. *Daedalus, 122,* 31–56.

11. Laurence Steinberg (1991). Developmental considerations in youth advocacy, in Jack C. Westman. *Who speaks for the children?* Sarasota. FL: Professional Resource Exchange, pp. 32–33. D.E. Gordon (1990). Formal operational thinking: The role of cognitive-developmental processes in adolescent decision-making about pregnancy and contraception. *American Journal of Orthopsychiatry, 60,* 346–356. For assisting adolescents in pregnancy decision making see: Paul V. Trad (1993). Adolescent pregnancy: An intervention challenge. *Child Psychiatry and Human Development, 24,* 99–113.

12. Jacquelyn Heard (1989). Make-believe teaches lesson: Project alive putting students in parents' shoes. *Chicago Tribune,* April 9, p. B1.

13. Stephen Small (1992). *The teen assessment project.* Madison, WI: Department of Child & Family Studies, University of Wisconsin-Madison.

14. Michael Sherraden (1990). *Individual developmental accounts.* Washington, DC: Corporation for Enterprise Development.

15. William Petersen (1990). Malthus: The reactionary reformer. *The American Scholar,* Spring: 275–282.

16. Franklin E. Zimring (1982). *The changing legal world of adolescence.* New York: Free Press.

17. Sandra Hoferth & Cheryl Hayes (Eds.) (1987). *Risking the future, Volume 2.* Washington, DC: National Academy Press, Table 3.3. Amara Bachu (1994). *Current Population Survey, June 1992, P20–470.* Washington, DC: Bureau of the Census, unpublished table. Joyce Dehli (1988). Study links drugs and early sex. *Wisconsin State Journal,* April 22. James M. Herzog (1984). Boys who make babies, in Max Sugar (Ed.), *Adolescent parenthood,* New York: SP Medical & Scientific Books, p. 71.

18. Freya L. Sonnerstein, Joseph H. Pleck, & Leighton C. Ku (1989). *At risk of AIDS: Behaviors, knowledge and attitudes among a national sample of adolescent males.* Presented at the Annual Meeting of the Population Association of America, March 31, Baltimore, MD. Joel W. Ager, Fredericka P. Shea, & Samuel J. Agronow (1982). Method discontinuance in teenage women: Implications for teen contraceptive programs, in Irving R. Stuart & Carl F. Wells (Eds.), *Pregnancy in adolescence: Needs, problems, and management.* New

York: Van Nostrand Reinhold, p. 237. The adolescent sense of invulnerability also is seen in the gay community in which a second wave of AIDS is appearing in 17 to 25 year olds in spite of awareness of the high risk of multiple partners: David Gelman (1993). The young and the reckless. *Newsweek*, January 11, pp. 60–61.

19. Moisy Shopper (1984). From (re)discovery to ownership of the vagina—A contribution to the explanation of nonuse of contraceptives in the female adolescent, in Max Sugar (Ed.), *Adolescent Parenthood*. New York: SP Medical & Scientific Books, p. 53. David E. Scharff (1982). *The sexual relationship*. London: Routledge, pp. 211–212.

20. Christine A. Bachrach (1986). Adoption plans, adopted children, and adoptive mothers. *Journal of Marriage and the Family*, *48*, 243–245.

21. Paul Robinson (1976). *The modernization of sex*. New York: Harper Colophon.

22. Sherrill Cohen & Nadine Taub (1988). *Reproductive laws for the 1990s*. Clifton, NJ: Humana, p. 5.

23. Ibid., pp. 381–384. Hyman Rodman, Susan H. Lewis, & Saralyn B. Griffith (1984). *The sexual rights of adolescents: Competence, vulnerability, and parental control*. New York: Columbia University Press.

24. Theodora Ooms (Ed.) (1981). *Teenage pregnancy in a family context*. Philadelphia, PA: Temple University Press, p. 43, p. 210.

25. *Poe v. Gerstein* (1975). 517 F. 2D 787; 5th Cir. *Hodgson et al v. Minnesota et al* (1990). U.S. Supreme Court Case No. 88–1125, June 25. *Ohio v. Akron Center for Reproductive Health et al* (1990). U.S. Supreme Court Case No. 88–805, June 25. Council on Ethical and Judicial Affairs (1993). Mandatory parental consent to abortion. *Journal of the American Medical Association 269*, 82–86.

26. Maris A. Vinovskis (1988). *An "epidemic" of adolescent pregnancy: Some historical and policy considerations*. New York: Oxford University Press, p. 211. Kristin A. Moore (1993). *Facts at a glance*. Washington, DC: Child Trends.

27. U.S. Bureau of the Census (1993). *Fertility of American women: June 1992, Current Population Reports P20–470*. Washington, DC: U.S. Government Printing Office.

28. U.S. General Accounting Office (1994). *Costs of welfare programs for families started by teenagers*. Washington, DC: U.S. Government Printing Office.

29. Ernie Lightman & Benjamin Schesinger (1982). Pregnant adolescents in maternity homes: Some professional concerns, in Irving R. Stuart & Carl F. Wells (Eds.), *Pregnancy in adolescence: Needs, problems, and management*. New York: Van Nostrand Reinhold, pp. 382–383.

30. For a description of the strengths and vicissitudes of teenage parenting see:

(1) Valerie Polakow (1993). *Lives on the edge: Single mothers and their children in the other America.* Chicago, IL: University of Chicago Press; (2) Ester Schaler Buchholz & Barbara Gol (1986). More than playing house: A developmental perspective on the strengths in teenage motherhood. *American Journal of Orthopsychiatry,* 56, 347–359; (3) Shelby Hayden Miller (1983). *Children as parents: Final report on a study of childbearing and child rearing among 12–15-year-olds.* New York: Child Welfare League; (4) Joelle Sander (1991). *Before their time: Four generations of teenage mothers.* New York: Harcourt Brace Jovanovich; and (5). Frank F. Furstenberg, Jr., J. Brooks-Gunn, & S. Philip Morgan (1987). *Adolescent Mothers in Later Life.* Cambridge, U.K.: Cambridge University Press.

31. Susan M. Fisher (1984). The psychodynamics of teenage pregnancy and motherhood, in Max Sugar (Ed.), *Adolescent Parenthood.* New York: SP Medical & Scientific Books. Judith S. Musick (1993). *Young, poor, and pregnant: The psychology of teenage motherhood.* New Haven, CT: Yale University Press.

32. Alice Schlegel & Herbert Barry, III (1991). *Adolescence: An anthropological enquiry.* New York: Free Press.

33. Theodora Ooms (1984). The family context of adolescent parenting, in Max Sugar (Ed.), *Adolescent parenthood.* New York: SP Medical & Scientific Books, p. 217.

34. Greg J. Duncan & Saul D. Hoffman (1990). Teenage welfare receipt and subsequent dependence among black adolescent mothers. *Family Planning Perspectives, 22,* 16–20. Patricia J. Dunston, Gladys Walton Hall, & Claudia Thorne-Henderson (1987). Black adolescent mothers and their families: Extending services, in Stanley F. Battle (Ed.), *The black adolescent parent.* New York: Haworth, p. 99. Melvin N. Wilson & Timothy F. J. Tolson (1988). Single parenting in the context of three-generational black families, in E. Mavis Hetherington & Josephine Arasteh (Eds.) *The impact of divorce, single parenting, and stepparenting on children.* Hillsdale, NJ: Erlbaum. For the Kinship Foster Family Program in New York City see: Office of Management Analysis (1993). *Selected child welfare trends in New York City.* New York: Human Resources Administration.

35. Minkler, Meredith & Roe, Kathleen M. (1993). *Grandmothers as caregivers: Raising children of the crack cocaine epidemic.* Newbury Park, CA: Sage Publications. Minkler, Meredith, Roe, Kathlees M., & Robertson-Beckley, Relda J. (1994). Raising Grandchildren from Crack-Cocaine Households: Effects on Family and Friendship Ties of African-American Women. *American Journal of Orthopsychiatry* 64, 20–29.

36. Herbert C. Quay (1981). Psychological factors in teenage pregnancy, in Keith G. Scott, Tiffany Field, & Evan G. Robertson (Eds.), *Teenage parents*

and their offspring. New York: Grune & Stratton, pp. 88–89. Jo Ann B. Fineman & Marguerite A. Smith (1984). Object ties and interaction of the infant and adolescent mother, in Max Sugar (Ed.), *Adolescent parenthood.* New York: SP Medical & Scientific Books.

37. Fank F. Furstenberg, Jr., Judith A. Levine, & Jeanne Brooks-Gunn (1990). The children of teenage mothers: Patterns of early childbearing in two generations. *Family Planning Perspectives, 22,* 54–61.

38. Michael D. Resnick, Robert William Blum, Jane Bose, Martha Smith, & Peter Toogood (1990). Characteristics of unmarried adolescent mothers: Determinants of child rearing versus adoption. *American Journal of Orthopsychiatry, 60,* 577–584.

39. S.D. McLaughlin, W.R. Grady, J.O.G. Billy, N.S. Landale, & L.D. Winges (1986). The effects of sequencing of marriage and first birth during adolescence. *Family Planning Perspectives, 18,* 12–18. J.R. Weeks (1976). *Teenage marriages: A demographic analysis.* Westpoint, CT: Greenwood. P. Glick & A. Norton (1977). *Marrying, divorcing and living together in the U.S. today.* Washington, DC: Population Reference Bureau, October.

40. Andrew Cherlin (1992). *Marriage, divorce, remarriage.* Cambridge, MA: Harvard University Press. William J. Wilson (1987). *The truly disadvantaged: The inner city, the underclass, and public policy.* Chicago, IL: University of Chicago Press, pp. 90, 92, 162.

41. Deborah L. Rhode (1993). Adolescent pregnancy and public policy, in Annette Lawson & Deborah L. Rhode (Eds.), *The politics of pregnancy: Adolescent sexuality and public policy.* New Haven, CT: Yale University Press, p. 314. Linda Gordon (1992). Teenage pregnancy: Morals, moralism, experts. MacArthur Foundation Conference on Morality and Health, Santa Fe, NM, June 22–23.

42. S. Philip Morgan, Antonio McDaniel, Andrew T. Miller, & Samuel H. Preston (1993). Racial differences in household and family structure at the turn of the century. *American Journal of Sociology, 98,* 799–828. Marian Wright Edelman (1992). *The measure of our success: A letter to my children and yours.* Boston, MA: Beacon Press, pp. 50–52.

43. Leon Dash (1989). *When children want children.* New York: Morrow, pp. 9–10.

44. John H. Ogbu (1990). Minority status and literacy in comparative perspective. *Daedalus, 119*(2) : 141–165.

45. Richard Majors & Janet Mancini Billson (1992). *Cool pose: The dilemmas of black manhood in America.* New York: Lexington Books.

46. James P. Comer (1972). *Beyond black and white.* New York: Quadrangle Books.

47. William Julius Wilson (1991). Poverty, joblessness, and family structure in

the inner city: A comparative perspective, Chicago Urban Poverty and Family Life Conference, October. For Puerto Ricans see: Nicholas Lemann (1991). The other underclass. *The Atlantic Monthly*, December: 96–110.

48. Angel Luis Martinez (1981). The impact of adolescent pregnancy on Hispanic adolescents and their families, in Theodora Ooms (Ed.), *Teenage pregnancy in a family context*. Philadelphia, PA: Temple University Press, pp. 335–336.

49. M. La Barre (1968). Pregnancy experiences among married adolescents. *American Journal of Orthopsychiatry, 38*, 47–55.

50. Kristin A. Moore, Sandra L. Hofferth, Richard F. Wertheimer, Linda J. Waite, & Steven B. Caldwell (1981). Teenage childbearing: Consequences for women, families and government welfare expenditures, in Keith G. Scott, Tiffany Field, & Evan Robertson (Eds.), *Teenage parents and their offspring*. New York: Grune & Stratton, p. 52. Rickie Solinger (1992). *Wake up little Suzie: Single pregnancy and race before Roe v. Wade*. New York: Routledge.

51. F. Furstenberg, Jr. (1981). Implicating the family: Teenage parenthood and kinship involvement, in Theodora Ooms (Ed.), *Teenage pregnancy in a family context*. Philadelphia, PA: Temple University Press, p. 217.

52. David Royse & Vernon R. Wiehe (1988). Impulsivity in felons and unwed mothers. *Psychological Reports, 62*, 335–336. Nancy A. Boxill (1987). "How would you feel. . .?": Clinical interviews with black adolescent mothers, in Stanley F. Battle (Ed.), *The black adolescent parent*, New York: Haworth, pp. 48–49. Search Institute (1993). *Youth in single-parent families: Risk and resiliency*. Minneapolis, MN: Author. Judith S. Musick (1990). Adolescents as mothers: The being and the doing. *Zero to Three, 11*(2) 21–28.

53. Sarah McCue Horowitz, Lorraine V. Klerman, H. Sung Kuo, & James F. Jekel (1991). Intergenerational transmission of school-age parenthood. *Family Planning Perspectives, 23*, 168–172. F.G. Bolton, Jr. (1983). *When bonding fails: Clinical assessment of high-risk families*. Beverly Hills, CA: Sage, pp. 150–155.

54. Richard J. Gelles (1989). Child abuse and violence in single-parent families: Parent absence and economic deprivation. *American Journal of Orthopsychiatry, 59*, 492–501. Nathan Hare & Julia Hare (1984). *The endangered black family*. San Francisco, CA: Black Think Tank. Nicholas Davidson (1990). Life without fathers: America's greatest social catastrophe. *Policy Review* Winter, 51, pp. 40–41. Rose, Harold & Mc Clain, Paula D. (1990). *Race, Place, and Risk: Black Homicide in Urban America*. Albany, NY: State University of New York Press, p. 198.

55. Lisbeth B. Schorr & Daniel Schorr (1988). *Within our reach: Breaking the cycle of disadvantage*. New York: Anchor Press, Doubleday, p. 15.

56. Sandra L. Hofferth & Cheryl D. Hayes (Eds.) (1987). *Risking the future: Adolescent sexuality, pregnancy, and child bearing, Volume I.* Washington, DC: National Academy Press, p. 2, p. 7, p. 138.
57. Elise F. Jones, Jacqueline Darrock Forrest, Noreen Goldman, Stanley Henshaw, Richard Lincoln, Jeannie I. Rosoff, Charles F. Wetsoff, & Diedre Wulf (1986). *Teenage pregnancy in industrialized countries.* New Haven, CT: Yale University Press.
58. Shelby Hayden Miller (1983). *Children as parents: Final report on a study of childbearing and child rearing among 12 to 15-year-olds.* New York: Child Welfare League, p. 112. For services that encourage "baby-making" see: Judith S. Musick (1993). *Young, poor, and pregnant: The psychology of teenage motherhood.* New Haven, CT: Yale University Press, p. 203.
59. Elise F. Jones, Jacqueline Darrock Forrest, Noreen Goldman, Stanley Henshaw, Richard Lincoln, Jeannie I. Rosoff, Charles Wetsoff, & Deidre Wulf (1986). *Teenage pregnancy in industrialized countries.* New Haven, CT: Yale University Press, p. 7.
60. J. Brooks-Gunn & F. Furstenberg, Jr. (1987). Continuity and change in the context of poverty: Adolescent mothers and their children, in J. Gallagher & C. Ramey (Eds.), *The malleability of children.* Baltimore, MD: Paul H. Brookes. Ronald B. Mincy & Susan J. Wiener (1990). *A mentor, peer group, incentive model for helping underclass youth.* Washington. DC: The Urban Institute.
61. *Carey v. Population Services International* (1977). 431 U.S. 678, p. 694.
62. Marie Winn (1983). *Children without childhood.* New York: Pantheon, p. 210.

10. A New Way of Thinking about Children

1. U.S. House of Representatives Select Committee on Children and Families (1989). *Report on the state of children in the United States.* Washington, DC: U.S. Government Printing Office.
2. Thomas S. Kuhn (1970). *The structure of scientific revolutions, 2nd Edition.* Chicago, IL: University of Chicago Press.
3. Robert Ornstein & Paul Ehrlich (1989). *New world, new mind: Moving toward conscious evolution.* New York: Doubleday.
4. Richard Harwood (1992). *Citizens and politics: A view from mainstreet America.* Dayton, OH: Kettering Foundation.
5. Daniel Yankelovitch (1992). *Coming to public judgment: Making democracy work in a complex world.* Syracuse, NY: Syracuse University Press.
6. William Damon (1988). *The moral child: Nurturing children's natural moral growth.* New York: Free Press.

7. Carl H. Nightingale (1993). *On the edge: A history of poor black children and their American dream*. New York: Basic Books.
8. For framing social claims to help children see: Joel Best (1990). *Threatened children: Rhetoric and concern about child victims*. Chicago, IL: University of Chicago Press.
9. Lisbeth B. Schorr & Daniel Schorr (1988). *Within our reach: Breaking the cycle of disadvantage*. New York: Anchor Press, pp. xxviii–xxix.
10. Michael B. Katz (1989). *The undeserving poor: From the war on poverty to the war on welfare*. New York: Basic Books, pp. 195–235.

11. A National Parenting Policy

1. John Stuart Mill (1859). On liberty, in Robert Maynard Hutchins (Ed.) (1952), *Great books of the Western world, Volume 43*. Chicago, IL: University of Chicago Press, p. 318.
2. Anne Tyler (1988). *Breathing lessons*. New York: Knopf, p. 182.
3. Barbara Dafoe Whitehead (1990). The family in an unfriendly culture. *Family Affairs, 3*, 1–6. Laurence D. Houlgate (1980). *The child and the state: A normative theory of juvenile rights*. Baltimore, MD: Johns Hopkins Press, p. 137. Robert Dingwall, John Ekelaar, & Topsy Murray (1983). *The protection of children: State intervention and family life*. Oxford, U.K.: Basil Blackwell.
4. Harriet L. Rheingold (1973). To rear a child. *American Psychologist, 28*, 42–46. Hugh La Follette (1980). Licensing parents. *Philosophy and Public Affairs, 9*, 182–197.
5. Daniel P. Moynihan (1986). *Family and nation*. San Diego, CA: Harcourt, Brace, Jovanovich, pp. 173, 192.
6. Richard H. de Lone (1979). *Small futures: Children, inequality, and the limits of liberal reform*. New York: Harcourt, Brace, Jovanovich.
7. Michael S. Wald (1976). State intervention on behalf of "neglected" children, in Margaret K. Rosenheim K. (Ed.), *Pursuing justice for the child*. Chicago, IL: University of Chicago Press. David A. Wolfe (1991). *Preventing physical and emotional abuse of children*. New York: Guilford. Clifford Grobstein (1988). *Science and the unborn: Choosing human futures*. New York: Basic Books, pp. 132–156.
8. Urie Bronfenbrenner (1987). Foreword, family support: The quiet revolution, in Sharon C. Kagan, Douglas R. Powell, Bernice Weissbourd, & Edward F. Zigler (Eds.), *America's family support programs: Perspectives and prospects*. New Haven, CT: Yale University Press, pp. xv–xvi.
9. For expanding employment opporunties for teenagers see: Sar A. Levitan & Frank Gallo (1992). *Spending to save: Expanding employment opportunities*.

Washington, DC: Center for Social Policy Studies, George Washington University. For education in the workplace see: (1) Forrest P. Chisman (1992). *The missing link: Workplace education in small business.* Washington, DC: The Southport Institute for Policy Analysis; (2) Laurie Bassi (1992). *Smart workers, smart work: A survey of small businesses on workplace education and reorganization of work.* Washington, DC: Southport Institute for Policy Analysis; (3) Southport Institute for Policy Analysis (1992). *Ahead of the curve: Basic skills programs in four exceptional firms.* Washington, DC: Southport Institute for Policy Analysis; and (4) John C. Coleman & Chris Warren-Adamson (Eds.) (1992). *Youth policy in the 1990s: The way forward.* London: Routledge. For the National Youth Service see: Donald J. Eberly (Ed.) (1991). *National youth service: A democratic institution for the 21st century.* Washington, DC: National Service Secretariat. U.S. Advisory Board on Child Abuse and Neglect (1991). *Creating caring communities: Blueprint for an effective federal policy on child abuse and neglect.* Washington, DC: U.S. Department of Health and Human Services.

10. Sheila S. Kamerman & Alfred Kahn (1980). Europe's innovative family policies. *Transatlantic Perspectives,* March, p. 12. Irwin Garfinkel & Sara S. McLanahan (1986). *Single mothers and their children: A new American dilemma.* Washington, DC: Urban Institute Press, pp. 181–185. Blankenhorn, David, Bayme, Steven, & Elshtain, Jean Bethke (1990). *Rebuilding the Nest: A New Commitment to the American Family.* Milwaukee, WI: Family Service of America, p. 253.

11. Irwin Garfinkel (1992). *Child support assurance.* New York: Columbia University School of Public Health. Irwin Garfinkel (1992). *Assuring child support: An extension of social security.* New York: Russell Sage Foundation.

12. Edward F. Zigler & Mary E. Lang (1991). *Child care choices: Balancing the needs of children, families, and society.* New York: Free Press, pp. 215–237.

13. Robert Halpern (1990). Poverty and early childhood parenting: Toward a framework for intervention. *American Journal of Orthopsychiatry, 60,* 6–18. John F. Rosen (1992). Effects of low levels of lead exposure. *Science, 256,* 294. Herbert L. Needleman (1992). Childhood lead poisoning: man-made and eradicable, *The PSR Quarterly, 2,* 130–134. Evelyn A. Mauss (1993). Commentary on childhood lead poisoning and social responsibility. *The PSR Quarterly, 3,* 4–7. Deborah Prothrow-Stith (1991). *Deadly consequences: How violence is destroying our teenage population and a plan to begin to solve it.* New York: HarperCollins.

14. For improving neighborhoods see: (1) John L. McNight & John P. Kretzmann (1990). *Mapping community capacity.* Evanston, IL: Center for Urban Affairs and Policy Research; (2) Wesley G. Skogan (1990). *Disorder and decline: Crime and the spiral of decay in American neighborhoods.* New York: Free

Press; (3) Robert Fisher (1984). *Let the people decide: Neighborhood organizing in America.* Boston, MA: Twayne; (4) Children's Defense Fund (1992). *Child watch update.* Washington, DC: Author; (5) David A. Hamburg (1993). *Children of urban poverty: Approaches to a critical American problem.* New York: Carnegie Corporation of New York; and (6). Roland Gilbert & Cheo Tyehimbay-Taylor (1993). *The ghetto solution.* Waco, TX: WRS Publications.

15. Karen J. Farestad (1991). Building a continuum of care and integrating service. *Protecting children, 8,* 13–16. U.S. Advisory Board on Child Abuse and Neglect (1991). *Creating caring communities: Blueprint for an effective federal policy on child abuse and neglect.* Washington, DC: U.S. Government Printing Office, Stock No. 017-092-00104-5. For individual and class child advocacy. see: Jack C. Westman (1991). *Who speaks for the children?* Sarasota, FL: Professional Resource Exchange, pp. 65–79.

16. Roland Hartley (1989). A program blueprint for neglectful families. *Protecting Children, 6,* 3–7. Sharon Kagan, Douglas Powell, & Bernice Weissbourd (Eds.) (1987). *America's family support programs.* New Haven CT: Yale University Press. Sylvia Ann Hewlett (1991). *When the bough breaks.* New York: Basic Books, p. 239.

17. Brigitte Berger (1988). Multiproblem families and the community, in James Q. Wilson & Glenn C. Loury (Eds.), *From children to citizens, Volume 3: Families, schools and delinquency prevention.* New York: Springer-Verlag, pp. 163, 276. Examples of mentoring programs are: the Institute for Urban and Minority Education in New York City; One to One in Washington, DC; One PLUS One in Pittsburgh, PA; the Education Commission of the States in Denver, CO: Public/Private Ventures in Philadelphia, PA; and The Baltimore Mentoring Institute in Baltimore, MD. For the Los Angeles EXCEL program in a safe apartment building equipped with a learning center see: Conversations on the Occasion of the Urban Institute's 25th Anniversary (1993). *The Urban Institute policy and research report, 23,* 1–4. Mary Lee Allen, Patricia Brown, & Belva Finley (1992). Missouri's parents as teachers (PAT), in *Helping children by strengthening families: A look at family support programs.* Washington, DC: Children's Defense Fund, pp. 48–53.

18. Edward Zigler & Susan Muenchow (1992). *Head Start: The inside story of America's most successful educational experiment.* New York: Basic Books.

19. B. Weissbourd & S. Kagan (1989). Family support programs: Catalysts for change. *American Journal of Orthopsychiatry, 59,* 20–31. Lisbeth B. Schorr & Daniel Schorr (1988). *Within our reach: Breaking the cycle of disadvantage.* New York: Anchor Press, Doubleday, pp. 292–293. Kathleen Linden & Robert B. Macfarland (1993). Community parenting centers in Colorado, *The Journal of Psychohistory, 21,* 7–19. Samuel J. Meisels & Jack P. Shonkoff (1990). *Handbook of early childhood intervention.* Cambridge, U.K.: Cam-

bridge University Press. Emily Fenichel (1991). Learning through supervision and mentorship to support the development of infants, toddlers and their families. *Zero to Three, 12*, 1–9, Washington, DC: National Center for Clinical Infant Programs. National Research Council (1993). *Effective services for young children*. Washington, DC: National Academy Press.

20. Richard Kagan & Shirley Schlosberg (1989). *Families in perpetual crisis*. New York: Norton. For an evaluation of seven demonstration projects for children living in poverty see: Mary Larner, Robert Halpern, & Oscar Harkavy (Eds.) (1992). *Fair start for children: Lessons learned from seven demonstration projects*. New Haven, CT: Yale University Press. For an intensive approach to treating parents and infants see: Paul V. Trad (1993). *Short-term parent-infant psychotherapy*. New York: Basic Books. For brief, solution-focused interventions see: Insoo Kim Berg (1993). *Family-based services: A solution-focused approach*. New York: W. W. Norton.

21. For an inventory of innovative programs see: Lisbeth B. Schorr & Daniel Schorr (1988). *Within our reach: Breaking the cycle of disadvantage*. New York: Anchor Press, Doubleday. For a frequently adopted program for disorganized families see: Gerald R. Patterson (1982). *A social learning approach, Volume 3: Coercive family process*. Eugene, OR: Castilia.

22. Jonathan Kozol (1985). *Illiterate America*. New York: Anchor Press, Doubleday.

23. National Foster Parent Association, Information and Services Office, 226 Kilts Drive, Houston, TX 77024.

24. National Center for Health Statistics (1972). *Handbook on marriage registration*. Rockville, MD: Department of Health, Education, and Welfare Publication No. (HSM) 72–111. Sylvester W. Trythall (1964). The premarital law: History and a survey of its effectiveness in Michigan. *Journal of the American Medical Association, 187*, 900–903.

25. Jeff Mayers (1992). Welfare test adds counties. *Wisconsin State Journal*, September 12, p. 1D.

26. Helen Gamble (1981). *The law relating to parents and children*. Sydney, Australia: The Law Book Company Ltd., pp. 20, 52–55. Cary Segall (1989). Homicide charge OK'd in fatal fetal injuries. *Wisconsin State Journal*, September 13.

27. Leonard Karp & Cheryl L. Karp (1989). *Domestic torts: Family violence, conflict and sexual abuse*. Colorado Springs, CO: Shepard/ McGraw-Hill. *In re Snyder* (1985). 532 P. 2d 278, 85 Wash. 2d 182.

28. Thomas A. Nazario (1985). *In defense of children: Understanding the rights, needs, and interests of the child*. New York: Scribner, p. 222.

29. David L. Chambers (1979). *Making fathers pay: The enforcement of child support*. Chicago, IL: University of Chicago Press.

30. Pamela Holcomb, Demetra S. Nightingale, & Jennifer M. Pick (1989). *Evaluation of the Western Interstate Child Support Clearinghouse Project.* Washington, DC: The Urban Institute. California Education Code 48900.1 and California Labor Code 230.7, 1989.
31. Quality Education Project (1992). *A system for student success through parental involvement.* Quality Education Project, 2110 Scott Street, San Francisco, CA 94115; (415) 921-8673.
32. Robert Pear (1990). Proposal links welfare funds to inoculations. *New York Times,* November 29, p. A15.
33. Wisconsin Statutes—Grandparents' Liability Law: Public Assistance Act 49.90, 2–13.
34. Mark Hardin & Patricia Tazzara (1981). *Termination of parental rights: A summary and comparison of grounds from nine model acts.* Washington, DC: National Legal Resource Center for Child Advocacy. and Protection, American Bar Association. For procedural protections for parents see: *Alsager v. District Court of Polk County, Iowa* (1976). 545 F.2d 1137 (8th Cir.).
35. Jack C. Westman & David Kaye (1990). The termination of parental rights as a therapeutic option, in Jack C. Westman (Ed.), *Who speaks for the children?* Sarasota, FL: Professional Resources Exchange, Inc.
36. Henry G. Grabowski & John M. Vernon (1983). *The regulation of pharmaceuticals.* Washington, DC: American Enterprise Institute.
37. Philip J. Hilts (1990). U.S. opens drive on lead poisoning in nation's young. *New York Times* December 20, pp. A1, A16.
38. San Francisco Society for the Prevention of Cruelty to Animals (1988). *Application for pet adoption.*
39. Benjamin B. Lindsey & Wainright Evans (1927). *The companionate marriage.* New York: Boni & Liveright, pp. v–viii.
40. Margaret Mead (1974). Marriage in two steps, in Robert F. Winch & Graham B. Spanier (Eds.), *Selected studies in marriage and the family, 4th Edition.* New York: Holt, Rinehart & Winston., pp. 507–510.
41. Beth Creager Fallon (1982). *Training leaders for family life education.* New York: Family Service Association of America. Carol Payne (Ed.) (1983). *Programs to strengthen families: A resource guide.* Chicago, IL: Family Resource Coalition. Lynne Ann De Spelder & Nathalia Prettyman (1980). *A guidebook for teaching family living.* Boston, MA: Allyn & Bacon. Pearl Karal (1984). *Parenting education for the young: A literature survey.* Toronto, Ontario: Ministry of Education. Dorothy Dolph Zeyen (1981). *Educators' challenge: Healthy mothers, healthy babies: A framework for curriculum development in responsible childbearing preschool through high school.* Alexandria, VA: Association for Supervision and Curriculum Development. Patricia A. Gorzka, Carol L. Blair, Arlene Steckel, & Lori Escallier (1991). Parenting: Categories for

anticipatory guidance. *Journal of Child and Adolescent Psychiatric and Mental Health Nursing*, *4*, 16–19. Marilyn Clayton Felt (1994). *Exploring childhood.* Newton, MA: Education Development Center, Inc. For the three Rs of parent education see: The Center for Population Options (1989). *Life planning education.* Washington, DC: Center for Population Options.

42. Harold Leitenberg (1987). Primary prevention of delinquency, in John D. Burchard & Sara N. Burchard (Eds.), *Prevention of delinquent behavior.* Newbury Park, CA: Sage, p. 324.
43. Hugh La Follette (1980). Licensing parents. *Philosophy and Public Affairs, 9*, 190.
44. D.P. Sommerfeld & J.R. Hughes (1987). Do health professionals agree on the parenting potential of pregnant women? *Social Sciences and Medicine, 24*, 285–288.
45. Lawrence Frisch (1981). On licentious licensing: A reply to Hugh La Follette. *Philosophy and Public Affairs, 11*, 173–179.
46. David T. Ellwood (1987). *Divide and conquer: Responsible security for America's poor.* New York: Ford Foundation, p. 43.
47. Karl Zinsmeister (1990). Growing up scared. *Atlantic Monthly*, June: 49–66.
48. Paul E. Peterson (1992). An immodest proposal. *Daedalus, 121*, 151–174.

12. Arguments against Licensing Parents

1. Benjamin F. Wright (Ed.) (1961). *The Federalist by Alexander Hamilton, James Madison, and John Jay.* Cambridge, MA: Harvard Library, p. 356.
2. Robert Proctor, (1988). *Racial hygiene: Medicine under the Nazis.* Cambridge, MA: Harvard University Press.
3. Tamar Jacoby (1988). Is sterilization the answer? *Newsweek*, August 8, p. 59.
4. The family as an institution is critiqued by: (1) Barrett, Michel & McIntosh, Mary (1991). *The Antisocial Family, 2nd Edition.* London: Verso; (2) Hayden, Delores (1985). *The Grand Domestic Revolution.* Cambridge, MA: MIT Press, pp. 1–29, pp. 47–49, pp. 96–105; and (3) Fraad, Harriet (1993). Children as an Exploited Class. *The Journal of Psychohistory, 21*, 37–51.
5. *In the Matter of the Welfare of Baby Boy May* (1976). 14 Wash. App. 765; 545 P.2d 25.
6. Denise B. Kandel & Victoria H. Raveis (1989). Cessation of illicit drug use in young adulthood. *Archives of General Psychiatry, 46*, 109–121.
7. *In Re East* (1972). 32 Ohio Misc. 65, 288 N. E. 2d 343.
8. Claudia Pap Mangel (1988). Licensing parents: How feasible? *Family Law Quarterly, 22*, 17–39, pp. 25–26. Doyle C. Pruitt & Marilyn T. Erickson (1985). The child abuse potential inventory: A study of concurrent validity.

Journal of Clinical Psychology, 41, 104–111. Michael J. Sandmire & Michael S. Wald (1990). Licensing parents—A response to Claudia Mangel's proposal. *Family Law Quarterly, 24*, 53–76. D.P. Sommerfeld. & J.R. Hughes (1987). Do health professionals agree on the parenting potential of pregnant women? *Social Sciences and Medicine, 24*, 285–288.

9. Jill Rachlin & Joseph P. Shapiro (1989). No pass, no drive. *U.S. News and World Report*, June 5, pp. 49–50.

10. Elinor Rosenberg (1992). *The adoption life cycle: The children and both their families through the years*. New York: Free Press.

11. Christine Bachrach, Kathryn London, & Penelope L. Maza (1991). On the path to adoption: Adoption seeking in the United States, 1988. *Journal of Marriage and the Family, 53*, 705–718. National Committee for Adoption (1989). *Adoption fact book*. Washington, DC: Author.

12. Ibid. Bureau of the Census (1991). *Curent Population Reports, Series P-20, No. 454: Fertility of American women, June 1990*. Washington, DC: U.S. Government Printing Office, pp. 29–31.

13. Beth Brophy (1989). The unhappy politics of interracial adoption. *U.S. News & World Report*, November 13, pp. 72–73. Maria Douglas, (1991). Fostering Black Adoptions: Private Agency Finds Lots of Willing Families. *Wisconsin State Journal*, November 17. Andrew Billingsley (1993). *Climbing Jacob's ladder: The enduring legacy of African-American families*. New York: Simon & Schuster.

14. Rita Simon & Howard Alstein (1987). *Transracial adoptees and their families*. New York: Praeger. Ruth McRoy & Louis A. Zurcher (1983). *Transracial and inracial adoptions*. Springfield, IL: Thomas. Arnold R. Silverman & William Feigelman (1990). Adjustment in interracial adoptions: An overview, in David M. Brodzinsky & Marshall D. Schechter (Eds.). *The psychology of adoption*. New York: Oxford Press, p. 199. Rita Simon & Howard Altstein (1991). *Adoption, race, and identity*. Westport, CT: Praeger, pp. 1–36. Child Welfare League of America (1988). *Standards for adoption service, revised*. New York: Author. The viscissitudes of transracial adoptions are described in: (1) Elizabeth Bartholet (1993). *Family bonds: Adoption and the politics of parenting*. Boston, MA: Houghton Mifflin; and (2) J. Douglas Gates (1993). *Gift children: A story of race, family, and adoption in a divided America*. New York: Ticknor & Fields.

15. Neil Alan Weiner & Marvin E. Wolfgang (1989). *Pathways to criminal violence*. Newbury Park, CA: Sage.

16. Jerome Kagan (1979). Family experience and the child's development. *American Psychologist, 34*, 886–891.

17. Phyllis L. Elickson & Robert M. Bell (1990). Drug prevention in junior high: A multi-site longitudinal test. *Science, 247*, 1299–1305.

18. Lee Thayer (1976). The functions of incompetence, in Ervin Laszlo & Emily Sellon (Eds.), *Vistas in physical reality*. New York: Plenum, p. 178.
19. Richard Carlson & Bruce Goldman (1990). *20/20 visions: Long view of a changing world*. Palo Alto, CA: Stanford University Alumni Association, p. 245.
20. Theda Skocpol (1992). *Protecting soldiers and mothers: The political origins of social policy in the United States*. Cambridge, MA: Harvard University Press.
21. John Barbour (1990). New groups are protecting land by buying it. *The Courier-Journal*, Louisville, KY, pp. D1–2.

Conclusion: Will the United States Value Parenting?

1. National Commission on Children (1991). *Beyond rhetoric: A new American agenda for children and families*. Washington, DC: U.S. Government Printing Office.
2. Committee for Economic Development (1989). *Children in need*. New York: Author. The Urban Institute (1992). Implications for future population changes. *Policy and Research Report, 22,* 17.
3. Metropolitan Court Judges Committee (1986). *Deprived children: A judicial response*. Reno, NV: National Council of Juvenile and Family Court Judges.
4. Phoebe H. Cottingham & David T. Ellwood (1989). *Welfare policy for the 1990s*. Cambridge, MA: Harvard University Press, p. 289. Howard Husock (1990). Fighting poverty the old-fashioned way. *The Wilson Quarterly, 14,* 79–91. Fay Lomax Cook & Edith J. Barrett (1992). *Support for the American welfare state: The views of Congress and the public*. New York: Columbia University Press. Michael B. Fabricant & Steve Burghardt (1992). *The welfare state crisis and the transformation of social service work*. Armonk, NY: M.E. Sharpe.
5. Midwest American Assembly (1990). *The future of social welfare in America*. Madison, WI: The Robert M. La Follette Institute of Public Affairs. The Assembly's conclusions are supported by the following publications: (1) National Center for Children in Poverty (1991). *Child welfare reform*. New York: Columbia University School of Public Health; (2) Michey Kaus (1992). *The end of equality*. New York: Basic Books; (3) Theodore R. Marmor, Jerry L. Mashaw, & Philip L. Harvey (1990). *America's misunderstood welfare state: Persistent myths, enduring realities*. New York: Basic Books; (4) Lawrence M. Mead (1992). *The new politics of poverty: The nonworking poor in America*. New York: Basic Books; and (5) Mary Jo Bane & David T. Ellwood (1994). *Welfare realities: From rhetoric to reform*. Cambridge, MA: Harvard University Press.

6. Anthony V. Bouza (1990). *The police mystique*. New York: Plenum.
7. Paul A. Krugman (1991). Myths and realities of U.S. competitiveness. *Science, 254*, 811–815.
8. Michael B. Katz (1986). *In the shadow of the poorhouse: A social history of welfare in America*. New York: Basic Books. Roger Cooter (Ed.) (1992). *In the name of the child: Health and welfare 1880–1940*. London, U.K.: Routledge.

Index

Protective
  factors in criminality and welfare
    dependency, 48
  services for children, 241–242
Prothrow-Stith, Deborah, 224
Psychoimmune system, 47
Psychomotor epilepsy, 59
Public
  education, 142
  health, 44
  policy changes, 272–273
Public Law 99–457, 227
Puerto Ricans, 189

Quality Education Project, 233
Quay, Herbert, 184
Quinton, David, 48

Racial hygiene, 251
Racism
  against African Americans, 111
  against African American girls, 194
  civil rights and, 145, 228
  sexism, ageism, and, 123,
Registering births, 239
Religious groups, 108
Removal of children from adoptive
    parents, 139–140
Restak, Richard, 59
Retrieval of switched baby, 140
Revel, Jean-François, 124
Rheingold, Harriet, 218
Rhesus monkeys, 49
Richette, Lisa, 74
Right to
  bear a child, 216
  conceive a child, 215
  the custody and rearing of a child, 216
Rights
  fear of according to children, 257–258
  restricting adults', 255–256
Risk
  of being a crime victim, 18
  prioritizing, 96–97
Robinson, Paul, 176

Robbery, 18, 19
Rockford Institute, 22
Roe v. Wade, 138
Roman Catholic Church, 254
Roman Empire, 8
Roosevelt, Eleanor, 150
Rothenberg, Michael, 128
Rousseau, Jean-Jacques, 47
Runaway Youth Program, 74
Rural
  neighborhoods, 60
  poverty, 39
  underclass children, 39
Rutter, Michael, 48

Sacred parent-child relationship, 252–254
Safety, 18–21, 56
Sagan, Leonard, 45
San Francisco Society for the Prevention
    of Cruelty to Animals, 236
Sanches, Jose, 67
Sandefur, Gary, 70
Save the Children Fund, 151
Scholastic Aptitude Score, 14
School dropouts, 13, 14, 93
Schor, Juliet, 22
Schorr, Daniel, 191, 211
Schorr, Lizbeth, 191, 211
Schweinhart, Lawrence, 62
Science achievement, 14
Sense of invulnerability, 171
Serotonin, 59
Sexism
  African American girls and, 194
  civil rights and, 145, 228
  racism, ageism, and, 123
Sexual behavior
  exploitation of children, 144
  harm of, 101–102
  "sexually active," 175
Sexually transmitted diseases
  epidemic of, 102
  incidence of, 16, 176
Shengold, Leonard, 66
Sipchen, Peter, 10